Andrew Murray
The Communist Party and Empire

A new history of the Communist Party
Volume One

Published by Manifesto Press Cooperative Limited 2025

© Andrew Murray 2025

All rights reserved. Apart from fair dealing, e.g. for the purpose of private study
or research, no part of this publication may be reproduced or transmitted,
in any form or by any means, electronic, photocopying, recording or otherwise, without
the prior permission of the publisher.
All rights reserved

ISBN 978-1-907464-68-3

Typeset in Bodoni and Gill
Printed by

Contents

v   Preface by Georgina Andrews

1   Introduction

5   *Chapter One*
       Joined at birth (1900-1917)

35   *Chapter Two*
       The World Revolution in Marxist Thought (1848-1914)

59   *Chapter Three*
       Lenin, Kautsky, and Connolly (1914-18)

82   *Chapter Four*
       Born Into Revolution (1920-1926)

117   *Chapter Five*
       The Challenges of Bolshevisation (1926-1929)

139   *Chapter Six*
       Against Social Democracy and Empire (1929-34)

173   Index

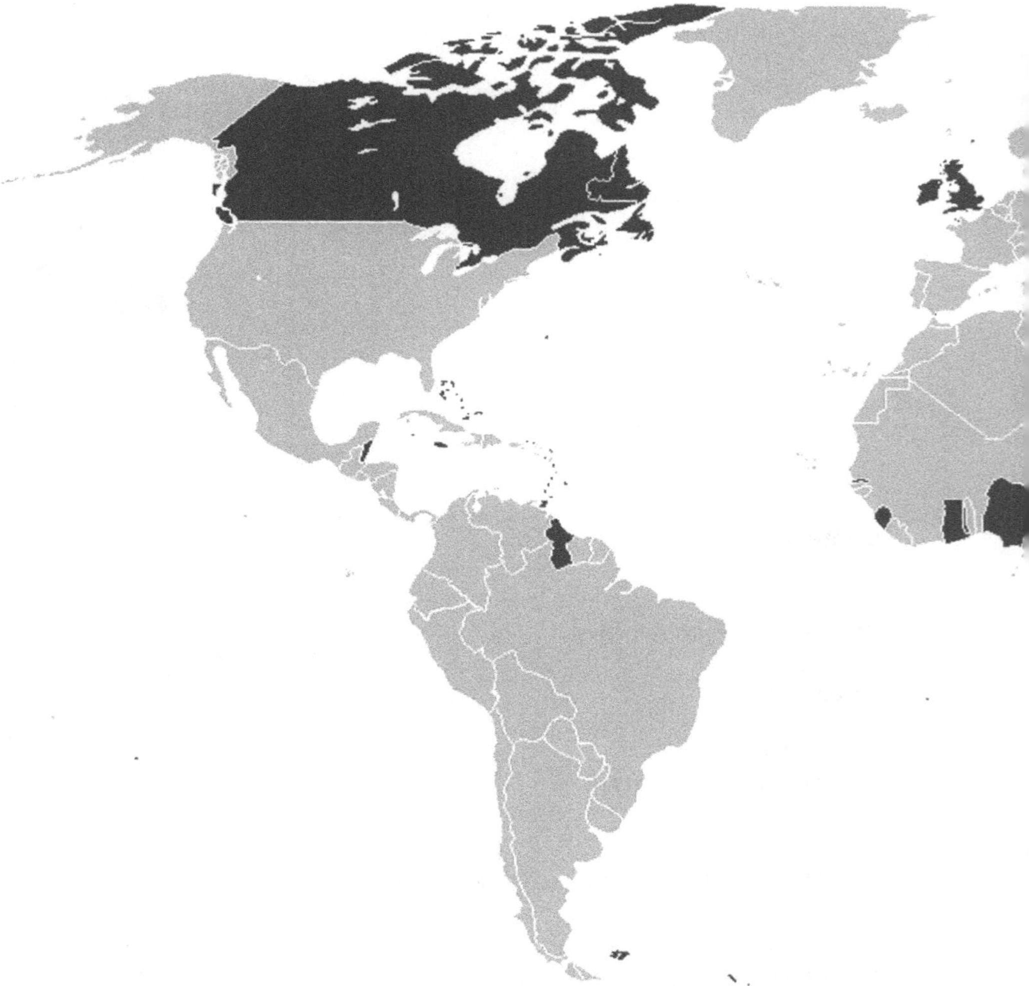

DAILY WORKER

LATE LONDON EDITION — Workers of the World, Unite!

Great Britain (British Section of the Communist International)
41, Tabernacle Street, E.C.   Telephone: Clerkenwell 0204

The Organ of the Communist Party of Editorial and Business Offices

One Penny

TO THE SQUARE ON SATURDAY!

No. 109   THURSDAY, MAY 8, 1930

Workers' Pledge to Indian Comrades

"Loyalty" is Doubted

UNITED FRONT IN FIGHT FOR SELF-DETERMINATION

Imperialist Repression Grows Rapidly in Ferocity

TWO INDIANS KILLED IN DELHI

INQUIRY INTO EXPLOSIONS

"A Searching Investigation" Says Clynes

EIGHT NOW DEAD

BIG DEMONSTRATION ON TOWER HILL

Hunger Marchers Call "Stand Firm" To Wood Strikers

WORKLESS FIGURES RISE

Nearly 40,000 Increase In A Month

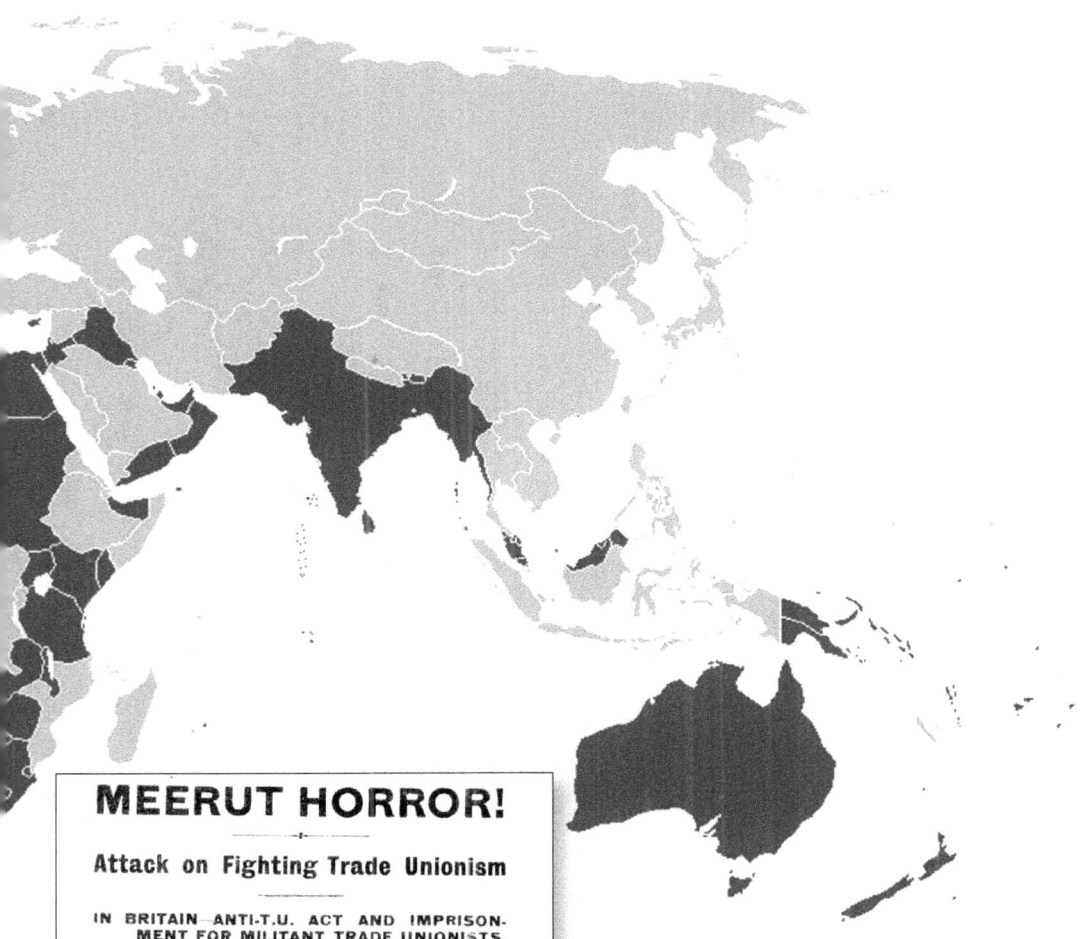

MEERUT HORROR!

Attack on Fighting Trade Unionism

IN BRITAIN—ANTI-T.U. ACT AND IMPRISONMENT FOR MILITANT TRADE UNIONISTS.

IN INDIA—TRANSPORTATION FOR SIMILAR ACTIVITY.

THE terrible sentences inflicted upon the Meerut prisoners affect every worker in this country.

Their crime was the organising of militant trade unions of the Indian workers, and the carrying through of strike struggles.

Kept in prisons for four years—for what?

For doing just what you have been doing every day of your lives, building up your organised strength, fighting for better trade union organisation in the class struggle.

SENTENCED FOR WHAT?

For saying what is said at trade union branch meetings in this country, that capitalism has got to go if the working class are to be free. Transportation and rigorous imprisonment for this.

FOR THE RIGHT TO COMBINE.

The Meerut sentences raise the whole question of the independent working-class right of organisation.

Workers of Britain, your unions have been built up in a century of painful struggles in Britain.

On you lies the duty and responsibility to stand up for the right of trade union and political organisation in India.

It is for you to use all your power and organised strength to annul these terrible sentences and secure the release of the prisoners.

DORCHESTER LABOURERS TRANSPORTED FOR SAME FIGHT.

The Trades Union Congress is preparing a solemn celebration of the hundred years anniversary of the Dorchester

"An empire on which the sun never set' was the imperial boast to which the Chartist Ernest Jones replied 'and the blood never dried.'

Below: Stowage of the British slave ship Brookes under the regulated slave trade act of 1788.,

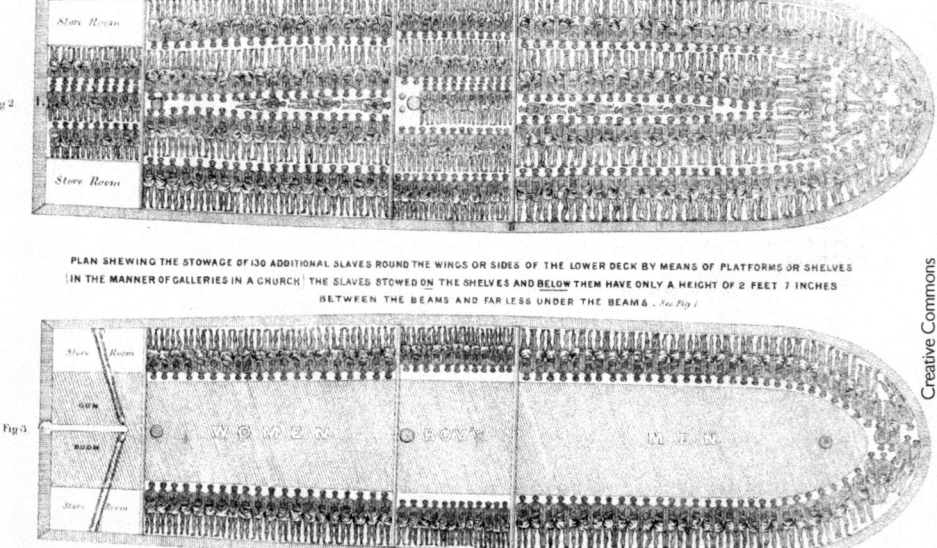

Preface

The Communist Party and Empire is a succinct and constructive text that offers insights into the development of the Communist Party in the material conditions of its foundation and early growth. Murray trails through this development in intertwining stages, reflecting on the state of domestic politics in Britain and in its empire and the influence of the USSR and colonial people on the Party's line. The weaknesses in the international outlook of the Party, especially during its beginnings, are analysed and the role of international meetings in advancing Party resolutions described. Also considered is the way in which the organisation of the Party evolved up to and including the publication of the *Daily Worker*, which gave members a tool and mechanism to organise in their communities and workplaces. The lessons that communists learnt 100 years ago are lessons that we can put into practice today – from challenging the influence of imperialist ideas in our organisations to the need for building the working class movement.

Andrew Murray covers the development of Marxist thought from 1848 and of the Communist Party of Great Britain to 1934, and analyses the impact of imperialism on the labour and progressive movement, with a reflection on its continuing role in shaping working class politics and trade union practice

Many of the arguments and actions of the Labour Party, and now government, in relation to arms manufacture and profit nowadays echo the the early pro-imperialist, pro-war arguments of Social Democratic Federation's founder Henry Hyndman and socialist campaigner Robert Blatchford.

These arguments pretend that arms manufacture and exports uphold international law and peace. As Murray maps – through the chronology of Marx and Lenin's thinking – it is clear that the support for imperialism and war in the British labour and progressive movement reflects still the privileges, the fruits of empire and imperialism, that the ruling class is still able to concede to workers.

The ruling class is still able to rely on trade union support for war spending and we have to tackle this especially in relation to the expansion of NATO and in the bloody and continuing Ukraine war.

Some unions have failed to oppose arms profiteering because they have members working in defence and aerospace industries. It is the logic of capitalism that the wages and conditions of workers in Britain come at the cost in blood of the men, women and children killed by weapons manufactured here.

Trade union consciousness arises spontaneously amongst workers but developing an anti imperialist political consciousness cannot be guaranteed without an effort on our part. It was then when the CPGB was formed and no less today that the task of communists and socialists is to be active in their trade union and fight to raise the political consciousness of workers by challenging the pro-imperialist sentiment in our organisations. This is the task that communists have had for over a century in Britain.

One of the challenges considered by Andrew Murray that is relevant to our newly elected government is its continuing 'pragmatism'. Keir Starmer has repeatedly rejected calls for the nationalisation of water, energy and railways in the name of pragmatic fiscal policies. Murray frames this in the context of the Labour Party traditionally concerning itself with a liberal agenda, working with the Liberals in its infancy to elect Labour MPs, rather than discussing and debating Marxism and socialism in the manner of other social democratic parties in Europe.

Starmer's approach to the Labour Party has been unambitious and full of arguments for a 'fiscally responsible' agenda that supposedly appeals to voters. In reality, Starmer's policy limits public expenditure and traps young and working people in poverty. The suspension – less than a month after the General Election – of seven Labour MPs who voted to scrap the two-child benefit cap that could have lifted an estimated 250,000 children out of poverty is a shameful case in point. This idea that the economy needs to grow before public expenditure can increase is a bald-faced lie peddled that draws attention away from the wealth that the ruling class in has accumulated. As Labour's Establishment seeks to limit trade union influence in the Labour Party and instead promote the interests of big business, the trade union and progressive movement has a big task ahead to build the United Front and challenge the Labour Party where it fails the working class.

Understanding our history is important for our new generation undertaking the vital work of the working class movement. We need to remind ourselves that whilst many people feel disappointed at the turn Labour has taken that the labour and progressive movement is again able to win concessions while the very crisis of capitalism raises again the necessity to fight for socialism.

This revolutionary optimism is touched upon by Andrew Murray where the early communists gave meaning to their lives through joining the socialist cause. This book is imbued with the passion and dedication of comrades that I and my generation strongly relate to and my heart is full with the knowledge that my revolutionary life is tied to the lives of thousands of people who have shared the same beliefs, revolutionary spirit and zeal for fighting for peace, jobs and socialism. We get to continue their legacy and traditions and build the future with their struggles and knowledge propelling us..

The Communist Party and Empire offers communists and fellow travellers an at times sobering but nevertheless productive analysis on the development of the Communist Party and its programme that puts our current political line into context as citizens of a leading imperialist nation. The lessons learned are still as pertinent in 2024 as they were around 100 years ago in ensuring the continual development of our work and achievements.

Georgina Andrews is general secretary of the Young Communist League

Introduction

WHY ANOTHER book on the history of the Communist Party of Great Britain? The influence of the CPGB on 20th century British history was famously well in excess of its membership figures, and still more so its degree of electoral success. Nevertheless, at no point in its seventy-one years did it look realistically likely to form a government, either as a result of the revolution it advocated or as a consequence of a general election.

This broad and crude fact has not staunched a flood of books covering the party's history in whole or part, the great majority published after its final demise in 1991. The literature is now more than considerable. The Party's own quasi-official history was eventually concluded in six volumes of varying quality and sympathy.[1] There are a number of one-volume histories, some of them merely pot-boilers, others sometimes grinding a particular ideological axe. To these one can add biographies – there are two worthwhile studies of the life of Harry Pollitt, probably the most significant single leader in British Communist history; there is one biography of Rajani Palme Dutt, the second most important figure, the scholarship of which is scarred by the author's hostility to his subject. Arthur Horner, Communist miners' leader, has had his life covered in a very detailed biography, and there are useful works on other Communists, including Bert Ramelson, Phil Piratin and Eric Hobsbawm, whose contributions lie outside the scope of the present volume. However, a number of very important Communist leaders have never been the subject of a biography, including Willie Gallacher, John Ross Campbell, and John Gollan.

Gallacher, the best-known of the handful of Communists elected to the House of Commons, left voluminous memoirs. His works, like other memoirs by prominent party members (including Pollitt), were considered as propaganda interventions addressed to the party's political needs of the time. Less well-known Communists, with no national profile but making a significant contribution in their own industries and communities, have also left a proliferation of memoirs, inevitably of varying quality but all with a warm sincerity and conviction of having given their life to something deeply worthwhile. Finally, there are serious and often deeply-researched studies dealing with particular aspects or periods of the Party's history – the "class against class" phase, the Popular Front, work in trade unions, relations with the Communist International and the Soviet Communist Party.

The present work draws on all of these, but has set out to do something different – describe the development of the CPGB's strategy and ideological assumptions, against the background of being part of a world revolutionary movement established on novel principles. This is a partisan work. This author first became interested in the CPGB's past while a member of it – trying to understand the sources of the decline into terminal ineffectuality that had set in well before I joined in 1977. My research, at a time when few of the books and archives available today were written or open, was hoping to contribute in a modest way to the party's renewal. That did not happen, but they did lead to a small book – *The Communist Party of Great Britain – a historical analysis to 1941* – eventually published in 1995. The present book draws on it in a few places but basically begins the work anew, and on a broader canvass with greater detail.

It aims, perhaps ambitiously, to locate the CPGB at the junction of several lines of analysis, or to integrate its place in history through different perspectives. This starts from assessing what the CPGB actually was. It was a revolutionary party, and by far the most significant to lay claim to that title in 20th century Britain – other pretenders have never been more than

Andrew Murray | 1

marginal in their impact. At the same time, it was not merely part of an international movement, but in significant ways the product of it. It was not just an affiliate of the Communist International in the period covered by this volume, and subject to the Comintern's discipline and often intrusive micro-management, it could not have come into being without world events acting as midwife.

At the same time, it was rooted in British conditions and the background of indigenous political traditions, many of which it worked to expunge in the name of superior international experience, but far from always successfully. One of the most salient of the circumstances shaping the CPGB was the obvious one – that it operated in Britain, a Britain which was in the years covered here still the mightiest imperialist power in the world, and a centre of international exploitation without historical precedent. Imperialism had shaped the British socialist movement from the outset, and it had grappled unevenly with the consequences of this throughout.

For the CPGB the question was more acute, however. The Communist International and its prevailing ideology, the Leninist development of Marxism, mandated a world revolutionary process of which the October Revolution was merely the first instalment. The implication of that mandate varied from one state in which Communist parties were newly-formed to another, but they could hardly be more consequential than in the country which sat at the centre of world imperialism which was the heart of the enemy. British Communists were required to integrate their efforts with the struggles of all those seeking liberation from British rule, numbering several hundreds of millions scattered across the face of the world. Playing its part in the world revolution meant not only seeking to secure the leadership of the British working class in the struggle to overturn capitalism, but assisting all efforts to undermine British rule in the colonies and semi-colonies. This aspect of the CPGB's mission is sometimes overlooked in the emphasis given to its relations with the Soviet Union, central though aligning with the first workers' state certainly was.

The present volume seeks to present the story of the CPGB through these lenses. The first chapter describes the entwined histories of imperialism and socialism in Britain before the first world war; the second follows debates and analyses around imperialism developed in the international (really European) socialist movement. These aim at providing context to what followed. Chapter three focuses on Lenin and Leninism, and the integrated theory of world revolution, giving a wholly new significance to colonial struggles, which developed after 1914, as well as tracing the work of those in Britain groping in the same direction.

Thereafter, we embark on the history of the CPGB itself. Chapter Four describes the formation of the Communist International and its British section, and how they started to grapple with the novel political requirements of world revolution. These were the nearest to a revolutionary situation seen in Britain since the years of Chartism, and we take them up to the landmark General Strike, which ended the period in which proletarian revolution could reasonably be imminently anticipated. Chapter Five deals with the CPGB, now relatively isolated from the rest of the British labour movement, reorienting itself under Comintern direction, embracing more closely the Bolshevik party model and an intransigent class-against-class perspective. The final chapter covers the controversial "third period" of the party's history, often dismissed as a sectarian aberration, but also the years in which the CPGB took a more definite shape and produced a strong network of revolutionary cadre.

The focus chosen here – the politics of world revolution and specifically of anti-imperialism – cannot entirely exclude intersecting with different framings. It would be impossible to render the story of the CPGB otherwise. So, this book covers events, like the General Strike, and issues, like left unity, militant trade unionism and unemployed campaigning too. It endeavours to present the party in the round, but it is primarily an account of ideological development and challenges, not a narrative history of the party's work and campaigns. There is therefore more Dutt than Pollitt here, not because the former was more important but because he played the larger part in those strategic debates. There are avenues left relatively unexplored here – communist women for example or relations with intellectuals.

The latter issue will be addressed more fully in the next volume, dealing with years in which the party became a significant force in such milieu. Greater attention will also be given to attitudes towards the USSR, again because the later 1930s were the time when that became the unequivocal touchstone of communist internationalism.

This may seem a touch arbitrary, a risk run by most attempts to periodise a history. Nevertheless, the conclusion of the present volume in 1934-5 has a logic beyond making the length of the book manageable. The advent of Nazism in Germany and the consequent reorientation of Soviet foreign policy and the strategy of the Communist international marked the definitive end of a whole epoch of world revolution. Essentially, the approach developed by Lenin in 1914-20 was played out, at least as an effective guide to day-to-day political action. There was no room any longer for the expectation of imminent revolutionary outbursts in Europe. But there was still more to the change – the seventh Comintern congress opened the way to a reconciliation with the bourgeois democracy reviled at its foundation in 1919, and to a demotion of anti-imperialism as an operational priority. The world revolution was not abandoned – that would not occur for many years yet – but it was punted into the middle distance as well as being redefined as to being closely associated with the expansion of the power of the USSR. As the future was to show, its further advance came either through the victories of the Red Army or through the militancy of a peasant-centred revolutionary nationalism in Asia.

None of this was clear at the time, of course. The Communist Party created by 1934 retained many critical features for decades subsequently (including very much the same leadership) but embarked on different strategic choices. That will be the subject of volume two.

In preparing this volume I have benefitted from the resources of the Labour History Museum in Manchester, the Working-Class Movement Library in nearby Salford, the Marx Memorial Library, and the British Library. I am grateful to the staff of all these institutions for their assistance. Thanks, too, to Nick Wright for his invaluable assistance in the design and publication of this work.

Andrew Murray London *November 2023*

Notes
1   All works referred to here will be referenced in the text where they are cited.

Illustration overleaf
Mural Depicting 1919 Amritsar Massacre - Jallianwala Bagh - Amritsar - Punjab - India
The Jallianwala Bagh massacre, also known as the Amritsar massacre, took place on 13 April 1919 when an anti colonial protest was met with sustained gunfire by troops under the command of Brigadier General REH Dyer

Chapter One
Joined at birth (1900-1917)

THE LABOUR CANDIDATE in the Woolwich by-election of 1903 could hardly have been clearer. Will Crooks, prominent trade unionist, Fabian, and municipal sponsor of the Greenwich foot tunnel through which pedestrians may walk beneath the Thames to this day, declared himself a supporter of "robust imperialism" and, for good measure, "an opponent of the claptrap of socialism."[1] He won a famous victory in Woolwich for the nascent Labour Representation Committee which three years later became the Labour Party. His outlook has, one could say, constituted a dominant trend in his party ever since, from Ramsay Macdonald to Tony Blair and Keir Starmer.

Crooks went on to distinguish himself by leading the singing of the national anthem in the House of Commons when war was declared in 1914. He was no aberration in his view of the Empire. John Burns, a still more eminent trade unionist – he had helped lead the great docks strike in London in 1889 – saw his opportunity when a consul-general (ruler in all but name) was needed in Egypt in 1907 to succeed that pioneer of bondholder imperialism Lord Cromer. "Appoint me, I will rule Egypt like a Pharaoh! You will not be disappointed,"[2] he told an aristocratic acquaintance. He was not given the chance to be the first trade union colonial overlord, but cabinet office was not far away nevertheless. A teachers' trade union MP, admittedly sitting for the Liberal Party, commended the idea of health insurance to the Commons as not "rank socialism, in reality it is first-class imperialism."[3]

There is another side to the coin though. Ernest Jones, a leader of the Chartists, Britain's first working-class political movement, had written as early as 1857 that "we do not believe that the British can prove a rightful claim to one single acre of ground…of Hindostan."[4] In 1896, when colonial issues first began to stir the emerging European labour movement, a leader of the more-or-less Marxist Social Democratic Federation in Britain, Belfort Bax[5], took issue with no less a figure than Eduard Bernstein, literary executor to the great Frederick Engels and still an associate of the then scarcely less-great (at the time) Karl Kautsky as well as a leader of the far stronger and unquestionably Marxist German SPD. Bernstein had argued that "…we will not condemn the idea that savages must be subjugated and made to conform to the rules of higher civilisation" and that "the freedom of an insignificant people in a non-European or semi-European region does not carry the same weight as the free development of the great and highly-civilised nations of Europe."

This was too much for Bax, who was a man considerably in advance of his time in his views on colonialism. He scorned the notion that "only those risings [in the colonial/semi-colonial world – AM] deserve the sympathy of the Socialists which are likely to result in the expansion of capitalist civilisation." Rather, it was "our duty as socialists…to fight tooth and nail against all advances of civilisation in barbarous and savage countries…their fight against the white man, against missions, traders, and settlers, is our fight. We recognise no rights, under any circumstances whatever, for a civilised power to subjugate races living in a lower stage of social development and to force civilisation upon them."[6] Bax's language bears of course all the marks of the age, but his policy proposal could scarcely have been further away from the eager support for Empire of Crooks and Burns.

Thus, battle was joined within the emerging labour and socialist movement in Britain over the matter of imperialism. A survey of British politics at the time by the panjandrum of Austro-Hungarian social democracy Otto Bauer posited that the Liberals were in danger of leaving the field to "...the two powers that will fight the decisive battle against each other: the Conservatives and the Labour Party, imperialism and socialism."[7] As an anticipation of the 20th century development of British parliamentary politics, Bauer's prediction was strikingly prescient. As an appreciation of the ideological alignment Labour would take, it was very far wide of the mark. Bax himself argued on the same lines: "capitalist-national imperialism is capitalism's reply to international Social Democracy...World history is now at the crossroads."[8] And a bloody crossroads it has proved to be.

Apogee of Empire

The issue itself was difficult to avoid at the turn of the century. The British Empire was everywhere, and the empire was everywhere in Britain. This was the time of *Land of Hope and Glory*. The tune was of course by Elgar, but lyricist A C Benson had his finger, perhaps instinctively, on the implacable dynamic of capital accumulation when he set Britain's imperial plans to song:

> "Wider still and wider shall thy bounds be set;
> God, who made thee mighty, make thee mightier yet"

Wider still and wider the Empire went indeed, adding four million square miles of territory between 1876 and 1915, more than any other colonial power. Writing at the end of the high imperial period – as, in fact, it was choking on the blood of millions – N.I. Bukharin listed in 1916 Britain's annexations since 1870. "Baluchistan, Burma, Cyprus, British North Borneo, We-han-Wei, the territories adjoining Hong Kong, increased Straits Settlements; Kuwait, the Sinai peninsula; annexed some islands in Australia; part of New Guinea, the Solomon Islands, the Tonga Islands, Egypt, part of Sudan, Uganda, Kenya, part of Somalia, Zanzibar, the two Boer Republics, Rhodesia, British Central Africa, Nigeria."[9]

He may have missed some too. This fantastic land-grab was added to an Empire which already embraced vast dominions of white settlement in Canada, Australasia and southern Africa, the Indian Raj (now directly governed from London in the name of a Queen-Empress no less, once the mercantilists of the East India Company had exhausted their role and their rule) and Ireland, formally a part of the metropolitan United Kingdom but in reality certainly the oldest and for long the most oppressively administered colony of all. "It was the largest Empire in history, comprising nearly a quarter of the land mass of the earth, and a quarter of its population." The British "...seemed to be arbiters of the world's affairs, righting a balance here, dismissing a potentate there, ringing the earth with railways and submarine cables, lending money everywhere, peopling the empty places with men of the British stock, grandly revenging wrongs, converting pagans, discovering unknown lakes, setting up dynasties, emancipating slaves, winning wars, putting down mutinies, keeping Turks in their place and building bigger and faster battleships," in Jan Morris's panoramic presentation.[10]

This was the Empire celebrated with choreographed pomp in 1897 to mark the diamond jubilee of Queen Victoria's accession to the throne of what had been, in 1837, a rather smaller operation. This was the Empire of song and stories, of the fashioning of a popular patriotism which could leave no class unscathed. But the Empire of colonial derring-do was, as Morris hints, only a part, and not the most important of that, of the whole imperial project. Morton and Tate offer a neat Marxist summary: "Down to 1914, Britain continued to occupy a unique and in some respects a dominating position in the world economy, a position which she owed to her earlier industrialisation, her maritime supremacy, the inheritance of a vast colonial empire from the mercantile phase of capitalism in the seventeenth and eighteenth centuries, and to the creation in the City of London of an unsurpassed international banking and financial mechanism."[11]

It is said that trade follows the flag. Capital, however, ran ahead of even the exponential march of the Union Jack in the thirty-plus years preceding the First World War. British investment overseas reached £4 billion by 1913 (more than £408 billion at 2016 values), or about 44 per cent of the global aggregation of foreign-owned capital. France, the runner-up, had around half as much. This yielded an income of just under £199 million. Britain continued to export a quarter of its manufacturing output, but "invisible income" from commercial services leapt ahead by 70 per cent from the mid-1880s to the eve of war. The balance of payments surplus advanced from £37 million in 1900 to £224 million in 1913. British investors, reassured by the certainties of the gold standard, kept more than one-third of Britain's total assets abroad, something rightly described by one historian as "an astonishing figure."[12]

The balance-of-payments surplus meant that huge funds were available for further overseas expansion. A Harvard economist has recently estimated that in this period "the average rate of return on British investments abroad was 50 to 75 percent higher than at home", which, in the words of one Winston Churchill, "give to the capital of the country a share in the new wealth of the whole world."[13] The 75 wars fought by Britain during Victoria's reign – Churchill was engaged in one or two himself – had not been without purpose or profit. Indeed, they secured an immense accretion of value extorted from millions of people around the world, flowing back to the metropolis year-in, year-out.

This was a different capitalism from the one which had powered (with more than a little assistance from the state, of course) the industrial revolution a century or so earlier. "Unlike the empires of the eighteenth century, the British Empire in the high Victorian era was an enabling system for global capitalist operations," writes Jürgen Osterhammel.[14] The storied "workplace of the world" had become the heart of a worldwide network of exploitation in which the banker, the investor, and the shipping magnate claimed place before the mill-owner. In John Darwin's words: "The era when Britain had been the unchallenged workshop of the world was over…Britain's share of world trade fell steadily …while Germany and the United States moved rapidly into the second generation of industrial products – electrical goods, chemicals, motor vehicles – Britain seemed to lag behind. Technological conservatism and excessive dependence upon 'old-fashioned' industries like cotton textiles, signalled an apparent loss of managerial dynamism, the onset of commercial sclerosis, and the triumph of a complacent upper-class amateurism over the scientific management demanded by the scale and scope of modern industry."[15] And yet the British "made themselves indispensable to the commercial prosperity not just of their empire but of most of the rest of the non-European world. To the empire coloured red on the map, the City had added an empire glued together by debt and defended by gold."[16]

This City's Empire reached – "wider yet and wider" – beyond even the red-coloured zones on the maps which hung in every late-Victorian classroom. No more than half of the capital invested abroad was to be found in the colonial empire, and that included self-governing areas like Australia and Canada. Huge sums were also placed in semi-colonial territories such as Egypt and China, while virtually all of the pre-1914 Latin American economy was under British suzerainty. Still more went to the USA and other industrial capitalist countries.[17]

A Chancellor of the Exchequer could boast that English banking was "on a crusading tour throughout the world...Banks abound whose familiar names in every variety suggest the one pervading fact of the marriage of English capital with foreign demand. There is the Anglo-Austrian bank, the Anglo-Italian bank, the Anglo-Egyptian bank. There is the English and Swedish Bank, there is the British and Californian Bank, there is the London and Hamburg Continental Exchange Bank; there is the London and Brazilian Bank, the London Buenos Aires and River Plate Bank, and even a London and South American Bank."[1] With British industry under increasing competitive pressure from more technologically-advanced rivals abroad "the City's international dominance gave it an authority in the economic affairs of the nation that was second to none," in Cain and Hopkins' words.[19] Or, as Osterhammel points out, London "...was not merely the economic centre of a formal colonial empire, or even of the much larger sphere in which Britain exercised political influence. It was a global control centre for flows of money and commodities, without rival until the rise of New York."[20]

The weight and import of these developments will be considered in the next chapter. However, it is plain that the economic transformation and colonial expansion of Britain in the late nineteenth and early twentieth centuries cannot but have had the most far-reaching impact on politics, including on the then-emerging socialist organisations and the wider labour movement, itself in a process of extensive development after a mid-Victorian generation of relative quietude marked by "the deep attachment of an elite of skilled workers and the labour leadership to the ethic of respectability", as one historian put it.[21]

Liberal imperialism and anti-imperialism
The great extension of British power embodied in the Empire was, to contemporary Tories, a process as natural as the rising of the sun which obligingly never set on the imperial estate, and one on which they were little given to reflect. With an ideology – although they would scourge the term – deeply marinated in the patriotism of property and with a preference for bellicosity matched by an ambivalence (to be generous) concerning democracy, what was there for them not to like? Empire, as the skilful manipulations of Disraeli showed, was also a means to extending the party's base among the middle classes, a necessity as the franchise haltingly extended through the male population in the course of the 19th century. That the Empire was about British power, patriotism, and profit needed no explanation or apology from the leaders of Conservative opinion. They were not above hypocrisy, of course – Lord Salisbury, a Blairite *avant la lettre*, described the Boer War as "a war for democracy", adding that Britain "seeks no goldfields, we seek no territory." The conflict nevertheless ended with no democracy for native South Africans but more gold and territory for Britain.[22] However, the Tories looked out upon the world of high Empire and found it good; given their ingrained scepticism about the perfectibility of people and about projects of improvement, they had no great desire to try to make it better.

Not so the Liberals. Not only was this the party of ethics, non-conformism, limited budgets, free thinking, free trade, and free enterprise, all of which seemed to militate somewhat against imperialism, it was also the party through which the emerging political voice of labour initially found its amplification. While working-class Toryism was a well-rooted political constituency, for reasons not substantially different to those satirised in the BBC sitcom *Till Death Us Do Part* three-quarters of a century later, the organised labour vote was largely and increasingly a vote for the Liberals. That did not in any sense make the Liberal Party a working-class organisation. Far from it – the Liberals were above all the party of the masters and the managers, of the self-confident bourgeoisie, but like the Tories, they too needed plebeian support at the polls.

As the imperial sun rose in the sky, the Liberal Party started to melt. It increasingly divided on the question of Empire (including Ireland), with its decisive sections coming to embrace a colonialism which mid-century Manchester liberalism would have regarded with a coldly cost-conscious eye. William Gladstone, the greatest prime minister of the Victorian era, marked the transition and embodied the contradictions. A man who made a political programme out of his moral compass he had, in the words of his biographer Roy Jenkins, "a sense...perhaps even a subconscious one of the superiority of Anglo-Saxon white men", of which he himself was a fine representative specimen."[23] His political oratory was critical in manufacturing the mist which convinced people that the Empire really was being acquired in a fit of absence of mind. Gladstone "...sought to free Ireland and deprived Egypt of freedom. Under the load of imperial responsibility he was forced into subterfuges and prevarications very unworthy of him...surreptitiously coming out upon his subject through a shrubbery of subordinate clauses, explaining to objectors why wealthy Britain could not afford to stop pushing opium on China."[24]

The "Grand Old Man" could on the one hand base a whole general election appeal on denouncing atrocities in the Balkans by foreign governments – the famous Midlothian campaign – while on the other ordering military intervention in Egypt to secure the interests of foreign bondholders, amongst whom he was himself to be numbered! This latter act of aggression in 1882 could perhaps be regarded as the moment Britain passed into the age of modern imperialism. Rajani Palme Dutt's judgement is severe but well-founded:

> "No sooner had he taken office than he continued and carried forward to new heights [Tory] imperialist foreign policy, with ruthless coercion in Ireland and with violent military aggression for the conquest of Egypt and the Sudan."[25]

Thus directed, "liberal imperialism" with its belief in Britain's "civilising mission" and the "white man's burden" came to definitively dominate the Liberal Party by the time Lord Rosebery (who had announced that the highest hopes of mankind rested on the British as early as 1883) became its leader at the turn of the century. The deepest split had been over the concession of Home Rule to the Irish, which led many Liberals into a "Unionist" coalition with the Tories. A 21st century historian catches the essence of that liberal and humanitarian outlook which blessed a policy of unending aggression: "The idea that the British were a tool of providence for the betterment of the world became a kind of ground bass among sections of the population whose gaze was directed beyond their own local sphere. Rather like the French after the revolution, the British felt themselves to be a kind of universal nation, both in their cultural achievements and in their resulting entitlement to spread them all around the world....This trope of a vocation to free other peoples from despotic rule and non-Christian superstitions rarely failed to produce its effect. Britain was the birthplace of humanitarian intervention, where the problem of human rights in relations between states was theorised... in a way that is still topical today."[26]

As we shall see, the new imperial dispensation and its underpinning assumptions met with only limited resistance from the representatives of labour. It was, however, opposed by a radical anti-imperialism within Liberalism itself. Just as liberal imperialism laid the foundations for a considerable quantity of the thinking of the Labour Party at its emergence and subsequently, so did the opposition to Empire in and around the Liberal Party inform the initial political challenge to imperialism within a labour movement as yet innocent of the analyses of Marx and Lenin.

Politically, this movement cut its teeth above all in opposition to the Boer War of 1900-03 in South Africa. In terms of its theoretical structure, it depended on the famous work by J.A. Hobson, *Imperialism*. Despite being no Marxist, Hobson started to put in place some of the concepts which came to inform Leninist anti-imperialism. His analysis was not anti-capitalist as such, but did address what he perceived as the mismanagement of the capitalist economy and the misbehaviour of some capitalists – financiers, essentially – who for their own interests exercised a baleful influence on state policy.[27] Hobson's underlying economic assumptions leaned heavily towards under-consumptionism (or over-saving). "It is not industrial progress that demands the opening up of new markets and areas of investment, but maldistribution of consuming power which prevents the absorption of commodities and capital within the country."[28] The clear answer to the problem thus posed was to raise the level of consumption in Britain itself, a position which would obviously recommend itself to trade unionism. Indeed, Hobson wrote that "Trade Unionism and Socialism are thus the natural enemies of Imperialism, for they take away from the 'imperialist' classes the surplus incomes which form the economic stimulus of Imperialism…by diverting to working-class or public expenditure elements of income which would otherwise be surplus savings, they raise the general standard of home consumption and abate the pressure for foreign markets." [29] As Bernard Porter has observed, the additional attraction of this line of reasoning for the labour movement, as against ethical liberal anti-imperialism, "was the way it dovetailed into preconceived notions about those who were doing labour down," blaming the whole problem on capitalists, although not capitalism.[30]

Instead of a prudent domestic-first approach by investors, Hobson saw the direction of the economy falling into the hands of those who preferred to reap easy profits abroad, and then browbeat the government into fighting for territory to guarantee them. He railed against "…the absurdity of spending half our financial resources in fighting to secure foreign markets at times when hungry mouths, ill-clad backs, ill-furnished houses indicate countless unsatisfied material wants among our own population." The home market, he argued was "capable of indefinite expansion," so it was not "inherent in the nature of things that we should spend our natural resources on militarism, war, and risky, unscrupulous diplomacy, in order to find markets for our goods and surplus capital."[31] Thus set out, this was a line of argument which could find support not only in the ranks of labour, but among sections of the capitalist class too. Indeed, elements of Hobson's work clearly anticipate what became known as Keynesianism, although the latter has never operated in Britain at the expense of 'militarism, war and unscrupulous diplomacy', but rather in tandem with it. In his own time, the Hobsonian view was all but endorsed by Lord Salisbury himself, who told a public meeting in Bradford in 1885 that if Britain meant "to hold our own against the efforts of the civilised powers of the world to strangle our commerce by their prohibitive finance we must be prepared to take the requisite measures to open new markets for ourselves among the half-civilised nations of the globe, and we must not be afraid if that effort, which is vital to our industries, should bring with it a new responsibility of empire and government." Salisbury thus offered his own anticipation of Leninism, improbably enough.[32]

Hobson also punctured the vanities of Liberal imperialism, counterposing the new imperialism with what he regarded as the "free, wholesome" colonialism of the areas of white settlement. "…the New Imperialism has increased the area of British despotism, far outbalancing the progress in population and in practical freedom attained by our few democratic colonies" (he is referring to Canada, Australia etc.) and added presciently that "…this large expansion of British political despotism is fraught with reactions upon home politics deserving of most serious consideration."[33] Indeed, the staunchest opponents of extending (or even maintaining) democracy in Edwardian England were the veterans of colonial governance, like Lords Cromer, Milner and Curzon. They believed that political parties and parliaments were encumbrances that a well-run empire could very well do without.[34] The Liberal Party leaders, having embraced imperialism and "…sold their party to a confederacy of stock gamblers and jingo sentimentalists, find themselves impotent to defend free trade, free press, free schools, free speech or any of the rudiments of ancient Liberalism."[35]

One further critical contribution of Hobson's has since entered into the mainstream of anti-imperialist agitation. That is the concept of "parasitism" which he develops towards the end of his book, and which Lenin reproduced extensively in his own subsequent work. Hobson warned of "…the gigantic peril of a western parasitism, a group of advanced industrial nations, whose upper classes drew vast tribute from Asia and Africa, with which they supported great tame masses of retainers, no longer engaged in the staple industries of agriculture and manufacture, but kept in the performance of personal or minor industrial services under the control of a new financial aristocracy. Let those who would scout such a theory as undeserving of consideration examine the economic and social conditions of districts in Southern England today." Reaching back into the favourite analogy of the fall of imperial Rome, he concluded: "This is the largest, plainest instance history presents of the social parasitic process by which a moneyed interest within the state, usurping the reins of government, makes for imperial expansion in order to fasten economic suckers into foreign bodies so as to drain them of their wealth in order to support domestic luxury. The new imperialism differs in no vital point from this old example."[36]

The weaknesses in Hobson's analysis are plain enough. He did not see the new imperialism as an inevitable development of a capitalism driven by the internal logic of accumulation to leave free enterprise behind in significant part, but rather as the product of the pressure of "the vested interests which…are shown to be the chief prompters of an imperialist policy… seeking their private commercial and financial gains at the expense and peril of the commonwealth."[37] This was, as Kiernan put it, "capitalism…led astray by the self-interest of dealers in arms, war contractors, financiers and stock-jobbers", almost empire-by-conspiracy.[38] Hobson believed therefore that the whole drive of imperialism could be obstructed by a return to a more democratic and enlightened capitalism. Expropriating the bourgeoisie or seeing that class as a whole as the social sponsor of imperialism, formed no part of his perspective. Additionally, the emphasis on the financier sometimes led Hobson and some of his co-thinkers into the shallows of anti-Semitism. Hobson himself at one stage described the Boer War as a "Jew-Imperialist design", although he later resiled from such an attitude.[39] For other radical anti-imperialists references to "financier" were too often preceded by the adjective "Hebrew."[40] The TUC itself in 1900 narrowly voted to condemn the war as aimed at securing "the gold fields of South Africa for cosmopolitan Jews most of whom had no patriotism and no country."[41] The racial trope aside, Hobson's presentation of the new phase in economic and political life clearly offered something for almost everyone – a basis for trade union redistributive demands, a summons to defence of democracy and a "healthy" British nationalism, the promotion of domestic consumption and, hence, local industry, and the advance of social reform without the need for the socialisation of the means of production. The subsequent development of the theory of the "anti-monopoly alliance" by sections of the world communist movement owes him a debt which is seldom acknowledged.

Radical (non-Socialist) anti-imperialism first really impacted on public opinion in the course of its opposition to the Boer War. In large part this was on account of the war's actual development and conduct which took the wind out of both nationalistic Tories, through being incompetently conducted and requiring three years and the expenditure of considerable treasure to crush two tiny Boer republics, and also at least some Liberal imperialists because it seemed to involve bullying small nations (white ones, it is not irrelevant to point out) and was moreover fought with methods which liberalism could scarcely explicitly countenance. The concentration camp for women and children made its deadly debut in this war. From this point onwards, Empire was a serious subject of controversy in domestic British politics and the left, radical-liberal and labour-socialist alike, had to start giving more applied consideration to foreign policy.

Labour meets Empire
So, what did the working-class believe about the Empire? Twenty years before the Boer War, Frederick Engels had few doubts, writing to Karl Kautsky: "You ask me what the English workers think about colonial policy. Well, exactly the same as they think about politics in general: the same as what the bourgeois think. There is no workers' party here, there are only Conservatives and Liberal-Radicals, and the workers gaily share the feast of England's monopoly of the world market and the colonies"[4]

Enlarging somewhat on this summary (and private) judgement a few years later, Engels dissected the state of the British working-class to Friedrich Sorge as follows: "The most repulsive thing here is the bourgeois "respectability" which has grown deep into the bones of the workers. The division of society into a scale of innumerable degrees, each recognised without question, each with its own pride but also its native respect for its "betters" and "superiors," is so old and firmly established that the bourgeois still find it pretty easy to get their bait accepted. I am not at all sure, for instance, that John Burns is not secretly prouder of his popularity with Cardinal Manning, the Lord Mayor, and the bourgeoisie in general than of his popularity with his own class. And Champion — an ex-lieutenant — has intrigued for years with bourgeois and especially with conservative elements, preached Socialism at the parsons' Church Congress, etc. Even Tom Mann, whom I regard as the finest of them, is fond of mentioning that he will be lunching with the Lord Mayor. If one compares this with the French, one can see what a revolution is good for after all. However, it will not help the bourgeoisie much if they do succeed in enticing some of the leaders into their toils. The movement has been far enough strengthened for this sort of thing to be overcome."[43]

Engels' concluding judgement here was surely over-optimistic. The material and ideological ties binding sections of the workers to the social order were strong, although the actual impact of either is disputed and hard to evaluate. The new imperialism did not, for one thing, impose itself on a society heaving with revolutionary spirit. The prosperity of the mid-Victorian era had spread modestly among many sections of society and had smothered much of what remained of the old Chartist militancy well before Gladstone took up arms for his fellow bond-holders. An "aristocracy of labour" had already emerged amongst skilled workers, which both dominated the craft trade unions (until the last decade of the century such unions were by far preponderant within the labour movement) and allied for the most part with the Liberal Party where they were not entirely apolitical. The groundwork for acquiescence in imperialism had therefore been laid, and its advocates were far stronger at the outset than the champions of socialism. Engels once more, writing in 1885 a new introduction to his classic work on the condition of the working-class in England in the 1840s:

> "…during the period of England's industrial monopoly the English working class have, to a certain extent, shared in the benefits of the monopoly. These benefits were very unequally parcelled out among them; the privileged minority pocketed most, but even the great mass had, at least, a temporary share now and then. And that is the reason why, since the dying out of Owenism, there has been no Socialism in England."[44]

So this was a "new imperialism" built on the foundations of an existing monopoly (albeit one beginning to crumble), with all the economic benefits, and political conformism as well, already accruing thereto.

Naturally, there was more to it than that. Imperialism renewed both the economic and ideological foundations for working-class acceptance of the status quo. At the very least, the fabulous flow of wealth from overseas, already described, afforded the establishment the wherewithal to make concessions to all domestic constituencies. The radical Liberal government of 1906 introduced reforms, like old age pensions, which could scarcely have been otherwise afforded. They constituted a belated and too limited attempt to prevent labour establishing its own independent political presence. In these respects, the fruits of imperialist plunder were shared with the whole of the working class. Particular industries or strata benefitted additionally. Hobson pointed out that "in many towns, most important trades are dependent upon government employment and contracts; the imperialism of the metal and ship-building centres is attributed in no small degree to this fact."[45] By government contracts, Hobson meant military expenditures above all, and such budgets do indeed have the effect of binding skilled sections of the working class to imperialism, as can be seen to this day.[46]

Whatever the exact economic benefits which workers obtained through citizenship in the mightiest capitalist state of the age, they needed to be supplemented by propaganda, reinforcing an imperial identity in which the working-class was incorporated with a sense of racial superiority, and a belief that things would go much worse in their industries if the colonies were lost. The great scientific achievements of Charles Darwin were perverted to present white Christians as the evolutionary peak of human development, a still largely religious country was assured from the pulpit that the Empire was God's work, and if all else failed what we might now call a Project Fear was deployed to paint a picture of economic doom and pauperisation if the so-recently world-conquering British industry was left to stand on its own domestic feet, unsupported by the additional proceeds of global brigandage.

The extent to which this worked, as with the mechanisms for "buying off" working people, is moot. According to Kiernan "how far the working class did succumb to the spell of empire is exceedingly hard to make out. On the whole it would seem that it let itself be persuaded that the empire was somehow a good thing for it, without troubling its head much about the matter or sharing the positive enthusiasm of the small middle classes. Amid the hysteria of the Boer War no anti-war speakers in working men's clubs were howled down, as they were outside." However, he adds that non-socialist workers, who were of course the great majority at this time, might simply elect to follow the lead given by "superior" social classes on this issue, as on others.[47]

An Indian historian agrees that "working-class opinion ignored jingoism and imperialism and was concerned primarily with social reform at home."[48] Hobsbawm fills out this view:

> "...imperialism encouraged the masses, and especially the potentially discontented, to identify themselves with the imperial state and nation, and thus unconsciously to endow the social and political system represented by that state with justification and legitimacy.... empire made good ideological cement. There is little doubt that in several countries imperialism was extremely popular among the new middle and white-collar strata, whose social identity largely rested on a claim to be the chosen vehicles of patriotism... There is much less evidence of any spontaneous enthusiasm of the workers for colonial conquests, let alone wars, or indeed of any great interest in the colonies (except those of white settlement). Attempts to institutionalise pride in imperialism, as by establishing the Empire Day in Britain, largely relied for their success on mobilising the captive audiences of school-children."[49]

Nevertheless, rooting imperial pride in the masses was an issue which the elite took seriously. It might have been comforted by the picture painted by Kautsky in 1902 "of a British working-class completely sunk in torpor and ignoble content, lost to anything higher than football or betting on horses",[50] an attitude which may have said more about Kautsky, who was arrogant and aloof long before he became revisionist, than about British workers; but little was left to chance. The idea that imperialism was "the most wholesome and effective antidote to democracy" would not have been particularly shocking at the time, but the fact that this sentiment was expressed by the then-Principal of the London Workingmen's College, C. P. Lucas, is worthy of note.[51] Every effort was made to extend Empire Day, an initiative taken by the high imperialist Lord Meath, beyond the schoolroom. Among those on the record as resisting this within the ranks of labour were the London Society of Compositors, the Poplar Labour League, the Paddington and Kensington Labour Council and the National Union of Clerks. The Gasworkers' Union – today the GMB – criticised the Empire Day's "undemocratic spirit", its "jingoism" and "the worship of a national fetish".[52] However, a demand from the British Socialist Party that the TUC call for all children to be withdrawn from school on the day in protest was not acted upon.

Imperialism may indeed be said to have the invention of modern propaganda among its accomplishments. It was the first social system to require the active assent – *in extremis* the mobilisation – of the mass of people for its successful prosecution. The old assumptions of religious conformity (or fear), the dull force of medievalism, the power of the press-gang were not likely to be sufficient to sustain the national effort required to conquer and secure a modern empire, still less to successfully fight the sort of war that arrived in 1914 but was in plain prospect for some years previously. The working-class had to be gingered up for the effort – it would not do to declare war and merely hope that "the scum of the earth", as the reactionary Duke of Wellington described his army during the Napoleonic Wars, would turn up. This propaganda was mediated through the social hierarchy to a large extent in the hope that, as Kiernan indicated, each class might follow its "betters" in the class directly above. Navy Leagues and other imperial mobilisation societies, fusing quasi-science with nationalist mysticism led the way. But it was hard to break down working-class indifference to projects which seemed to have little real bearing on their lives, and securing a reliable working-class was an enduring elite anxiety. Baden-Powell had initially sought to make his Boy Scouts pledge loyalty to their employers as well as to God and Country, but later had to think better of it.

The Labour Party emerged into this environment. When it did, the dominant role was played by trade unions rather than by socialists. This base amongst organised workers affiliated through their union is an historic distinctive mark of the Labour Party, different from all other social-democratic parties in the advanced capitalist countries of the time. This gave it a different ideological outlook (the very idea of having any such outlook at all was anathema to pragmatic trade unionism), being for the most part distant from the debates on the application of Marxism which wracked the German SDP, for example. The tone was set by trade unionists concerned first of all with economic questions and with the freedom to organise without state restriction, and either barely interested in more general questions, like the Empire, or else informed on these matters by the traditions of liberalism rather than by the developing ideas of socialism. Labour MPs were first elected as Liberals, and then with Liberal support, only forming a distinct Labour Party (which even then depended in significant measure on electoral arrangements with the Liberals for its successes) in 1906. In parliament, it was "moderate, pragmatic and without ambition"[53] and in the last years of the 19th century Labour MPs never once raised colonial issues in the House of Commons. However, by 1901 things had improved somewhat, to the extent that Keir Hardie and John Burns, who we have already encountered, did vote to cut appropriations for the administration in British Somaliland, in the Horn of Africa, on grounds of its brutal conduct.[54] By then, of course, the Boer War was making indifference to Empire no longer sustainable, but such Labour MPs as raised colonial questions still tended to dwell on "labour" problems among the subject peoples – the treatment of Chinese "coolies" in Transvaal for example – rather than the broader political issues of sovereignty, self-determination, and the link between empire and war. It was a start, nevertheless. "The 'capitalist exploitation' argument became Labour's special contribution to the Edwardian public debate about Empire", Bernard Porter writes.[55]

Hardie did give a lead on the Boer War, dissenting from the proposal to vote Lord Roberts, British Commander-in-Chief in the conflict, £100,000 for his eventually successful efforts to vanquish the enemy – worth nearly £11 million today, a quite extraordinary amount.[56] Most Labour MPs merely abstained. Chinese historian Tingfu Tsiang wrote later that "as one reads the speeches of the acquiescent majority of Labourites, one gets the impression that they would have liked to oppose the war more vigorously than they actually did, a failure more of moral courage than of intellectual conviction."[57]

This general indifference could not, of course, extend to the Irish question. The Irish people were entwined with the working-class in Britain and directly represented in the House of Commons, so Labour could scarcely avoid taking a stand. That stand was to support the constitutional nationalism of John Redmond's parliamentary nationalist party, which sought Home Rule through the British parliament, and which held almost all of the Irish constituencies in the House of Commons outside the Protestant settler areas of the north-east. As such, Labour led by Ramsay MacDonald opposed the Curragh mutiny, which saw British Army officers in Northern Ireland decline to act to curb Edward Carson's putative insurrection against the Liberal government's Home Rule proposal. However, Lenin's conclusion on this episode – "this lesson will not be lost on the British labour movement, the working class will now quickly proceed to shake off its philistine faith in the scrap of paper called the British law and constitution which the British aristocrats have torn up before the eyes of the whole people" [58] – was definitely on the optimistic side. Ramsay MacDonald was a long way from being ready to abandon his "philistine faith" in the British constitution.

This appearance of apathy could perhaps be extenuated by the argument that the colonies were not then engulfed in the mass struggles for freedom which began to develop between the world wars and reached a crescendo in the years after 1945. This, however, understates the degree of resistance to British rule already emerging among the subject peoples. The Ashanti people alone, in what is now Ghana in West Africa, fought no less than eight wars against the British.[59] The Sudanese had heroically resisted British occupation in the 1880s, earning the approbation of William Morris at the time. Like Belfort Bax, he took an advanced view on the question – "…the Mahdi is the representative of his countrymen in their heroic defence of their liberties…As to his fanaticism (which it seems must be condemned in him though praised in Gordon) you should remember that any popular movement in the East is bound to take a religious form…Surely it must be considered an article of faith with us to sympathise with all popular revolutionary movements though we may not agree with all the tenets of the revolutionaries". [60] Morris, writing 130 years ago, offers an approach worthy of robust emulation today.

On a smaller scale, episodes like the Dinshawai incident in Egypt, which saw brutal collective punishments meted out to villagers after they had scuffled with British officers, the latter being engaged in a lawless hunting expedition which had included the shooting of an Egyptian woman, pointed to a developing resistance which would in time become one of the defining movements of the twentieth century. Labour's general opposition to the conduct of colonial wars never led to an identification with the struggle of the oppressed. This was the limitation of the Christian-ethical and radical anti-imperialism which, in the absence of an ideologically formed socialist anti-imperialism, at least with any resonance in Britain, dominated the labour and progressive approach on the question. As was true on other issues, "the British labour movement derived its original understanding of imperialism from outside its own ranks", in the words of Stuart MacIntyre,[61] exemplifying the disjuncture between the growing organisation of the working-class in trade unions on the one hand, the strengthening of a class awareness and class attitudes, and a willingness to resist the depredations of the British ruling class at home, and on the other the small impact of socialist thought and indeed a reluctance to engage in the larger questions of politics and social organisation in any systematic way at all.

Or, as Karl Marx asserted back in 1870, the English had all they needed for socialism except "a sense of generalisation and revolutionary passion."[62]

The emergence of socialism

As Engels put it at the time: "…Today, there is indeed 'Socialism again in England', and plenty of it – Socialism of all shades, Socialism conscious and unconscious, Socialism prosaic and poetic, Socialism of the working class and of the middle class, for, verily, that abomination of abominations, Socialism, has not only become respectable, but has actually donned evening dress and lounges lazily on drawing-room causeuses." [63]

Engels, it is fair to say, had a dash of scepticism about the socialist organisations which emerged in Britain in his old age, preferring to focus his hopes on the great mass movement of workers in London's East End which from the late 1880s onwards laid the foundations for general trade unionism. His characterisation of the socialist movement cited above, written in 1892, betrays an exasperation born with intimate acquaintance of many of the leading personalities within it. The lazily-lounging, evening-dressed, middle-class socialists are easy to identify. They were surely members of the Fabian Society. Since the Fabians were not only middle-class themselves, but entirely oriented their activities towards shaping not merely middle-class but even ruling-class opinion, their outlook will be considered in the next section. If the work of socialists was to strive to effect the dialectical fusion of an ideology (socialism) with an agency (the working-class) then it is clear the Fabians were playing a different game altogether. They were representatives of a rival fusion, fairly described as social-imperialism.

The attitude of the rest of British socialism to the colonial question is well-captured in the resolution the British delegation (including representatives of both the Independent Labour Party and the Social Democratic Federation, discussed below) to the 1904 Congress of the Second International submitted to the Colonial Commission of the Congress: "Congress recognises the right of the inhabitants of civilised countries to settle in lands where the population is at a lower stage of development. However, it condemns most strongly the existing capitalist system of colonial rule and urges the Socialists of all countries to put an end to it...Since England has had most success in subjugating foreign nations, the effects on British India have been correspondingly greater and more formidable....Congress calls on the workers of Great Britain to compel their government to abandon its prevent infamous and degrading colonial system and to introduce the perfectly practicable system of self-government for the Indian people under English sovereignty."[64]

Here are all the contradictions, ambiguities, and downright errors of early British socialist thought on the matter. The citizens of "civilised" countries have the right to settle where they will (since everywhere else would be at a 'lower level of development') but an end must be put to "capitalist colonial rule" at the same time, even though, in keeping with the theory of stages of social development hegemonic among Marxists of the era, it was precisely capitalism which bestowed the higher level of civilisation! At any event, present colonial policies, at least in India (the Amsterdam Congress heard an unprecedented plea for freedom from an Indian representative) should be abandoned and replaced by self-government, even while British sovereignty is maintained for no very obvious purpose. This was neither an endorsement of the status quo nor a manifesto for liberation. Twentieth century events considerably overtook its provisions, of course, notwithstanding that the outlook expressed was far ahead of mean British working-class opinion of 1904.

Chapter Two will trace the evolution of the international socialist debate on imperialism and colonialism in general. Here we look at the emerging politics of the organisations which contributed to the drafting of this submission from British socialism, organisations now long departed from political life, leaving a heritage which has marked all subsequent efforts to establish revolutionary and anti-imperialist politics in the soil of the oldest imperial power. By way of a general contrast of the two principal organisations concerned, Otto Bauer's judgement represents something of a consensus: "...being incapable of uniting the broad masses of the English working class into a great political party, the English socialists were only able to build small propaganda-groups: the SDP (Social-Democratic Party) which propagated the ideas of Marxian socialism; the Independent Labour Party, which lagged far behind the SDP in theoretical clarity but knew better how to adapt its agitation to England's special conditions and to impart socialist ideas to the broad masses..."[65]

For Engels' "socialism of the unconscious", British workers had the Independent Labour Party. The ILP's motto might have been The Only Way is Ethics. Founded in 1893, the ILP "in their educational work among the trade unionists, hardly ever referred to revolution and class warfare, but started from the ethical, nonconformist and democratic sentiments which appeal most to British workmen,"[66] according to a contemporary socialist writer. In the more severe but basically complementary judgment of a Soviet historian the ILP's "brand of socialism was essentially a summary of ideas and wishes in respect of ethical reforms, acceptable to a great many people in Britain who were far from, and even hostile to, Marxism."[67] As for the Empire, "ILP thought on imperial questions was eclectic," Nicholas Owen writes, "but perhaps best distinguished as internationalist and pacifist…in its leanings."[68]

The ILP affiliated to the Labour Party from the outset and supplied not merely much of the early socialist thought in a federation otherwise dominated by trade unionists of limited political horizons, but also two of the party's most eminent leaders, Keir Hardie and Ramsay Macdonald. The one's reputation is covered in a roseate glow of principle, while the other has become a byword for betrayal. As far as the British Empire was concerned the two differed, but perhaps not by as much as one would have thought. Hardie was, in general, opposed to imperialism as he was opposed to capitalism. "Modern imperialism is in fact to socialists simply capitalism in its most predatory and militant phase," he wrote.[69] Macdonald was more verbose but in his own way no less clear: "So far as the underlying spirit of imperialism is a frank acceptance of national duty exercised beyond the nation's political frontiers, so far as it is a claim that a righteous nation is by its nature restless to embark on crusades of righteousness wherever the world appeals for help, the spirit of imperialism cannot be condemned…the compulsion to expand and assume world responsibility is worthy at its origins."

Restless for righteousness as he clearly was, MacDonald wrote a book on *Labour and Empire* in which he advocated a "socialist imperialism", no less, based on "pride of race" which "to its subject-races…desires to occupy the position of a friend." The Empire was a "historical fact" which must be accepted, he opined, in a fine example of that pragmatism for which the British labour movement was to become notorious in most other parts of the world. He had, however, resigned from the Fabian Society over the latter's support for the Boer War, one of several well-timed gestures which allowed Britain's first Labour Prime Minister to preserve for a generation a reputation as a man of integrity which was thoroughly undeserved.[70] Edward Said's judgement that MacDonald was "a critic of British imperialist practices but not opposed to imperialism as such," would come to seem a little on the generous side, if anything.[71]

Hardie took the greater interest in colonial issues, to the displeasure of the governing elite. The wife of the Viceroy of India, Lady Minto, strongly deprecated Hardie's visit to the Raj in 1908 – "It is monstrous these men coming out and trying to create further agitation". Her husband instructed that the Labour MP should be barred from addressing "inflammable populations" (or British troops) and bemoaned the lack of any legal grounds for immediately deporting him. Their worries were exaggerated: Hardie offered himself as an intermediary between the authorities and moderate Indian nationalists and when he returned to Britain went no further in the columns of the ILP's Labour Leader than urging Lord Minto (who had 'won golden opinions') to take a further bold step by appointing "an educated Indian gentleman as one of his private secretaries". Hardie had not, it seems, taken the full measure of the situation.[72]

MacDonald too offered himself as an intermediary in India. Minto was told by Lord Morley, India Secretary in the imperial government in London, that he was "a…Labour member of very superior quality", needing only to be "set on the right path". Morley was wiser than Minto, who still regarded the future head of the National Government of the 1930s as a liability on account of his association "with agitators of the worst type." MacDonald again wrote a book on the subject. The very title – *Awakening of India* – is question-begging. His analysis centred on religion and caste, in the finest orientalist fashion.[73]

The Independent Labour Party was not large by the standards of many continental Social-

Democratic parties of the time, but it had considerably more members than any of the other socialist parties in Britain of the time. Its paid-up membership doubled during the Boer War and its aftermath to around 10,000 and continued to rise thereafter. [74] Up until 1918 the Labour Party had no individual membership so the ILP largely played the part occupied thereafter by the Constituency Labour Parties, as the means through which people not content – or eligible – to be represented in the Party solely through their trade union could play their part. This gave it great weight in shaping the party's ideological orientation. The common ground of, and the limited differences between, MacDonald and Hardie defined not just the tone and template for Labour on the Empire question, but for its approach to the state and the ruling class in years to come.

There were socialists outside the ILP. Most of them were in the Party which set itself up as the organisation for Marx's followers in Britain, the Social Democratic Federation (later Party). The SDF's influence did not match that of the ILP (or the Fabian Society for that matter) but it did constitute, after much uniting, splitting, and re-unifying, the core of the Communist Party of Great Britain when the latter was eventually founded in 1920. Therefore, its strengths and weaknesses need some consideration since they tended to re-emerge in the history of the CPGB and the wider socialist movement down through the century.

Study of the SDF has long been inseparable from study of its founder and principal leader, Henry Myers Hyndman. He loomed far too large over its proceedings from its formation in 1881 until its split in 1916 over support for the First World War. Perhaps this was inevitable for a man who "may be the only Marxist leader in history who has played county cricket as a Gentleman."[75] If most of the leadership of the labour movement emerged politically from the embrace of the Liberal Party, Hyndman vaulted directly from Toryism to Marxism, or at least as far as his own understanding of the doctrine. His relationship with Marx himself was poisoned from an early stage after he presented a popularisation of Marxist political economy as his own work, without acknowledging its source. This was aggravated for Marx, and Engels too, for many more years, by doubts regarding his real political value to the movement. Anyone whose world view can fairly be described as going "…beyond Tory democracy (before Tory democracy was proclaimed) to Tory socialism; a socialism that had a strong colouring of nationalism, a deep belief in the liberal principles of the rights of small nations, more than a touch of Germanophobia, and a profound belief in the British navy"[76] was never likely to secure their undiluted approval.

Hyndman united in himself a dedication to the propagation of a socialism that at least owed enough to Marx for most British Marxists to rally around the SDF together with a lofty aversion, not shared by all the SDF membership, to engagement in the practical struggles of the working-class. These he regarded as irrelevant at best and an actual diversion from the argument for socialism at worst. Industrial action he had no more time for than would a *Daily Telegraph* leader writer. He wrote in 1903 that the SDF was "opposed to strikes altogether", and in 1907 argued that "we…are opposed to strikes in principle…political action is far safer, far better and far less costly." In 1912 after the great strike wave had started to roll through British industry from 1911 on, he was still at it: "…can anything be imagined more foolish, more harmful, more…unsocial than a strike? I have never yet advocated a strike."[77]

And then there was the British nationalism. In a Soviet view Hyndman's opinions "were a peculiar mixture of occasional Marxist concepts and imperialist and even racist notions. He regarded the Social Democratic Party as the elite of the working-class movement and acted to prevent closer contacts with the masses of workers."[78] All true, although Professor John Foster has persuasively argued that Hyndman was not always the chauvinist he later became. Indeed, in 1883 he denounced England as "the vampire of nations, the master of a system which forced foreign countries to exhaust alike their soil and their inhabitants by paying heavy tribute for loans to the capitalist class of Great Britain." [79] Nevertheless he carefully tended his obsession with the Royal Navy ("not an anti-democratic force" in his view), apparently desiring "a powerful Britain with a big navy so that when she became socialist she could spread enlightenment throughout her empire, and use her vast influence among the nations in favour of socialism."[80] The idea of world socialism being spread by the Royal Navy now seems absurd, but similar concepts, if less extremely formulated, were to endure on the left in Britain for another half-century or more. By the time the Boer War came Hyndman all-too easily persuaded himself that the SDF would be better off not pushing active opposition, despite having told an international congress that the conflict filled "us English socialists with mourning and shame". [81] The shame and mourning, it transpired, were for the edification of foreign socialists, his private views were different. "I fear the decay of our Empire has begun in earnest," he wrote in 1901, the key word here clearly being "fear". And later: "I begin to doubt whether we shall win this South African war; whether, in fact, it will turn out the beginning of the downfall of the British Empire."[82] Anti-war campaigning was a waste of effort.[83]

This vacillation was covered by a certain amount of anti-Semitism on Hyndman's part — blaming the war on Jewish finance — which, as we have seen, could easily dovetail both with extraneous elements that Hobson introduced into his analysis of imperialism and with sections of public opinion.[84] Blaming Jews clearly allowed Hyndman to bridge his sympathy with the small, struggling Boer nations on the one hand and his British nationalism on the other. The ruling class was in the hands of "their masters, the capitalist Jews" and their "Jew-jingo press". [85] This deplorable anti-Semitism did not go unchallenged within the SDF. Belfort Bax, and ultimately the party itself, dissociated themselves from anti-Semitism and went further, critiquing not just Hyndman's racist attitudes, but his sectarian politics, which often held the SDF aloof from working-class struggle, and his lack of an eye for the revolutionary opportunity. Bax regretted that: "Comrade Hyndman…should allow the weak and beggarly elements of British chauvinism within him run away with his feelings," while Russian exile Theodore Rothstein ridiculed the idea "that to fight against coercion in Ireland or the manifestation of famine in India or the war in South Africa is not the proper business of socialists, but their proper business is… 'to spread socialism'…it is not by preaching the gospel of discontent but by fighting the cause of the discontented that socialism becomes the all-conquering living force that it is."[86]

One James Connolly was even more scathing about the contents of *Justice*, effectively the SDF's newspaper, during the war:

> "…instead of grasping the opportunity to demonstrate the unscrupulous and bloodthirsty methods of the capitalist class, [it] strove to divert the wrath of the advanced workers from the capitalists to the Jews…until the paper became positively unreadable to any fair-minded man who recognised the truth, viz., that the war was a child of capitalist greed and inspired by men with whom race or religion were matters of no moment."[87]

The approach of Rothstein and Connolly dovetailed with arguments being developed by Lenin in Russia at the same time, although they could not have been aware of it.

These disputes underline that there was more to the SDF than Hyndman alone. The Falkirk branch of the party showed a very different spirit in greeting the victory celebrations at the end of the war, reporting that "while on all sides of the street the harlot, Capitalism, was decked in horrible array of all possible and impossible colours, there was projected from the windows of the SDF a transparency of five feet, giving the statistics of deaths in war, deaths in concentration camps, the number of paupers, the number of unemployed in Britain, the famine deaths in India, and the famine deaths, emigration and evictions in Ireland."[88] The different perspectives in the Party clashed frequently. Lenin wrote a contemporary review of the debate on foreign policy at the Party's 1911 conference, which pitted an internationalist left against Hyndman and the SDF executive. Hyndman "…allowed himself to be scared by the screams of the British bourgeois press about the 'German menace' and went so far as to assert that Britain had to arm for defence, that she had to have a powerful navy, that Wilhelm was the aggressive party." Zelda Kahan, a leader of the left in the Party, supported a resolution "calling for a determined struggle against all increases in armaments, and opposing all colonial and financial aggression." Lenin quotes her as telling delegates that "the British navy is kept to maintain the Empire. Never had the SDP made a bigger mistake than in identifying the Party with the jingoist warmongers."

However, "the entire Party Executive Committee, including Harry Quelch – we have to confess with shame – supported Hyndman." They moved an amendment arguing for "the maintenance of an adequate navy for national defence. Then, of course, it goes on to repeat all the 'good old words' – about combatting imperialist policy, about war against capitalism etc. All this honey, of course, was spoiled by a spoonful of tar, by the phrase recognising the need for an 'adequate' navy, a phrase that is bourgeois both in its evasiveness and in its pure chauvinism." Lenin accused Quelch – who he otherwise rather admired – of "miserable sophistry" for arguing that "if [the SDF] believe[s] in national autonomy, we must have national defence and that defence must be adequate, or it is useless. We are opposed to imperialism, whether British or German; the small nationalities under Prussian rule hate her despotism, and the small nations threatened by her regard the British Navy and German social-democracy as their only hope…" Hyndman's position narrowly prevailed on this occasion, and the *Daily Mail*'s welcome of his policy doubtless justified Lenin pointing out "how quickly those who step on the slippery slope of opportunism slide to the bottom!"[89]

Still, the SDF climbed back up, in an uneven ascent. Later the same year it united with an element of the much smaller Socialist Labour Party (a purist group, mainly strong in Scotland, which followed the tactical prescriptions of the US socialist sectarian Daniel De Leon), some ILP left-wingers and other socialist groups to form the British Socialist Party. The Socialist Unity conference report records the unanimous passage of a resolution expressing "its disgust and detestation at the acts of brigandage being committed by the Governments of France, Spain, Germany and Italy upon the inhabitants of North Africa. It includes in that condemnation the British Government, which has neglected to use its influence to prevent the war between Italy and Turkey and the protection of indigenous peoples." The resolution added that "all European governments are in reality controlled by an international gang of financial criminals, who use the force of their respective countries to shoot and kill foreign people."[90] The next year, at the first conference of the BSP proper, Harry Quelch clashed with Willie Gallacher, later to be one of the most eminent leaders of the CPGB and a Communist MP from 1935 to 1950. Quelch's attempts to separate good patriotism from bad imperialism were scorned by the delegate from Paisley. Gallacher said it "was no use juggling with the word patriotism…they could not have a Citizen Navy. They should condemn all idea of patriotism and all idea of militarism, unless it took the form of shooting down those who exploited them. They must stand as internationalists, and not trouble about nationalism."[91]

In these recurring debates we can see the emergence of the internationalist trend in British Marxism, which only grew in salience during the greater political conflicts concerning the First World War. There are other grounds on which the work of the SDF/BSP has been criticised, but it was only on the matter of imperialism and war that the contradictions within the party could become acute enough to generate the divisions which allowed it to lead the formation of the Communist Party. Other socialist organisations also played their part in that development. The diminutive SLP, with very limited purchase outside Scotland, was unequivocal in its condemnation of militarism and war, but its refusal to engage in any form of political action, preferring the promotion of industrial trade unionism, and its sectarian fissiparousness retarded its influence among the mass of workers. Nevertheless, its hostility to reformism in all its manifestations obviously pre-figured the division in the international socialist movement of which the formation of the Communist International was the eventual consummation.[92]

Social-Imperialism

Thus far we have described two of the great political currents of thought of the early twentieth century. Liberalism, the classical ideology of the bourgeois class, had fractured into liberal-imperialism, adapting to the exigencies of the latest stage of capitalist development, and radical anti-imperialism which, while far from rejecting capitalism in toto, stood out against the new dispensation and exerted a certain influence on the labour movement as the latter developed its political muscles at last. Socialism was fast gaining strength, despite being imperfectly disentangled from liberalism and as yet insufficiently rooted in the working-class and its struggles.[93] In the absence of a real Marxist appreciation of imperialism, both liberal-imperialism and radical anti-imperialism found their echoes among socialists, the latter obviously being preferable to the former. The third political position was social-imperialism, through which both Toryism and its ally Liberal Unionism tried to extend and embellish its political base in a way consistent with the shifting focus of the propertied interests they had long represented, as well as with neutralising the incipient threat of working-class socialism.[94]

Others had identified the clash of the age as being the opposition of socialism and imperialism. The genius of social-imperialism was that it tried to effect a coagulation of the two. This work could be approached from different directions. Great business interests could promote it to supply a solid material foundation of mass support for a modernising imperialist capitalism, while socialists could champion it, in one variant or another, as a means of providing the wherewithal for social reforms which obviated the need to expropriate the bourgeoisie, with all the associated disorder and difficulties that would entail. From either perspective it appeared to offer a way of avoiding the immense unpleasantness and upsets of class struggle. The founding idea of social imperialism was therefore the collaboration of classes in a common endeavour of promoting moderate reform and immoderate empire, and its social base was the better-off sections of the workers and the more sophisticated sections of the capitalists. There was no fixed dividing line between social-imperialism and the reform sections of liberal-imperialists, other than that the siren appeal of protectionism was greater for the former. Both agreed on the need for social improvements funded by the proceeds of an imperial business policy, the disagreement was over whether this funding should come from tariffs or from taxation.[95] It therefore constituted a broad and thorough programme for government, entrenching

Britain's place in the world and the place of the workers in Britain through state-led efficiency and investment, while also averting the problems associated with the relative industrial decline which was then starting to become both apparent and alarming to the British elite.[96]

From the conservative point of view, the classic expression of imperialism as a solution to the "social problem" was that voiced by the colonial adventurer Cecil Rhodes, who was famously quoted in Lenin's *Imperialism* as having returned from a visit to London's East End "…more than ever convinced of the importance of imperialism…My cherished idea is a solution of the social problem…In order to save the 40 million inhabitants of the UK from a bloody civil war, we colonial statesmen must acquire new lands to settle the surplus population, to provide new markets for the goods produced in the factories and mines. The Empire, as I have always said, is a bread and butter question. If you want to avoid civil war, you must become imperialists."[97]

Rhodes, however, was not at the centre of the British establishment. One who was, Tory minister George Wyndham, put in plainly after the 1906 general election had swept his party from office. "Two ideals, and only two, emerge from the vortex: 1. Imperialism, which demands unity at home between classes, and unity throughout the Empire…2. Insular socialism and class antagonism."[98]

The leading politician advocating a form of social-imperialism was Joseph Chamberlain, who migrated from the radical wing of the Liberal Party to becoming its leading Unionist, which by the end of the 19th century meant alliance with the Conservatives under the arch-imperialist Lord Salisbury. A municipal reformer in his home city of Birmingham, (clearing slums, taking control of the water supply, building libraries and other amenities) Chamberlain championed a policy of imperial tariffs on the national stage, in opposition to the entrenched dogma of free trade. He said of the Empire "our trade, the employment of our people, our very existence depend on it". He was at one and the same time the Colonial Secretary and the leading social reformer in the Conservative government.[99] In one historian's estimate he "…hated injustice and human suffering. He also hated inefficiency and it is sometimes difficult to tell which he hated more, injustice or inefficiency."[100] While Chamberlain struggled to turn the balance of the ruling class away from at least a general commitment to free trade at that stage, he immediately established an ideological base for cooperation with sections of labour and the socialist movement. Bernard Porter records that "many Labour MPs allied themselves with 'social imperialists' on issues of social reform."[101]1

The drift of Henry Hyndman into overt chauvinism has been described. He was, however, by no means the first nor the most significant social-imperialist from the socialist[102] side of the equation during this period. The leading individual on the left championing empire was Robert Blatchford, and the principle organised body was of course the Fabian Society. Blatchford was a journalist and campaigner who associated with but never really absorbed himself in the different socialist organisations. He had "the principle quality of flair – it was the secret of his audience among the masses."[103] His book, *Merrie England*, based on articles he had written for the *Clarion* newspaper he edited, sold two million copies in Britain and the USA, and has a fair claim to be the first mass popularisation of socialism in England – a socialism which, Blatchford was keen to underline at every turn, owed nothing at all to Marx. "I do not wish to stir up class hatred," he assured readers in another of his bestsellers *Britain for the British*.[104]

During the Boer War he made his position unambiguous: "When England is at war, I'm English. I have no politics and no party. I am English." He scorned those in the labour moment who took a different view. In 1908, he said that "Britain must defend her Empire or lose it", making his own preference plain, since loss "would be a bloody, a ruinous and horrible business."[105] The German socialist Georges Ledebour caused a stir at the 1907 Congress of the Socialist International in Stuttgart by accusing Blatchford of "making his daughter play 'Rule Britannia' on the piano to him every evening during the South African war."[106] True or not, it was indisputable that Blatchford, like Hyndman, "allied with some of the most reactionary elements in the country, endorsing the arms manufacturers' age-old plea, that guns and bigger guns alone could safeguard the peace."[107]

This was a socialism – and a very ably popularised socialism – unabashed about its alliance with the imperial nation-state. In 1909, Blatchford published a series of articles in the *Daily Mail* depicting German war preparations in lurid terms – "...I believe that Germany is deliberately preparing to destroy the British Empire and... I know that we are not able or ready to defend ourselves against a sudden and formidable attack."[108] The Executive of the Labour Party disavowed Blatchford's views as "absurd and wicked." So too did the SDP, with Zelda Kahan declaring that "if the SDP does not speedily...repudiate such bourgeois imperialist views then goodbye to it as a serious force in the national and international socialist movements." Of course, the opposition to Blatchford's warmongering was not that clear cut. Labour's alternative, at least according to MacDonald, included seeking an imperial accommodation with Germany in Asia Minor while Hyndman, SDP policy notwithstanding, continued to urge a £100 million increase in naval spending in the columns of the Conservative *Morning Post*.[109] However, it would be a mistake to assume that Blatchford's popularity rested on his chauvinism. It was his argument that only "better educated, better governed, better trained and better treated" masses could sustain the Empire which recommended his imperialism to working people, while it was the advantage to the Empire of such a policy which recommended his socialism to the elite, the *Daily Mail* editors included.[110]

Blatchford offered his popular audience a social-imperialism of the heart. The Fabian Society aimed at conquering the head, with its famous strategy of "permeation" of the elite with their ideas. This was not socialism through class struggle, indeed it was not a socialism that prioritised working-class organisation or agency at all.[111] The Fabians, never more than a few hundred intellectuals, mainly London-based, set as their aim the influencing of the ruling parties, Tory and Liberal (Labour only came later), in the direction of rational and scientific policies which would improve the lot of ordinary folk, for their own good and that of the Empire as a whole. Sidney Webb's belief that one could "further the socialist cause by gradually extending municipal enterprise, that is, by gas and water collectivism"[112] made for a natural fit with Chamberlain, who had terrified the Birmingham middle class "because of his far-reaching measures of socialisation"[113] during his time as Mayor, according to Baumgart. And there was nothing at all in Fabian thinking which would have hesitated at imposing the same benefits of sound bureaucratic governance on any other peoples fortunate enough to fall under British rule. "In England there was a 'Fabian imperialism' which saw no harm in Europe bestowing its civilisation on tropical lands and receiving their products in return: a fair exchange of glass beads for gold could not be called robbery," Victor Kiernan commented, acidly.[114]

In *Fabianism and the Empire*, published in 1900, the Society argued pragmatically that "the partition of the greater part of the globe among such Powers is, as a matter of fact that must be faced, approvingly or deploringly, now only a question of time; and whether England is to be the centre and nucleus of one of those Great Powers of the future, or to be cast off by its colonies, ousted from its provinces, and reduced to its old island status, will depend on the ability with which the Empire is governed as a whole." [115] Its leading eminences were of one view, George Bernard Shaw asserting that "a Fabian is necessarily an imperialist" while Sidney Webb threw his support behind the Liberal imperialist Lord Rosebery as the man most likely create a "collectivist, imperialist opposition party," clearly combining notions of socialism with the practice of empire. [116] Later, Webb derided the hands-off approach of the Indian Civil Service in running the Raj, urging instead "a bold policy of government exploitation", including state control of the railways, establishing government-run factories, and imposing a tobacco monopoly. Many of the standard remedies of Labour reformism were thus first advocated as a mechanism for intensifying colonial exploitation and development (the two notions were so often deliberately confounded in social-democratic rhetoric).[117]

The Fabians asserted during the Boer War that "states with a higher civilisation had a right to take over backward states" and Shaw argued for good measure that "if the Chinese themselves cannot establish order in our sense, the Powers must establish it for them," at a time when a condominium of the world's great powers was putting down the Boxer Rising in Beijing with exemplary ferocity.[118] The Fabians, however, seldom gave in to "jingo", and did not promote private interests, and that was their strength. They instead offered a rational and indeed an internationalist and public-spirited case for imperialism, which reached parts of the metropolitan democratic market which could not have been conquered by the blustering patriotism of Tory nationalism, nor easily seduced by the pieties of a Gladstonian liberal-imperialism. Shaw put it thus: "The notion that a nation has a right to do what it pleases with its own territory, without reference to the interests of the rest of the world, is no more tenable from international socialist point of view…than the notion that a landlord has a right to do what he likes within his estate without reference to the interests of his neighbours." Years later, and nearing the time when Labour was to be first entrusted with the seals of Her Majesty's Government, Chancellor-to-be and ILP stalwart Phillip Snowden was still leaning on the same argument – China had no right to "deprive the rest of the world of access to her natural resources" and "by no moral right may the ownership and control of the natural and material resources of a territory be regarded as the absolute monopoly of the people who happen to be settled there." [119]

That the social-imperialism of Blatchford and the Fabians, echoed as it was by the Hyndmanites in the SDF and accepted more passively by a number of trade union and ILP leaders, was well-adapted to its political environment can be measured in the fact that its underpinning arguments can still be heard today in almost every international crisis.

The first measure of the strength of these conflicting trends in the working-class movement – and there have been many since – was soon upon them.

And so to War

Improbable as it may now seem, the leadership of the British labour movement briefly came close to opposing the outbreak of the First World War on clear class lines. On August 1 1914 Keir Hardie and the more respectable Arthur Henderson (to be in the war cabinet before long) issued a declaration on behalf of the British Section of the Bureau of the Second International: "Hold vast demonstrations against war in every industrial centre…Workers, stand together therefore for peace! Combine and conquer the militarist enemy and the self-seeking Imperialists today, once and for all…Down with class rule. Down with the rule of brute force. Down with war…"[120]

This spirited rhetoric was, of course, as good as it was to get for some time to come. When the war explicitly foreseen by international socialism did indeed break out in 1914 as inter-imperialist jockeying passed from diplomacy, tariffs, and colonial conquests to the direct confrontation of arms, British labour, and British Socialists for the most part fell in line with their government, aping faithfully the attitude of every Socialist Party across Europe (the Russian and Serbian aside) including of course the mighty German SPD, lodestar of the International. Of all the vacillations and outright capitulations among the socialists of the warring powers in 1914, that of the British was among the least surprising. At the 1907 Congress of the Socialist International, to which we will return, a British delegate named Russell Smart had bluntly told the assembly:

> "No British government is capable of conducting a war without the consent of the overwhelming majority of the working class. But if the public were whipped up into a nationalist frenzy, then a military strike would be pure lunacy. In the struggle against war, therefore, under no circumstances can the British Social Democracy go beyond peaceful activity in Parliament, at conferences and in the streets…British soldiers do not shoot at the people…British freedom allows us to discuss this question without the least danger."[121]

There was little for the bourgeois parties in Westminster to fear in such an approach, the more so since the anticipated "nationalist frenzy" was indeed whipped up. Little street resistance or parliamentary opposition was mobilised, and no industrial action. The Labour and trade union leadership acquiesced in the outbreak of war, perhaps more with resignation than enthusiasm, and gave full practical support to the Liberal government in waging it. The final Labour Party statement contented itself with noting that the party had opposed the policy which had led to the war and expressing the hope that peace could be restored as soon as possible. When the Trades Union Congress considered the matter a few months later, it agreed (by 600 votes to seven) that the position of Britain and her allies was "completely justified and expresses its horror at the atrocities which have been committed by the German-Austrian military authorities…and hereby pledges itself to assist the government as far as possible in the successful prosecution of the war." [122] There was dissent within the movement from this endorsement of the conflict, but it did not include the leadership of the British Socialist Party which, under Hyndman's influence, declared its support for the war against the despised Germans whom he had spent so much time agitating against. Hyndman wrote that "…it was quite impossible for us to fail to recognise that, as a nation, we were bound…by solemn international treaties and international declarations…to declare war against the aggressor and disturber of Europe…"[123] The BSP followed this up with a manifesto urging support for the campaign to enlist in the armed forces, a move which, in the words of the Party's subsequent official history, "set the Party aflame" with resolutions of both support and opposition pouring in, starting an inner-party conflict which continued for nearly two years, and was in essence a continuation of the pre-war divisions over imperialism already described.[124]

Socialist resistance to the war was slow to develop. Hardie told his constituents in Merthyr Tydfil that "a nation at war must be united…With the boom of the enemy's guns within earshot the lads who have gone forth to fight their country's battles must not be disheartened by any discordant note at home." Ramsay MacDonald, who opposed the declaration of war on quasi-pacifist grounds, was likewise anxious to establish his patriotism above all else, and declared, four days in, that "whatever our view may be on the origin of the war, we must go through with it".[125] Manny Shinwell, then a Clydeside militant and later a Labour minister, was to write years later that MacDonald left his audiences hearing "a man who loathed past wars, regarded future wars with abhorrence, but carefully evaded giving his opinion on the basic question of the current one."[126] Although the small SLP did come out with an unequivocal denunciation of the war, the future Soviet Foreign Affairs Commissar Maxim Litvinov, then living in Britain, was justified in writing to Lenin in early 1915 that "in England a left tendency does not exist."[127]

As opposition did eventually grow, it was still anxious to appear as respectable as possible. The ILP was pushed into supporting an anti-conscription movement by a rank-and-file infused with pacifism. It spent some energy on formulating hypothetical democratic peace plans to end the conflict, but it neither broke with the Labour Party leadership nor, under MacDonald's guidance, tried to build a campaign to stop the war.[128] The struggle within the BSP was sharper, as the more securely-grounded anti-capitalism of its membership pushed back against Hyndman's increasingly noxious chauvinism.[129] The BSP Executive by a narrow majority supported the Zimmerwald conference in 1915, summoned by anti-war (but not, in their majority, revolutionary) opponents of the war in the international socialist movement, a decision which the Hyndmanites continued to publicly oppose. The British government prohibited delegates from attending the conference in Switzerland, and in October 1915 the BSP was still qualifying its view that "the continuation of the war…imperils the future of socialism" with a pledge that "all action should be rigorously avoided calculated to endanger national defence", but the dam was starting to break.[130]

On the Clyde, John Mclean (a BSP member) led the anti-war fight in spite of his party's line. He was the most remarkable socialist leader in Britain of the period, self-sacrificing and unswerving in his commitment to the working-class cause, and deeply versed in Marxism. In the assessment of Willie Gallacher, Chair of the Clyde Workers Committee and a comrade of MacLean in Glasgow during the war, "MacLean never dealt in 'abstract' Marxism of the Kautsky variety. He applied his Marxist knowledge to the events around him and used all that was happening to show the truth of Marxism. He demonstrated in the clearest manner that the war was a war for trade and brought out into full relief the sinister robber forces behind it."[131] The Clyde Workers Committee was an 'unofficial' body which united the workers in the key factories (and across the BSP/ILP/SLP division of socialists too) in campaigning against the economic and industrial consequences of the conflict, although not against the war itself until fairly late in the day. Its merit was that, in contradistinction to the leadership of the labour movement, it was not prepared to suspend or play down the struggle around economic and social demands on account of the war. MacLean himself was perhaps the only leading British socialist of the period who displayed consistent revolutionary will and grasped the changing nature of the world struggle, and he was duly persecuted by the authorities again and again for his pains. In east London Sylvia Pankhurst, broadening her perspective from women's suffrage to socialism, also led mass campaigns uniting the basic demands of the workers with anti-war agitation.[132]

The main clash of opinions was within the British Socialist Party. However, it was not until 1917 that the anti-war agitation which eventually overwhelmed the Hyndman leadership of the BSP began to take hold on significant sections of the wider working class – the BSP debates initially only engaged a small minority. The Party leadership's position was strictly in line with what became the precepts of Kautsky – the war was unfortunate, but Socialists could do nothing about it, even if they wished to, so they must guard their unity "ready to resume our work in the class struggle when peace shall be proclaimed," in the words of an editorial in Justice.[133] This position now seems a surpassing stupidity. However, it was the one advocated at the time not by the out-and-out social-chauvinists but by the champions of Marxist orthodoxy, who believed domestic social combat required global peace, and could not see imperialism and war as a front-line – the front-line – of class struggle, making the ruling elites more vulnerable to revolutionary overthrow than ever before. From this view it was easy to take the further step and believe that the best conditions for "class struggle" would be created by the victory of one's own Empire. Even Belfort Bax, whose advanced views on colonial issues have already been noted, succumbed. "Prussia-ridden Germany is now the enemy of not only democracy and Socialism but of the entire human race. Is it not time that the apologists for Prussian militarism and its inhuman and dastardly crimes were eliminated from the ranks of Socialist bodies?" he wrote. Articles such as this led party activist Joe Vaughan, later the Communist mayor of his east London borough of Bethnal Green, to describe *Justice* as "a dirty rag" and Maclean to establish his own paper, *Vanguard*, in opposition to it.[134]

Vanguard, supporting Maclean's view that "the only war worth waging is the class war", was by the end of 1915 demanding not only a sharpening class struggle and the preparation of "drastic revolutionary action" but also raising the need to "purify our parties" and criticising the vacillations of the anti-war elements in the BSP leadership who nevertheless trimmed in the interests of party unity.[135] The split eventually came at Easter 1916 (while the Irish rising was gripping Dublin) when the increasingly super-heated chauvinism of the Hyndmanites, who had established their own British Workers Defence League, was finally repudiated by the majority of delegates. Hyndman led his supporters out of the conference, both they and the cheering majority singing the 'Red Flag' in opposition to each other. This, however, did not lead to the kind of revolutionary anti-war movement advocated by Maclean. The BSP instead adopted a broadly pacifist position and took its main task as being the education of "…the workers so that when the hour of the social revolution strikes, they will have the necessary training and discipline to accomplish their emancipation", while avoiding "hunger revolts which will lead to the transformation of our towns and cities into bloody shambles" and "ill-directed demonstrations of the workers" in the words of Chairman Sam Farrow.[136] Kendall seems fair in describing this position as political disarmament before the ruling class. Nevertheless, the BSP – now an affiliate to the Labour Party after an earlier sectarian hiatus – increasingly united the majority of anti-war and anti-imperialist activists in campaigning, in the midst of the world slaughter, for both peace and socialism. It was to take the Russian example to move things on a stage further, in terms not only of preparedness for revolutionary action but also in opening up before British socialists a much broader and more dialectical view of the world struggle in the age of imperialism. We will trace the emergence of these perspectives in the next chapter.

Conclusion

Eric Hobsbawm's later stricture, that "…the left never wavered in its condemnation of colonial wars and conquests.…Yet, with the rarest exceptions …western socialists did little actually to organise the resistance of colonial peoples to their rulers, until the era of the Communist International"[137] is justified. Even prior to the Russian revolution and the formation of the Comintern, the most advanced socialists in Britain were moving to a new understanding, but this was a hesitant process and by no means reflected a majority position among British socialists, still less the labour movement as a whole.

Two positions predominated among socialists and trade unionists alike. The first was frank support for the Empire and the state, while reserving the right to criticise and condemn particular excesses or brutalities and holding out the eventual prospect of a greater degree of self-rule by colonial populations than the imperialist elite might admit. This view, the majority one, was underpinned not just by an attitude of capitulation to imperialist culture and propaganda, but also by a conviction that the strength of the Empire, and British capitalism in general, was essential for the prosperity of the working class at home. It was unequivocal, therefore, in supporting the British Empire in the 1914-18 war.

The second outlook – not all that far from the first in practical application – opposed imperialism on both ethical (ILP) and economic (Hobson) grounds. Both were grounded less in socialism than a radicalism itself ultimately sourced in the Liberal party – radical liberalism being in general the political point of departure for the nascent labour movement of the early twentieth century. This held that Britain itself would be better off, or more true to its own liberal ideals, without colonialism. This position could easily be swayed to an opposition to the War, but only of the most passive and cautious kind, neither exactly wiling the Empire's victory nor its defeat.

The third position, of working to bring down the Empire in a struggle of unity with movements for resistance and independence in the colonies, and of looking at the war as an opportunity for revolution, rather than a reason for its postponement, was only adhered to by a vanishingly small section of the left. Despite the red shoots identified above, this only really started to change in 1917, with the Russian revolutions, which showed the possibility of a serious challenge to the ruling classes, and the apparent intractability of the war (and the impossibility of it being ended by any other methods) starting to impose new perspectives.

Notes
1   *The Origins of British Bolshevism* by Raymond Challinor (London:1977) p21
2   *Marxism and Imperialism* by Victor Kiernan (London: 1974) p x. Burns, to be sure, did go on to oppose the First World War, unlike Crooks, resigning as President of the Board of Trade at the outbreak.
3   *Insurgent Empire* by Priyamvada Gopal (London: 2019) p.4
5   *The Making of British Socialism* by Mark Bevir (Princeton/Oxford: 2011) devotes a chapter to the neglected figure of Bax, exploring his unusual philosophical approach to Marxism. Alas, his anti-imperialism is not specifically considered. See pp 45-64
6   *Discovering Imperialism* by Richard B. Day and Daniel Gaido (eds) (Leiden/Boston: 2012) pp 11-13
7   *Ibid* p 411
8   Kiernan, (1974) p 7
I9 *Imperialism and World Economy* by Nikolai Bukharin (London:1972[1916]) p 85
10 *Pax Britannica* by Jan Morris (London:1992 [1968]), pp1-2; this is the second volume of Morris's history of the British Empire, probably the pinnacle of bourgeois-inflected writing on the question
11 *The British Labour Movement* by A.L. Morton and George Tate (London:1956) p 133
12 *Unfinished Empire* by John Darwin (London:2012) p 185; statistics are taken from here, and from *The Empire Project* by John Darwin (Cambridge:2009) pp 274-77
13 *Global Capitalism* by Jeffrey A. Frieden (New York: 2006) p.50
14 *The Transformation of the World* by Jürgen Osterhammel (Princeton, N.J.: 2014) p 454. This is a panoramic survey of global 19th century history by a contemporary German historian
15 Darwin (2009) p. 273
16 Darwin (2012) p. 185; "…Britain was quite unlike its main economic rivals. It was not just an industrial state, but an agency state (providing commercial services) and a rentier state as well, drawing a huge proportion of its wealth from these latter functions where the growth of international competition was much less acute," he writes in Darwin (2009) p 275
17 These figures from Bukharin (1972) p 43; Eric Hobsbawm in *Age of Empire* (London:1987) p 355 gives the following proportions for British overseas investments in 1911-13: Empire 46%; Latin America 22%; USA 19%; Europe 6%; elsewhere 7%.

18 George Goschen cited in *British Imperialism 1688-1914* by P.J. Cain and A.G. Hopkins (London/New York: 1993) pp 172-3. Goschen was speaking in the 1880s, when this expansion was still in its earlier phase.
19 Cain/Hopkins (1993) p 84
20 Osterhammel, (2014) p 458. The Austro-Marxist leader Otto Bauer broadly agreed, writing in 1907, but correctly introducing industrial capital into the equation: "Great Britain…is more and more turning from an industrial state into a rentier state. The newly-accumulated capital does not flow to domestic production in order to export goods to foreign countries, it is rather invested in other continents. It builds railways in America and canals in Egypt; it develops gold mines in South Africa. Behind imperialist policy stand not only the stock-exchange' great banks and holders of foreign and colonial bonds, but also great industrial capitalists, especially the heavy-iron industry…."; in Day and Gaido (2012) p 316
21 *The Growth of Working-Class Reformism in Mid-Victorian England* by Neville Kirk (Beckenham:1985) p 174
22 *Humanitarian Imperialism* by Jean Bricmont (New York: 2006), p 29. The witticism is allegedly attributable to Bertrand Russell in its original form
23 *Gladstone* by Roy Jenkins (London: 1995), pp 500-1
24 This judgement is to be found in The Lords of Human Kind by Victor Kiernan (Harmondsworth: 1972), p xxx
25 *The Crisis of Britain and the British Empire* by R. Palme Dutt (London: 1953) p 277
26 Osterhammel, (2014) p451; Rosebery himself mixed God and Mammon in different proportions, defining his Liberal imperialism as about 1) maintaining the Empire; 2) extending it to relocate surplus population, 3) suppressing the slave trade and 4) developing Britain's commerce; see *Imperialism* by Winfried Baumgart (Oxford 1982 [1975]) p 170
27 Nor indeed was Hobson actually anti-imperialist. His focus was not really on imperialism at all but on policies for social reform in Britain and his book was, like Lenin's later work, very much a political intervention, in his case into debates on the origin of the Boer War.
28 *Imperialism* by J.A. Hobson (London: 1902) p 85
29 *Ibid* p 90-1
30 *The Absent-Minded Imperialists* by Bernard Porter (Oxford: 2004) p 218
31 Hobson (1902) pp 86, 88
32 Bogdanor (2022) p 71
33 Bogdanor (2022) p 71
34 See *The Imperial Controversy* by Andrew Murray (Croydon: 2009) pp 44-46 for detail
35 Hobson (1902) p 143
36 *Ibid*, pp 364, 367
37 *Ibid* p 142
38 Kiernan (1974) p 3
39 Day and Gaido (2012) p 14; in *Imperialism* Hobson asks rhetorically "does anyone seriously suppose that a great war could be undertaken by any European state, or a great State loan subscribed, if the House of Rothschild and its connexions set itself against it?", (op cit. p 57) , a formula which has launched a thousand conspiracy theories, unexhausted to this day. This deplorable aspect of Hobson's thinking hit the headlines in 2019 when the fact that Jeremy Corbyn had written a foreword to an edition of *Imperialism* was adduced as further evidence of his alleged anti-Semitism as part of a broad anti-Labour campaign. It is fair to say that Hobson's anti-Semitism, while reprehensible, only accounts for the smallest part of this work, and is entirely peripheral and superfluous to its analysis.
40 See *Empire* by Niall Ferguson (London: 2003) pp 280-82 for examples. However, even Ferguson, an uber-apologist for Britain's Empire, largely in the hope of persuading the USA to operate on similar principles in the present century, does allow that the radical anti-imperialists were "not entirely wide of the mark" in suggesting that private finance was manipulating government policy for its own ends at the time.
41 Bogdanor, (2022) p 341
42 *Collected Works of Marx and Engels* (Moscow/London: 1975-2004) vol 46 p 322
43 *Ibid* vol 48 p 418
44 *Condition of the Working-Class in England* by Frederick Engels (London: 2009 [1845]) p 47

45 Hobson, (1902) p 97
46 See the 2022 TUC resolution urging a trade union campaign for increased military spending, passed by a small majority.
47 Kiernan (1974) p 56
48 *Imperialism and the British Labour Movement 1914-1964* by P. S. Gupta (London/Basingstoke: 1975) p 12
49 Hobsbawm, (1987) p 70
50 Kiernan (1974) p 55
51 Porter (2004) pp203-7. Lucas's view was that the College should aim "not to…enable the workers to climb the social ladder, but merely to make the poor man happier with his lot."
52 *Empire* by Denis Judd (London: 1996) p. 209; Porter (2004) p 209
53 Francois Bedarida in *Histoire Generale du Socialisme* tome 2 edited by Jacques Droz (Paris: 1974) p 385.
54 *Labour and Empire* by Tingfu F. Tsiang (New York/London: 1923) p 85
55 Porter (2004) p 218
56 Roberts was clearly worth it – he had also played a key part in the suppression of the great Indian uprising against British rule in 1857. Nevertheless, history must record that British MPs voted a considerable fortune in thanks to the man who first developed the concentration camp. As for Hardie, he advocated the vote for black men in Cape Colony and Natal, but not in Transvaal and the Orange Free State.
57 Tsiang (1923) pp 82-3. "The predominant characteristic of the reaction of British labour to British imperialism in Africa from 1880 to 1920 is acquiescence." (p 95)
58 Lenin, *Collected Works* volume 20 p 228
59 See *Empire or Democracy?* by Leonard Barnes (London: 1939) p 125ff for details
60 *The Blood Never Dried* by John Newsinger (London: 2006), pp 97-98. This is an excellent brief study of the unvarnished history of the British Empire.
61 'Imperialism and the British Labour Movement in the 1920s '(*Our History Journal* 64) by Stuart MacIntyre (London: 1975) p 3
62 *Marx/Engels* vol 21 pp118-19
63 Engels (2009) p 48
64 *History of The International* volume one by Julius Braunthal (New York: 1967 [1961]) p 312
65 Day and Gaido (2012) p 404
66 *A History of British Socialism* volume two by Max Beer (London: 1919) p.
67 *The International Working-Class Movement* volume three by Boris Ponomarev et al (eds) (Moscow:1983) p 336
68 Nicholas Owen in *The Twentieth Century* (Oxford History of the British Empire) by Judith Brown and Wm Roger Louis (eds) (Oxford: 1999) p 191
69 Dutt (1953) p 322
70 Newsinger (2006) p 146
71 Gopal (2019) p 31
72 Kiernan (1974) p x; *The British Left and India* by Nicholas Owen (Oxford: 2007) p 55
73 Owen (2007) pp 92, 89
74 *British Workers and the Independent Labour Party* by David Howell (Manchester: 1983) pp328ff
75 *British Workers and the Independent Labour Party* by David Howell (Manchester: 1983) pp328ff
76 Bill Baker in *Our History* 59 (Summer 1974), a publication of the CPGB, p 3
77 *The Revolutionary Movement in Britain 1900-21* by Walter Kendall (London: 1969) pp 28-29. At the same time as Hyndman was denouncing strikes, the head of Special Branch was warning the Cabinet that Britain was heading for a revolution "unless there was a European war to divert it"; See Porter (2004) p 219. Hyndman proved to be on the side of diversion rather than revolution.
78 Ponomarev et al (1983) p 336
79 John Foster in *Marx Memorial Library Bulletin* (Autumn 1984), which includes the text of his lecture on "The Merits of the SDF", p 33
80 Baker (1974) p 4; on another occasion Hyndman wrote that "it is sad to witness the decay of any great nation; it is saddest to witness the deterioration of our own"; see *Propaganda and Empire* by John MacKenzie (Manchester: 1984) p 229
81 Braunthal (1967) p 309

82 *Ibid.* p 10
83 In the dry judgement of Paul Kennedy: "…Marxist rhetoric was, moreover, blended into the more traditional Radical-pacifist thought of the British left, and together they ensured that the movement as a whole remained critical of the ententes (particularly with Russia), demanded an end to the naval race, sought to control Grey's diplomacy and sent frequent messages of goodwill to their German opposite-numbers." See *The Rise of Anglo-German Antagonism* (New York: 1980) p 331
84 For example, 83 Trade union officials condemning Boer War claimed that "the capitalists who brought up or lured the Press both in South Africa and in England to clamour for war are largely Jews or foreigners;" Gupta (1975) p 10
85 *Ibid.* p 6
86 *Ibid* p 11. Theodore Rothstein was the father of Andrew Rothstein, an important figure in the CPGB's history, and a member from its beginning to its end.
87 Challinor (1977) p 14
88 *Ibid.* p 15
89 *Ibid.* p 15
90 Official Report of the Socialist Unity Conference, 1911, p 14
91 *The First Annual Conference of the British Socialist Party 1912 Official Report*, p 20
92 See Kendall (1969) pp 75-75 and also Challinor (1977) for a more positive view of the SLP. *Pioneering Days* by Thomas Bell (London: 1941) gives a feel for the work of the SLP by a working-class activist later prominent in the CPGB.
93 "The establishment of the British Socialist Party was definitely a step forward in the development of the socialist movement in Britain. However, the Socialists failed to lead the mass upsurge of the working-class movement or have any serious impact on it." Such is the verdict, generally not contested, in Ponomarev (1983) p 338
94 This was explicit. In 1910 Conservative election propagandist J.L. Garvin – an early spin-doctor – set as the party's aim winning over working-class voters on the basis of the compatibility of "their dream…Socialism and the earthly paradise…" and "our dream – imperial strength and industrial security based upon Tariff Reform." See M.E. Chamberlain in *British Imperialism in the Nineteenth Century* by C.C. Eldridge (ed) (London/Basingstoke: 1984) p 165
95 See Baumgart (1982) pp 165-177 for a discussion of this.
96 Polish Socialist Julian Marchlewski, writing on the subject of British imperialism in 1904 pointed out that "… 'the decline of British industry' has become a slogan for the imperialist agitators to bait the masses. For England's working class, the decline of British industry would undoubtedly be a fearful danger…" In Day and Gaido (2012) p 305
97 *Imperialism, the Highest Stage of Capitalism* by V.I. Lenin (Moscow: 1952 [1916]) pp 93-94. Lenin's quotation is not entirely accurate. The original rendering, which has been tracked down, has Rhodes declaring still more colourfully "if you have not to be cannibals, you have got to be imperialists." See Max Beer in Day and Gaido (2012) p 104-5
98 Bogdanor (2022) p 839
99 Day and Gaido (2012) p 105
100 M.E. Chamberlain in Eldridge (1984) p 155
101 *British Imperial* by Bernard Porter (London/New York: 2016) p 65. "…the British Empire even had a number of professed socialists running it…At the turn of the twentieth century, socialist imperialism along these lines was fairly common: based on the idea, not of abolishing the Empire, but turning it into a socialist commonwealth;" *ibid.* p 31
102 In this context the use of the term "socialism" and its derivatives relates to the professed aspirations of people like Blatchford, a profession taken as sound currency by millions at the time. It is of course fair to argue, as we will subsequently, that the socialist side of social-imperialism was in fact slight to non-existent. That is something which only became apparent rather later, as socialism itself became refined in both theory and practice.
103 Bedarida in Droz (1974) p 377
104 Challinor (1977) pp 20-21. Curiously, "Britain for the British" was the slogan which Harry Pollitt (who did wish to stir up class hatred) wanted to see the CPGB adopt in September 1939 at the start of World War Two, doubtless recollecting the socialist literature of his youth in the movement.
105 *Class or Nation* by Neil Redfern (London/New York: 2005) p 25
106 *The Second International* by James Joll (London/Boston: 1974[1955]) p 125

107 Kendall (1969) p 51
108 *Ibid.* p 52
109 Tsiang (1923) pp141-42; Kennedy (1980) p 331; Kendall (1969) . p 52
110 Kennedy, op. cit. p 331. This episode may represent the only time the *Daily Mail* has given such space – nine articles – to a self-declared socialist. Blatchford renounced socialism after the war, but never nationalism.
111 It was not in fact socialism at all, although many regarded it as such at the time.
112 Bevir, (2011) p 186. "Webb saw no need for a radical break with capitalism or a sudden shift in the underlying constitution of social life. Socialism would evolve gradually." (*ibid*)
113 Baumgart (1982) p 174
114 Kiernan (1974) p 7; similarly Nicholas Owen writes that "…some Fabians saw imperialism as a necessity in an era of fiercely competing nation-states, to be pursued in the name of 'national efficiency' and turned, where possible, into progressive channels;" Brown and Louis (1999) p 191
115 Dutt (1953) p 323
116 Redfern (2005) p 25
117 Owen (2007) p 98
118 Gupta (1975) p 11; Day and Gaido (2012) p 22
119 Cited in *Labour – A Party Fit for Imperialism* by Robert Clough (London: 1992) pp 40, 42
120 *Hesitant Comrades* by Geoffrey Bell (London: 2016) p 3
121 *Lenin's Struggle for a Revolutionary International* by John Riddell (ed) (New York: 1984) pp 75-6
122 Tsiang (1923) pp 176-77, 180.
123 *Social-Democracy in Britain* by H.W. Lee and E. Archbold (London: 1935) p 222. This official history, produced by the remnants of the SDF years later, presents the Hyndman case throughout. The authors' lack of perspective is illustrated by the fact that, immediately after the passage quoted, they discuss staffing problems at the Party's printing operation!
124 *Ibid.* p 227
125 Challinor (1977) p 124; Morton and Tate (1956) p 256
126 *Under Siege* by Ian Bullock (Edmonton, Canada: 2017) p 44
127 *War on War* by R. Craig Nation (Chicago: 2009 [1989]) p 51
128 *Ibid..* pp 119-120
129 He denounced in 1916 mildly anti-war articles in the ILP press as having been paid for by German money.
130 Riddell (1984) p 436; Kendall (1969) p 97
131 *Revolt on the Clyde* by Willie Gallacher (London: 1978 [1936]) p 37.
132 Such is the view of Walter Kendall: "British history before 1917 contains no trace of a Bolshevik will to power except in the revolutionary ardour of John MacLean, nor, indeed, in the latter's case, of any slight indication of Bolshevik organisational conceptions," Kendall (1969) p 234. On this point, he seems correct. For the activities of Pankhurst see *Sylvia Pankhurst* by Katherine Connelly (London: 2013) pp 67-86 in particular.
133 Kendall (1969) p 86
134 *Ibid* p 94-6
135 *Ibid* p 99
136 *Ibid* p 173
137 Hobsbawm (1985) p 72

Illustration overleaf
VI Lenin

Chapter Two
The World Revolution in Marxist Thought (1848-1914)

WHEN THE Communist Party of Great Britain was established in 1920, it was as a section of the Communist International (Comintern), the party of world revolution. The road to the Comintern was the second inheritance of the CPGB, and it brought with it several novelties and inputs quite absent from the traditions of the British labour and socialist movements, already outlined. The distinctive features of this inheritance were also preponderantly to do with imperialism and how Marxist socialism should respond to its development as the pivotal element of world capitalist economics and politics over the generation before the First World War.

The debates we trace here also gave shape to the concept of "world revolution" as a response to the new politics of the imperialist age, and invested that term, already familiar to the workers' movement, with a fresh content and usage. Prior to the First World War, it would only be a small exaggeration to say that when socialists spoke of a "world revolution" they really meant the more-or-less simultaneous victory of the proletariat in the developed parts of Europe and perhaps North America, a sort of 1848 writ larger. The rest of the world, from peasant Europe to the colonies and semi-colonies, would follow in the train of the industrialised heartlands, which represented the *vanguard* of human progress and thus held a monopoly on political initiative. Even those on the radical left who seriously grappled with the question of imperialism in the decade or so before the great conflict remained to a large extent prisoners of this outlook. Rosa Luxemburg, the most passionate critic of capitalist colonialism, wrote as late as 1916, in her celebrated *Junius* pamphlet, that "only from Europe, only from the most modern capitalist states, when the hour is ripe, can the signal for social revolution and the liberation of humanity emerge. Only the English, French, Belgian, German, Russian and Italian workers can collectively lead the army of exploited and enserfed peoples of the seven continents."[1] These ideas were to be hard a-dying, in part because they were not entirely wrong – when the signal came it was indeed from Russia, the least developed of the six countries Luxemburg listed. But the Europe-first perspective was only by stages and through struggle enriched with that new understanding of revolution – democratic, national, and socialist entwined – which imperialism made not just possible but essential.

Marx and Empire

The word "imperialism" does not occur in the works of Karl Marx. A lively and continuing argument debates whether the concept does, at least in any meaningful form.[2] Much of this debate cannot usefully inform our present purpose, since it relies on the assessment of documents, including copious notebooks, which were not published in Marx's lifetime or for many years after and were therefore as unknown to the socialist movement of the late 19th and early 20th centuries as were the *Grundrisse* or the "Paris Manuscripts". Indeed, the arguments of those, like Kevin Anderson and Lucia Pradella, who claim that Marx *did* have a well-worked out theory of imperialism rest heavily on access to notebooks written in Marx's last years which are only now available for study, in the 21st century, courtesy of the immense MEGA project.[3]

So, in tracing the emergence of socialist anti-imperialism and the contribution of Marx and Engels to this, we must rely on such of their writings as were available to Kautsky, Lenin, Hilferding, Luxemburg and the rest (including those socialists who tried to use Marx's works to justify, rather than oppose, capitalist colonialism).

On the one hand, Marx wrote a lot about colonialism and colonial wars, and also about Ireland and Poland, two oppressed (and European) countries marginal to industrial development in the 19th century. Much of this was in his journalism published in the *New York Tribune*. On the other hand, he definitely ceased his great theoretical labours before the development of modern imperialism, including the systemic export of capital and the wholesale division of the world, became the leading dynamic in the world economy. Naturally, his views on the impact and consequences of colonialism matured over the years. On this matter, Marx's Hegelian inheritance was at best a mixed blessing, given Hegel's ingrained eurocentrism and disdain for the Indian and other "historyless" peoples.[4] Hegel was, amongst his many other views, inclined to racism. Africa, he wrote "...is no historical part of the world; it has no movement or development to exhibit. Historical movement in it...belongs to the Asiatic or European world....What we properly understand by Africa is the unhistorical, undeveloped Spirit, still involved in the conditions of mere nature..."[5] Nor did Asia fare any better: "The English, or rather the East India Company, are the lords of [India]; for it is the necessary fate of Asiatic Empires to be subjected to Europeans; and China will, some day, be obliged to submit to this fate." The "diffusion of Indian culture is only a dumb, deedless expansion" and in India itself "...neither morality, nor justice, nor religiosity is to be found."[6] More: "Deceit and cunning are the fundamental characteristics of the Hindoo. Cheating, stealing, robbing, murdering are with him habitual."[7] There is no space here to do justice to the full richness of Hegel's theory of history, the school in which Marx's own views ripened, but it suffices to say that he saw most of humanity as requiring the external animating intervention of European civilisation in order to hit history's highway.

There is no question of Marx having taken over these views wholesale. Nevertheless, the general civilizational argument of Hegel was not "stood on its head", along with the master's philosophical method, as sharply as it might have been. The early Marx tended rather to invest the history and progress of nations with materialist content without fully addressing the underlying assumptions about the legitimacy of the domination of the more advanced systems, whether they owed their position to the workings of Hegel's World Spirit or to the forces of production.

This legacy certainly contributed to the celebration of bourgeois progress over "barbarian" people in *The Communist Manifesto* of 1848 and to Marx's ambivalence in his early writings on British colonialism. Famously, he wrote of British rule in India in 1853 (before the great rebellion):

> "England, it is true, in causing a social revolution in Hindostan, was actuated only by the vilest interests, and was stupid in her manner of enforcing them. But that is not the question. The question is, can mankind fulfil its destiny without a fundamental revolution in the social state of Asia? If not, whatever may have been the crimes of England she was the unconscious tool of history in bringing about that revolution."[8]

He elaborated extensively on this viewpoint in a further article the same year: "The introduction of railroads may be easily made to subserve agricultural purposes by the formation of tanks, where ground is required for embankment, and by the conveyance of water along the different lines. Thus irrigation, the *sine qua non* of farming in the East, might be greatly extended, and the frequently recurring local famines, arising from the want of water, would be averted....

> "I know that the English millocracy intend to endow India with railways with the exclusive view of extracting at diminished expenses the cotton and other raw materials for their manufactures. But when you have once introduced machinery into the locomotion of a country, which possesses iron and coals, you are unable to withhold it from its fabrication...the railway-system will therefore become, in India, truly the forerunner of modern industry...

> "The Indians will not reap the fruits of new elements of society scattered among them by the British bourgeoisie, till in Great Britain itself the now ruling classes shall have been supplanted by the industrial proletariat, or till the Hindoos themselves shall have grown strong enough to throw off the English yoke altogether....

> "When a great social revolution shall have mastered the results of the bourgeois epoch, the market of the world and the modern powers of production, and subjected them to the *common control of the most advanced peoples* [emphasis added], then only will human progress cease to resemble that hideous, pagan idol, who would not drink the nectar but from the skulls of the slain."[9]

These passages identify the tensions within Marx's thought on the question at that stage in his work: The priority given to imported technical development as the engine of progress, the supposed inertia of traditional society being broken up by a bourgeoisie acting in its own self-interest (and with considerable brutality), the requirement for the means of production to be controlled by the "advanced peoples", the idea of class societies developing by way of stages through which all must pass culminating in capitalism, and yet also the clear implicit support for the Indian people to throw off British rule – this last became more pronounced after the uprising of 1857. Some of this was purely illusory. The hope that imperial railroads would put an end to famine in India proved to be entirely misplaced – they may indeed have exacerbated the danger of starvation by expediting the imposition of the requirements of market relations in place of those of human subsistence.[10] Other aspects remained part of the heritage of the socialist movement down to the world war and indeed beyond. All this seems to justify V.G. Kiernan's observation that "in Marx...there can be felt an unreconciled dualism between a historical scheme which made nearly all revolts useless or...worse than useless, and an impulse to applaud every struggle against oppression, as Marx did in 1857."[11] Certainly, Marx can never be found on the wrong side of a struggle between the oppressed and their oppressors, from India and Ireland to the American Civil War. But for the most part, the Socialists of the Second International could also find comfort in his published works for the view that industrial capitalism was the measure of progress (social as well as economic) for all peoples, and that its export was an inevitability against which resistance was ultimately an historical fatuity.

Some Marxist and anti-imperialist critics have been harsher. The eminent writer Edward

Said summarised Marx's position as "the idea that even in destroying Asia, Britain was making possible there a real social revolution" and as holding conceptions that "are Romantic and even messianic: as human material the Orient is less important than as an element in a Romantic redemptive project. Marx's economic analyses are perfectly fitted thus to a standard Orientalist undertaking, even though Marx's humanity, his sympathy for the misery of people, are clearly engaged." [12] By aligning with the struggle of the oppressed Marx clearly went beyond Hegel, but still within a system that owed too much to an idea of unilinear progress, with the line to be followed being determined in Western Europe.

Robert Biel argues that Marx and Engels "…never fully surmounted the view that colonialism was regrettable for all its atrocities, but still a force objectively making for progress. They didn't recognise that the only progressive element is embodied in the **resistance** to which colonialism gives rise."[13] In fact, Marx did start to move towards that view, although Biel is right that his overcoming of the attitude that anti-colonial struggles were of a secondary order was an uneven process. As is well known, Marx wrote to Engels in 1869, modifying his views on agency priority in relation to Ireland at least:

> "For a long time, I believed it would be possible to overthrow the Irish regime by English working-class ascendancy…Deeper study has now convinced me of the opposite. The English working class will never accomplish anything before it has got rid of Ireland. The lever must be applied in Ireland. This is why the Irish question is so important for the social movement in general."[14]

Indeed, Marx argued for support for the Irish Fenians within the counsels of the First International, a pioneer example of attempting to integrate the demands of the national question with the struggle of the workers' movement that was, unfortunately, scarcely generalised from for forty years or more. Moreover, he later circumscribed his view of the historical inevitability of capitalism by indicating that the then-new system may apply to Western Europe alone, in the course of addressing the possibilities presented by the Russian village commune for an original transition to communism.[15]

And as early as 1858, Engels had worried that the socialist revolution would be "bound to be crushed in this little corner (Europe), considering that in a far greater territory the movement of bourgeois society is still on the ascendant,"[16] a view which pointed towards an understanding of the need for the unity of the struggles against colonialism with the working-class movement in Europe. Yet years later, Engels was still writing in narrower terms to Eduard Bernstein about the anti-colonial war developing in Egypt: "…we can perfectly well enter the arena on behalf of the oppressed fellaheen without sharing their current illusions (for a peasant population has to be fleeced for centuries before it learns from experience), and against the brutality of the English without, for all that, espousing the cause of those who are currently their military opponents."[17] This latter position could scarcely be characterised as anti-imperialist – it would have more in common with later Labour Party attitudes between (and after) the world wars, of condemning imperial abuses while not supporting full and immediate independence.

To that extent, Marx and Engels did not really bequeath a comprehensive theory of world revolution (or at least one that outlasted their immediate epoch) in the works published during their lifetime. Marx did move away from the idea that all countries would have to pass along the path described in *Capital* later in his life, but this was largely acknowledged only in private correspondence. An integral theory of global struggle suitable for the forthcoming age of imperialism eluded them, even though they left behind the materials from which one could be fashioned. They were too dismissive of the potentiality of the peasantry in the colonial and semi-colonial world playing a historically progressive role, not merely in fighting for their own human dignity against oppression, but in laying the groundwork for alternative forms of social development beyond those mandated by industrial capitalism. Instead, they relied on images of economic stagnation, primitive religious beliefs, barbaric social practices and so on to sustain a view that for all their brutality and hypocrisy, the capitalist empire-builders were doing history's work.[18]

A connected debate rumbles on over the extent to which Marx's abstraction of the inner workings of the capitalist system, spread across the three volumes of *Capital* and beyond, anticipates the necessary development of imperialism later in the nineteenth century. Pradella, for example, claims that "Marx didn't just develop a critique of imperialism – he also saw processes of imperialist expansion as being subordinated under the overall tendencies of capitalist accumulation, under the law of the impoverishment of the working class in particular."[19] This is set against the more orthodox view that Marx's model in *Capital* (volume one at least) [20] was of a national capitalist economy as a largely self-contained entity, if only for the purposes of abstraction. Of course, the existence of colonial plunder plays a significant part in the passages on the genesis of capital, while the world market hovers as a background assumption throughout. But when Marx discusses wage-labour and exploitation, it is very firmly centred on the industrial capitalist (British) economy and assumes a common value of labour-power and an equalising rate of surplus value, something that has never yet developed in the world capitalist economy. Pradella is right, though, to argue that Marx anticipates monopoly capitalism very clearly in his discussions on the concentration and centralisation of capital.

In fact, he had foreseen the emergence of capitalist monopoly earlier still, in a typically dialectical fashion. "In practical life we find not only competition, monopoly and the antagonism between them, but also the synthesis of the two, which is not a formula, but a movement. Monopoly produces competition, competition produces monopoly. Monopolists compete among themselves; competitors become monopolists...the synthesis is such that monopoly can only maintain itself by continually entering into the struggle of competition" he wrote in *The Poverty of Philosophy* in 1847.[21] Clearly, this anticipates Hilferding and Lenin to some extent, but Kiernan, perhaps the most thorough and erudite analyst, in English at least, of the Marxist understanding of imperialism, still argues that "several scattered observations by Marx...suggest that he was willing to think of imperialism as a morbid excrescence on capitalism rather than (as Lenin...considered it) an integral, inescapable part of capitalism."[22]

In Volume Three of *Capital* Marx did push his argument further when he addressed the various factors that worked against the tendency for the rate of profit to fall. Prominent among these were the attractions of surplus profit to be earned in the colonies. "As far as capital invested in the colonies etc. is concerned, however, the reason why this can yield higher rates of profit is that the profit rate is generally higher there on account of the lower degree of development, and so too is the exploitation of slaves and coolies etc."[23] However, the fact that this passage is in a section headed (either by Marx or by the editor of the volume, Engels) "Foreign Trade" rather reinforces the view that the model in use was a national capitalist system rather than world economy.

This whole debate has, of course, been vastly enriched by the access to so much more of Marx's writings over the last hundred years or so. However, in considering the development of the understanding of imperialism in the workers' movement of Western Europe at the start of the twentieth century, the published works left by Engels and himself bestowed an ambiguous legacy, not fully fit-for-purpose. The changing world economy was not grasped as a contradictory unity, and the struggles against colonialism remained on the periphery of a political field of vision focussed on the development of industry and its concomitant, the proletariat, as the universal precondition for socialism. The shoots of a more integral perspective, of an International really uniting the human race in the words of Poitier, could be identified; but it would fall to the next generation of socialists to try to ripen and harvest them, with uneven results. Certainly, the problems left unsolved by the founders of scientific socialism dogged the CPGB, in one form or another, throughout its history.

The Second International meets imperialism

International Social Democracy's first serious argument about the problem of imperialism was held in the shadow of defeat – the electoral setback suffered by its premier section, the German SPD, in early 1907. Until then, the story of the SPD had been one of gradual but uninterrupted electoral advance. Allied to the theory of inevitable capitalist breakdown, this was the underpinning of the Kautskyite theory – then the Marxist orthodoxy – of the advance to working-class power and socialism. The Reichstag election of 1907 was a traumatic setback.

The election had been called by German Chancellor Bernhard von Bulow in order to secure a free hand for the colonial policy of the Reich, untrammelled by the parliamentary opposition of the SPD (and the Catholic Centre Party). The poll became known as the "Hottentot election" in honour of German imperialism's policy of expansion in Africa, and was conducted in an atmosphere of nationalism and chauvinism. In fact, the SPD's vote held up, but its parliamentary representation fell from 81 seats to 43, as a result of the bourgeois Progressive Party no longer supporting it in the run-off phase in the constituencies, so desirous was the latter of disassociating itself from the 'anti-national' SPD. [24]

The right-wing of the SPD – an increasingly-divided party behind its official Marxist rectitude – immediately urged the abandonment of its anti-colonial (and revolutionary) rhetoric, for which proposal they had the general support of party founder and icon August Bebel. The young Karl Liebknecht, to the contrary, demanded a strengthening of anti-militarist and anti-war agitation. In this debate, Kautsky generally inclined to the left and the powerful German trade unions to the right.

When an issue exercised the SPD it could not but affect the International. The outcome of the "Hottentot election" helped ensure that the colonial question would be at the head of the agenda when the International met for its congress in Stuttgart later in 1907, and that the German right-wing would try to use the occasion to dilute or reverse the International's previous condemnations of colonialism. Every national delegation arrived at the Congress divided over the colonial question (and the closely-related one of militarism) and their arguments prefigured those of August 1914 and, indeed, echo down to those around the 21st century "war on terror."

The first clashes were in the Colonial Commission of the Congress, where German delegate Edgar David bluntly stated that "Europe needs colonies. It does not have enough of them. Without colonies we would be comparable from an economic standpoint to China". This view was echoed by Belgian representative Modeste Terwange, speaking for the chauvinist minority in his Party:

> "For us Belgians the question is: should we leave the Congo in its current state, or do we want better conditions there?...If from one day to the next colonial production were ended, industry would be seriously damaged. It logically follows that men utilise all the riches of the globe, wherever they may be situated."

His amendment proposing that Congress "...does not reject in principle every colonial policy; under socialism, colonisation could be a force for civilisation" was carried in the Commission, over the objections of the German left-winger Georg Ledebour who urged that "the resolution must emphasise that we do not expect capitalist colonisation to exercise any civilising mission. We are principled opponents of all exploitation and oppression in our own countries, and as such must fight against the much greater exploitation in the colonies."[25]

The Commission's conclusions were challenged on the floor of Congress. Ledebour joined with other delegates to move a replacement formula: "The Congress considers that by its inherent nature, capitalist colonial policy must lead to enslavement, forced labour, or the extermination of the coloured people of the colonised regions. The civilising mission that capitalist society claims to serve is not more than a veil for its lust for conquest and exploitation. Only socialist society will offer the possibility to all peoples of developing fully to civilisation."

The right did not accept this without a fight. Dutch delegate Hendrick van Kol encapsulated the "Marxist" argument of the inevitability of going through the capitalist stage and pressed it into colonial service:

> "Surely Ledebour will agree that capitalism in Europe was unavoidable – a necessary and inevitable stage of development. Should the same not also be true about capitalism in the colonies?...We Dutch are one of the oldest colonising peoples. But we have reached the point where murder, torture, burning and plundering are no longer everyday occurrences in the Dutch colonies…As long as humanity has existed there have been colonies and I think that they will exist for a long time yet…Perhaps [Ledebour] can also tell us what he would do about the overpopulation of Europe. Where would the people who must emigrate go, if not to the colonies? And does he as a Social Democrat want to shirk his duty to work continually for the education and further advancement of the backward peoples?"

Van Kol's satisfaction that "murder, torture, burning and plundering" no longer happened every day in the Dutch colonies was perhaps a low point of the debate (he was to sink still lower, as we shall see), but nevertheless it was a position that most of the British delegates did not neglect to applaud.[26]

Eduard Bernstein and Karl Kautsky, the antagonists of the "revisionist controversy" which had shaken international socialism a few years earlier, resumed their political opposition over the issue. "We must get away from the utopian notion of simply abandoning the colonies. The ultimate consequence of such a view would be to give the United States back to the Indians," Bernstein joked, a scenario which for his fellow-revisionist David would mean not humane rule in the colonies "but a return to barbarism...The colonies as well must go through a stage of capitalist development. There too you cannot simply leap from savagery to socialism." Kautsky refuted the argument that Marx would have endorsed colonialism, argued that "a colonial policy is fundamentally detrimental to the ability to play a civilising role" and that Bernstein was arguing "the postulate of all despotism" – that there are people born to rule and those born to be ruled.[27]

The Polish socialist Julian Marchlewski (Karski) challenged the prevailing Eurocentrism, telling the Congress that "we socialists understand that there are other civilisations besides simply that of capitalist Europe. We have absolutely no grounds to be conceited about our so-called civilisation, nor to impose it on the Asiatic peoples with their ancient civilisations." India could do perfectly well without the British, he added; a position endorsed by an Indian delegate (a rare sight at Second International events). Bhikajee Kama told of "the brutal yoke of British despotism" and the price India paid for "British capitalist rule" – thirty-five million pounds a year flowing from India to Britain. This was all too much for the hapless Van Kol, who allowed Kautsky to provoke him into a reply of notably racist content:

> "...Today, to be sure, colonial policy is imperialist. But it does not have to be. It can be democratic as well...Suppose that we bring a machine to the savages of central Africa, what will they do with it? Perhaps they will start up a war dance around it or increase by one the number of their innumerable holy idols. Perhaps we should send some Europeans to run the machines...perhaps Kautsky and I will make the attempt... Perhaps the natives will destroy our machines. Perhaps they will kill us or even eat us...If we Europeans go there with tools and machines, we would be defenceless victims of the natives. Therefore, we must go with weapons in hand, even if Kautsky calls that imperialism."[28]

Happily, Congress did not endorse this outburst, and the amendment advanced by Ledebour passed, but only by 128 votes to 108. The amended resolution then carried, with the Dutch delegation abstaining and the German voting in favour, after the defeat of a manoeuvre by David to secure a negative vote. The resolution condemned "the barbarous methods of capitalist colonialism and demands, in the interests of the development of the productive forces, a policy based on peaceful cultural development and one which develops the world's mineral resources in the interests of the whole of humanity" and urged Socialist MPs to fight for reforms to better the lot of colonial peoples and "do everything possible to educate them for independence." Only in 1928 did the Socialist International finally go so far as to explicitly call for self-government and independence in the colonies.[29]

Lenin, a delegate to the Congress from the Russian party, applauded this outcome. In his review of the Congress he for the first time linked up opportunism in the workers' movement with the effects of imperialism – a subject he was to return to very substantially a few years later.

> "This vote on the colonial question is of very great importance. First, it strikingly showed up socialist opportunism, which succumbs to bourgeois blandishments. Secondly, it revealed a negative feature in the European labour movement, one that can do no little harm to the proletarian cause, and for that reason should receive serious atten-

tion…The non-propertied, but non-working, class is incapable of overthrowing the exploiters. Only the proletarian class, which maintains the whole of society, can bring about the social revolution. However, as a result of the extensive colonial policy, the European proletarian *partly* finds himself in a position when it is not his labour, but the labour of the practically enslaved natives in the colonies, that maintains the whole of society. The British bourgeoisie, for example, derives more profit from the many millions of the population of India and other colonies than from the British workers. In certain countries this provides the material and economic basis for infecting the proletariat with chauvinism. Of course, this may only be a temporary phenomenon, but the evil must nonetheless be clearly realised and its causes understood in order to be able to rally the proletariat of all countries for the struggle against such opportunism."[30]

Chauvinism and opportunism in the workers' movement were far from being a "temporary phenomenon" as things turned out. However, battle was now joined over these pathologies, and above all in the German SPD. The SPD's retention of Marxism as its guiding ideology (something not formally repudiated until 1959) masked a widening divergence between its pragmatic parliamentarians and trade union officials on the right, a left around Rosa Luxemburg committed to the revolutionary mass strike, and a centre represented above all by the most authoritative Marxist of the times, Karl Kautsky. Kautsky had led the denunciation of the revisionist ideas of Eduard Bernstein, who had sought to discard key postulates of Marxism in favour of an explicit reformism and neo-Kantianism (as well as imperialism), at the turn of the century.[31]

Kautsky took up the issue of imperialism most comprehensively in his 1909 work *The Road to Power*, a book which turned out to be his last major writing as a revolutionary (and one which the SPD Executive was considerably embarrassed by). It has been argued that his handling of imperialism significantly prefigures Lenin's own treatment of the subject.[32] In fact, this is not correct – Kautsky in several places refers to imperialism as a "policy" of capitalism, rather than a phase tied up with monopoly, and identifies it more-or-less exclusively with colonialism. These were to become principal lines of demarcation between what became the Leninist handling of the question and its opponents. That said, Kautsky clearly took an anti-imperialist orientation in the book. "The imperialism of a great power means…a policy of conquest. It means also hostility toward the other great powers that wish to conduct the same policy of conquest in the same areas," he wrote.[33]

"The colonial policy of imperialism is based on the assumption that only the peoples possessed of European civilisation are capable of independent development. The men of other races are considered children, idiots, or beasts of burden according to the degree of unfriendliness with which one treats them; in any case as beings having a lower level of development, who can be directed as one wishes. Even socialists proceed on this assumption as soon as they want to pursue a policy of colonial expansion, an ethical one, of course. But reality soon teaches them that our party's tenet that all men are equal is no mere figure of speech, but a very real force."[34]

Indeed, Kautsky went further in identifying the importance of the unity of struggles against European colonialism in Asia, the Middle East and Africa with the movement for socialism in Europe. "The Boers are terrible slave drivers; the rulers of Japan are the worst persecutors of socialists; and the Young Turks have already felt themselves compelled to take action against striking workers. Thus we must not view the opponents of capitalism outside of Europe uncritically. *That does not in any way alter the fact that they are weakening European capitalism and its governments and introducing an element of political unrest into the whole world".* (emphasis added) And: "because of the policy of colonial expansion, however, the Orient – taking this word in its widest meaning – is linked politically and economically so intimately with the Occident that the political unrest of the East will have that of the West as one of its consequences." [35] This must count as one of Kautsky's most far-sighted political evaluations. He also correctly assessed that imperialism was the only politically-attractive counter-offer which the ruling classes could make to the masses as against socialism: "…the more the idea of imperialism becomes bankrupt, all the more does the Social Democratic Party become the only party still championing a great idea, a great goal, one that is able to unleash all the energy and devotion that flow forth from such a goal." [36] The relative weight of the two projects in the sympathies of the people was shortly to be tested and, like Lenin, the Kautsky of *The Road to Power* erred only in his excessive short-term optimism about where that balance would lie. But the connections were at least starting to emerge – the simultaneous entwining and opposition of socialism and imperialism; and the unity of the democratic and proletarian struggles against the latter.

Finance Capital

Events like the Boer War and the 'Hottentot election' forced the socialist movement to take a political attitude on imperial matters, a requirement which opened up the divisions we have noted. In parallel to this, a relatively small number of socialists undertook the serious work of attempting to interpret the new phase in the development of capitalism. This was an endeavour which, for our present purposes, can be held to culminate in the appearance of Lenin's *Imperialism, the Highest Stage of Capitalism* in 1918, two years after it had been written. Naturally, these two endeavours – political positioning and economic analysis – could not proceed independently. Their synthesis lay in the requirement to reassess the strategy for socialist revolution in the light of the coming together of the world economy under the pressure of capitalist colonialism and neo-colonialism. This development united different prevailing modes of production, not to mention different peoples with their diverse democratic struggles, in a single knot, which we call imperialism, or the "new imperialism" to differentiate from the imperialism of the early twentieth century (which has been sustained with important modifications ever since) from the many earlier variations of empire.

Max Beer, an itinerant German socialist journalist, was one of the first to take up the nature of the new epoch in any depth. In an essay in 1902 on 'imperialist policy' he first of all identified it in a broadening of the nation-state into a union of culturally related states (Great Britain with Canada and Australia, for example). More interestingly, he then wrote that: "the second characteristic of imperialism is the drive towards colonies, protectorates and spheres of influence, in short towards a world policy. Only those states that engage in a world policy are great powers. The essence of the world policy can be best understood through a comparison with the national state and mercantilist colonial policy. The latter served above all the demands of production in the mother-country, the creation of favourable monetary balance, the largest possible export of metropolitan commodities to foreign lands…The world policy has other purposes: it serves above all the interests of investment-capital and loan-capital through the opening up of territories for surplus capital, the extraction of tribute from foreign races, and the creation of a 'favourable' balance of trade. It further serves to dispose of the surplus intelligence and energies of the ruling classes, and finally to extract raw materials, especially iron, coal and bullion…"[37]

Beer continued by outlining the growing division of the world into spheres of influence, identifying particularly US expansion into the Pacific, that the US "ultimately regards itself as heir to the British Empire", before adding that "the only disturbing element is Germany", a "comet among fixed stars".[38] One can see in Beer's writings some of the elements later enhanced by Hilferding, Luxemburg, and finally Lenin.

The breakthrough, however, was made by Austrian Marxist (later reformist Finance Minister in the Weimar era in Germany, ultimately a victim of the Gestapo) Rudolf Hilferding, in his great and controversial work *Finance Capital*, first published in Germany in 1910. The debt owed to this work by Lenin – and hence the communist movement he initiated – to the analyses in *Finance Capital* is considerable and evident.

Hilferding's foundational argument was that the growth of fixed capital could not readily be reallocated in the event of falling prices, so large firms became more dependent on banks in adjusting to short-term market changes, while banks in turn protected their investments through forming trusts and cartels. These then developed greater credit requirements, promoting a mutual centralisation of capital. From this base, *Finance Capital* introduced many of the ideas Lenin would later develop in *Imperialism*, including his famous five distinctive features of the new imperialism, distinguishing it from the earlier liberal, free-market capitalism.

First, Hilferding sketches the fusion of bank and industrial capital in the new dispensation in Germany:

> "I call bank capital, that is, capital in money form which is actually transformed in this way into industrial capital, finance capital. So far as its owners are concerned, it always retains the money form; it is invested by them in the form of money-capital, interest-bearing capital, and can always be withdrawn by them as money capital. But in reality the greater part of the capital so invested with the banks is transformed into industrial, productive capital (means of production and labour power) and is invested in the productive process. An ever-increasing proportion of the capital used in industry is finance capital, capital at the disposition of the banks which is used by the industrialists. Finance capital develops with the development of the joint-stock company and reaches its peak with the monopolisation of industry….It is clear that with the increasing concentration of property, the owners of the fictitious capital which gives power over the banks, and the owners of the capital which gives power over industry, become increasingly the same people."[39]

While Hilferding reserves use of the term "imperialism" to his concluding chapter, and even there uses it more for propagandistic than scientific purposes,[40] his concept of finance-capital makes the point clear: "The policy of finance capital has three objectives: 1) to establish the largest possible economic territory; 2) to close this territory to foreign competition by a wall of protective tariffs, and consequently 3) to reserve it as an area of exploitation for the national monopolistic combinations."[41]

He places the export of capital front and centre in this process. "By 'export of capital'

I mean the export of value which is intended to breed surplus value abroad. It is essential from this point of view that the surplus value should remain at the disposal of the domestic capital....the precondition for the export of capital is the variation in rates of profit, and the export of capital is the means of equalising national rates of profit."[42] This formulation, while accurate in itself, does not yet introduce the concept of surplus-profit to be secured by the intensified exploitation of labour power in the colonies and semi-colonies. Hilferding sees the export of capital as integral to capitalist production but in too limited a sense: "While at one time colonies and new markets were established mainly to provide new articles of consumption, new capital investment is now directed principally to branches of production which provide raw materials for industry. As domestic industry, which supplies the requirements of capital export, grows, so the exported capital is applied to the production of raw materials for the industry. In this way the products of the exported capital find a market in the home country, and the narrow sphere in which production moved in England undergoes a great expansion as domestic industry and the products of exported capital nourish each other."[43]

However, Hilferding did foreground the role of the state in sustaining this new phase of capitalism, from the introduction of tariffs to organised violence, again anticipating Lenin's later formulations:

> "As has always been the case, when capital first encounters conditions which contradict its need for valorisation, and could only be overcome much too slowly and gradually by purely economic means, it has recourse to the power of the state and uses it for forcible expropriation in order to create the required free wage proletariat. In the early days of capitalism this was the fate of the European peasants and of the Indians of Mexico and Peru, and today the same is happening to the Negroes of Africa."[44]

Here Hilferding stands firmly on the ground of *Capital*, but he goes further: "Since the new markets are no longer simply outlets for goods, but also spheres for the investment of capital, this has also brought about a change in the political behaviour of the capital-exporting countries...The risks involved in building railways, acquiring land, constructing harbours, opening and operating mines, in a foreign country, are much greater than in the mere buying and selling of goods." Legal systems must be changed by force if necessary.

> "Violent methods are of the essence of colonial policy, without which it would lose its capitalist rationale. They are just as much an integral part of it as the existence of a propertyless proletariat is a condition sine qua non of capitalism in general. The idea of pursuing a colonial policy without having to resort to its violent methods is an illusion to be taken no more seriously than that of abolishing the proletariat while maintaining capitalism in existence."[45]

"At the same time the competition for the newly-opened spheres of investment produces further clashes and conflicts among the advanced capitalist states themselves." Capitalism also promotes in subjected people "...the ideal that was once the highest aspiration of the European nations; namely the formation of a unified national state as an instrument of economic and cultural freedom. This independence movement threatens European capital precisely in its most valuable and promising areas of exploitation"[46]

This last idea is of great importance. Hilferding raises the connection between the struggles for national independence in the colonies with those of the labour movement against capitalism in the heartlands of empire. Yet, like Kautsky earlier, Hilferding does not really develop the point. Instead, his focus is on how this new finance capital would lead to war *between* the great powers: "...the protective tariff has become an offensive weapon which the cartels employ in the competitive struggle, thus intensifying the price war, while at the same time they seek to strengthen their competitive position by recourse to the machinery of the state and to diplomatic intervention"[47] and "the drive for colonial acquisitions thus leads to a steadily-growing conflict among the large economic territories and has major repercussions upon the relations between individual states in Europe."[48]

"This struggle is intensified the more developed finance capital is and the more vigorous its efforts to monopolise parts of the world market for its own national capital; and the more advanced this process of monopolisation, the more bitter the struggle for the rest of the world market becomes...This is a situation which is bound to intensify greatly the conflict between Germany and England and their respective satellites, and to lead towards a solution by force." [49]

This was the programme of a bourgeoisie which had exhausted all its progressive ideals and potential, and was instead a global force for reaction, racism, and authoritarianism – the very forces which would, in Nazi guise, murder Hilferding thirty years later. Indeed, in a striking passage, Hilferding anticipates Hitlerism in all its essentials as a product of finance capital and imperialism:

"The demand for an expansionist policy revolutionises the whole world view of the bourgeoisie, it ceases to be peace-loving and humanitarian. The old free traders believed in free trade not only as the best economic policy but also as the beginning of an era of peace. Finance capital...has not faith in the harmony of capitalist interests, and knows well that competition is becoming increasingly a political power struggle. The ideal of peace has lost its lustre, and in place of the idea of humanity there emerges a glorification of the greatness and power of the state....The ideal now is to secure for one's own nation the domination of the world, an aspiration which is as unbounded as the capitalist lust for profit from which it springs...Since the subjection of foreign nations takes place by force...it appears to the ruling nation that this domination is due to some special natural qualities, in short to its racial characteristics. Thus there emerges in racist ideology, cloaked in the garb of natural science, a justification for finance capital's lust for power...An oligarchic ideal of domination has replaced the democratic ideal of equality."[50]

All this good sense did not, however, stop Hilferding from sharing in the core illusion of Kautskyism, then starting to emerge – that all these developments could be avoided by a more far-sighted approach by the bourgeoisie, that such a shift in policy had an objective foundation in common interest and that the labour movement could impose such a shift on the ruling class.

"The export of capital itself gives rise to tendencies which militate against such a solution by force..." he wrote, explaining that the intertwining of capital produces "various tendencies...which make for solidarity among international capitalist interests" and that "...the socialist movement has inspired a fear of the domestic political consequences which might follow from a war."[51]

The policy which the socialist movement – the powerful socialist party of Germany above all – should follow was Hilferding's final preoccupation:

"...however strong [the proletariat's] conviction that the policy of finance capital is bound to lead towards war, and hence to the unleashing of revolutionary storms, it cannot abandon its implacable hostility to militarism and the war policy, nor can it in any way support capital's expansion on the ground that this policy may prove to be, in the end, the most powerful factor in its own eventual triumph. On the contrary, victory can only come from an unremitting struggle against that policy, for only then will the proletariat be the beneficiary of the collapse to which it must lead, a collapse which will be political and social, not economic; for the idea of a purely economic collapse makes no sense.

"The response of the proletariat to the economic policy of finance capital – imperialism – cannot be free trade, but only socialism. The objective of proletarian policy cannot possibly be the now reactionary ideal of reinstating free competition by the overthrow of capitalism. The proletariat avoids the bourgeois dilemma –protectionism or free trade – with a solution of its own...socialism, the organisation of production, the conscious control of the economy not by and for the benefit of capitalist magnates but by and for society as a whole..."[52]

Like Lenin later, he believed that the new phase of capitalism had pushed society to the very eve of socialist revolution.

"The tendency of finance capital is to establish social control of production, but it is an antagonistic form of socialisation, since the control of social production remains vested in an oligarchy. The struggle to dispossess this oligarchy constitutes the ultimate phase of the class struggle between bourgeoisie and proletariat. The socialising function of finance capital facilitates enormously the task of overcoming capitalism" and "finance capital...is the climax of the dictatorship of the magnates of capital. At the same time it makes the dictatorship of the capitalist lords of one country increasingly incompatible with the capitalist interests of other countries, and the internal domination of capital increasingly irreconcilable with the interests of the mass of people, exploited by finance capital but also summoned into battle against it. In the violent clash of these hostile interests the dictatorship of the magnates of capital will finally be transformed into the dictatorship of the proletariat."[53]

We have outlined Hilferding's views at some length in order that, in highlighting what Lenin took from them, we can later foreground what he did not. The main elements of Lenin's underpinning analysis of imperialism are to be found in *Finance Capital*. Hilferding, however, did not, in Brewer's words ... "put [the] arguments into a definite concept of imperialism,"⁵⁴ crediting Bukharin for this later forward movement. Of course, Hilferding was writing before the outbreak of the war, and he took the analysis of imperialism as far as anyone did before the conflict broke out. He did not develop a theory of world revolution although, as we have seen, he skirted around the possibility in one or two passages. Nevertheless, the fact that he anticipated not just most of the economic analysis in Lenin's *Imperialism* but also some of the political lessons that the latter drew is consequential in that it shows that Leninism did not appear as an ideological tendency out of thin air, as it were. Some of its political suppositions, while raised to a new pitch of clarity by the split in socialism occasioned by the war, were already part of the currency of at least the advanced sections of the European socialist movement. When Lenin wrote *Imperialism* he was both standing upon Hilferding's work but also fighting against it, in that *Finance Capital* provided ammunition not just for revolutionary socialism but also for what was by then its Kautskyite negation. This lies not so much in Hilferding's failure to conceptualise a new perspective for revolution out of his analysis of finance capital as in his view of imperialism as ultimately a policy which could be avoided under the right conditions, and his embryonic projection of what Kautsky would come to call "ultra-imperialism" – a new and possibly peaceful fusing of national monopoly capitals as a logical extension of the emergence of monopoly in the advanced capitalist nation-states, expedited through cross-investment in each other's countries and colonies.⁵⁵ He foresaw an "organised capitalism" based on an unlimited cartelisation ending in a world where the entirety of capitalist production would be "consciously regulated" in all spheres. Lenin described this later as Hilferding endeavouring to reconcile Marxism with opportunism on the basis of these formulae, but this was not argued when *Finance Capital* was first published, six years previously.

Rosa Luxemburg

The idea that imperialism was a policy adopted by the bourgeoisie, under pressure from its most reactionary elements – a policy with real roots in the changes in capitalism but which could either be abandoned under pressure or superseded by another, more peaceful, phase of capitalism – died hard in the European labour movement.⁵⁶ The first worked-out presentation which moved beyond these assumptions is to the credit of Rosa Luxemburg, then a leader of the left in the German SPD, later a martyr of the German revolution, murdered by right-wing army officers in 1919. Her flawed masterpiece *The Accumulation of Capital* sought, through a critique of the underpinning assumptions of *Capital*, to create an understanding of the inevitability of imperialism. Indeed, in 1911, two years before her book appeared, she had already referred to imperialism as "the highest and last stage of capitalist development."⁵⁷

Luxemburg's central argument was that Marx's model for the accumulation of capital as set out in *Capital* was unworkable because surplus-value could not be sufficiently realised either through sales to workers or to capitalists themselves and that it was therefore only possible to accumulate the capital required for expanded reproduction through sales in non-capitalist markets. It therefore followed that to avoid collapse, capitalism depended on indefinite expansion into non-capitalist areas of the world. The more this expansion met its spatial limits the more intense would be the struggle for markets and for areas for investment between the great imperial powers, leading to "a string of political and social disasters and convulsions." ⁵⁸

It is not necessary here to submit this argument to a detailed critique – this was done at the time and has been repeated endlessly since. Indeed, to some extent Luxemburg's key arguments were refuted many years earlier, unbeknownst to her, in Lenin's polemics with the economic theories of the Narodniks (populists) in Russia.[59] Our concern here is the extent to which she contributed to the emergence of an integrated theory of world revolution, building on the new connections forged by the development of the imperialist phase.

Like Hilferding, she recognised that those connections indeed exist. At the most fundamental level she asserted – the first time a leading socialist had done so – that "capital…must be able to mobilise world labour power without restriction in order to utilise all productive forces of the globe – up to the limits imposed by a system of producing surplus value."[60] The introduction of the concept of "world labour power" – and this was at the heart of her solution to her self-invented "accumulation problem" – could only lay the foundation for the development of a community of class interest between metropolitan worker and colonial worker, and this Luxemburg attempted to set out:

> "Capital increasingly employs militarism for implementing a foreign and colonial policy to get hold of the means of production and labour power of non-capitalist countries and societies. The same militarism works in a like manner in the capitalist countries to divert purchasing power away from the non-capitalist strata. The representatives of simple commodity production and the working class are affected alike in this way. At their expense, the accumulation of capital is raised to the highest power, by robbing the one of the productive forces and by depressing the other's standard of living. Needless to say, after a certain stage the conditions for the accumulation of capital both at home and abroad turn into their very opposite – they become conditions for the decline of capitalism. The more ruthlessly capital sets about the destruction of non-capitalist strata at home and in the outside world, the more it lowers the standard of living for the workers as a whole…"[61]

Once she had got past her lengthy examination of Marx's supposed errors – passages which were "a shocking muddle" in Lenin's estimation [62] – Luxemburg wrote powerfully about the crimes of imperialism and militarism as they worked to displace natural economy with commodity economy across the globe. However, she continued to regard socialism as essentially the work of the proletariat in Europe alone. Her analysis of the common burdens borne by workers in the "North" and the toilers of the "South" has nothing to say about the greater exploitation of labour power in the latter, nor about the transfer of this surplus value to the metropolitan countries, and the use of some of this super-profit to ameliorate conditions for working people there.[63] Her relative neglect of the connection between capital and the state further inhibited the emergence of a full theory of imperialism. [64] But above all, and most famously, Luxemburg turned her back on the issues of democracy and national liberation, asserting that neither could be attained under the capitalist system – in Trotsky's later pithy summation, she believed that "national self-determination under capitalism is impossible, and under socialism it is superfluous."[65] This effectively foreclosed any major emancipatory role for the struggles of the millions of oppressed in the colonies and made any support for such struggles by the labour movements in the great centres of Empire a matter of chance or charity. Her much-quoted aphorism that the world faced the choice of "socialism or barbarism" effectively left little or no space for struggle for anything short of socialism which, in turn, was only on the order of the day in the developed centres of capitalism, mostly in Europe.

In 1909 she wrote – mainly in relation to oppressed European nations held captive within the Empires of the day (Russian, Ottoman, Austro-Hungarian, British) – that:

> "the idea of ensuring all 'nations' the possibility of self-determination is equivalent to reverting from Great-Capitalist development to the small medieval states, far earlier than the fifteenth and sixteenth centuries….There literally is not one social area, from the coarsest material relationships to the most subtle moral ones, in which the possessing class and the class-conscious proletariat hold the same attitude, and in which they appear as a consolidated 'national' entity."[66]

In her celebrated "Junius pamphlet" published pseudonymously in 1916, she explicitly extended this outlook to cover the non-European colonies too, as we have already noted. These ideas have been shown by history to be wrong, but they were the errors of a passionate opponent of imperialism, and it was in that sense of being misguided comrades, but comrades still, that Lenin argued against Luxemburg and her co-thinkers later on.

Contemporary socialists tended to prefer Hilferding's work to Luxemburg's. However, Luxemburg's strengths were also acknowledged. Anton Pannekoek wrote:

> "We disregard now the fact that her economic analysis is incorrect and that it can therefore prove or explain nothing, because the thesis she has built upon it is correct…expanding capitalism does need a constant expansion of markets for sales, of areas of non-capitalist production. This necessity has always been a driving force in the world policy of the capitalist states, and this world policy, based on the necessity of ever newer markets for sales…We would…like to denote by imperialism the striving of modern capitalist powers to bring the largest possible areas of foreign continents directly or indirectly under their political control and to combine them in a world empire. This imperialism finds its economic explanation not in the necessity of new markets for sales or in the interests of selling commodities, but in capital-exports."[67]

Indeed, some of Luxemburg's theories anticipate much later developments in world capitalism. As Anthony Brewer has noted Luxemburg's "real contribution…is to insist that the mechanisms of primitive accumulation, with the concomitant use of force, fraud, and state power, are not simply a regrettable aspect of capitalism's past, but persist throughout the history of capitalism at the margin where capitalist and pre-capitalist economic systems meet. This margin is not geographic but social, it exists within countries rather than between them, and if a capitalist form of organisation has triumphed completely in a few places…the unequal struggle still goes on in vast areas of the world."[68] In that sense, as in many others, Rosa Luxemburg is still with us today.

Bukharin and *World Economy*

The final major Marxist work concerning imperialism which preceded Lenin's synthesis on the question was written by a member of his own party, N.I. Bukharin. Bukharin was a young and talented Bolshevik theoretician who headed the "left Communists" in Russia after the revolution, before moving to lead the right wing of the Party, presiding for a time over the work of the Communist International and ultimately being executed by the Soviet regime in 1938 after a trial at which he confessed to all manner of fanciful or non-existent crimes.

How much his book *Imperialism and World Economy*, written in late 1915, actually impacted on Lenin's own thinking is somewhat open to doubt. The Party leader wrote a foreword to the work, from which it is not at all clear that he endorsed all the arguments therein, since he went no further than praising the author for his detailed assembly of data. At the time Lenin and Bukharin were definitely on opposing sides on the issue of national self-determination. The traces of Bukharin's ideas in Lenin's *Imperialism* are certainly fainter than the impress of Hilferding or Hobson. [69]

However, *Imperialism and World Economy* stands in its own right as a major contribution to the developing consideration of imperialism in the socialist movement, a consideration which had, by the time Bukharin wrote, moved from being merely urgent to entirely inescapable as a consequence of the Great War for empire engulfing Europe, the Middle East, and parts of Africa. That war had, in all the contending powers to one extent or another, given a great impetus to the involvement of the state in the management of the war economy, and the direction of private monopoly by state interests. "Capitalism has attempted to overcome its own anarchy by pressing it into the iron ring of state organisation. But having eliminated competition within the state, it let loose all the devils of a world scuffle."[70] This appeared to add a fresh dimension to the concentration and centralisation of capital stressed by Hilferding, which was "creating a very strong tendency towards transforming the entire national economy into one gigantic combined enterprise under the tutelage of the financial kings and the capitalist state, an enterprise which monopolises the national market and forms the prerequisite for organised production on a higher non-capitalist level. It follows that world capitalism, the world system of production, assumes in our time the following aspect: a few, consolidated, organised economic bodies ('the great civilised powers') on the one hand, and a periphery of undeveloped countries with a semi-agrarian or agrarian system on the other."[71]

Bukharin's focus on *world* capitalism and production was a fruitful one.

> "In various ways there…takes place the transfusion of capital from one 'national' sphere into the other; there grows the intertwining of 'national capitals'; there proceeds the 'internationalisation' of capital. Capital flows into foreign factories and mines, plantations and railroads, steamship lines and banks; it grows in volume; it sends part of the surplus value 'home' where it may begin an independent movement; it accumulates the other part; it widens over and over again the sphere of its application; it creates an ever thickening network of international interdependence."[72]

This "ever-thickening network" had an impact on the development of the international working-class, too.

> "When a Russian city obtains a loan from London capitalists and pays interest on the loan, then this is what happens: part of the surplus value expressing the relation that exists between the English worker and the English capitalist is transferred to the municipal government of a Russian city; the latter, in paying interest, gives away part of the surplus value received by the bourgeoisie of that city and expressing the production relations existing between the Russian worker and the Russian capitalist. Thus, connections are established both between the workers and the capitalists of the two countries."[73]

Here Bukharin, like Hilferding before him, comes close to expressing the new basis for world revolution in the immediate entwining of the interests of the workers of different lands, but again does not draw any particular political conclusions.

Bukharin also identified the developing possibility of a community of interest emerging between sections of the working-class in the imperial powers with their own rulers, and at the expense of the colonial peoples. He pointed out the fact, sadly unavoidable for revolutionary socialists in 1915, that:

> "...the end of the nineteenth century, which to a large degree destroyed the bond of unity between capitalists and workers, which placed against each other those classes and their organisations as classes...has not yet destroyed the bond of unity between the working class and the greatest organisation of the bourgeoisie, the capitalist state" adding that "the bill for [colonial] policy is paid, not by the continental workers, and not by the workers of England, but by the little people of the colonies. It is in the colonies that all the blood and filth, all the horror and shame of capitalism, all the cynicism, greed and bestiality of modern democracy are concentrated. The European workers, considered from the point of view of the moment, are the winners, because they receive increments to their wages due to 'industrial prosperity.' All the relative 'prosperity' of the European-American industry was conditioned by nothing but the fact that a safety valve was opened in the form of colonial policy. In this way the exploitation of 'third persons' (pre-capitalist producers) and colonial labour led to a rise in the wages of the European and American workers."[74]

Nevertheless, he also wrote, not unreasonably if perhaps optimistically:

> "The additional pennies received by the European workers from the colonial policy of imperialism – what do they count compared to millions of butchered workers, to billions devoured by war, to the monstrous pressure of brazen militarism, to the vandalism of plundered productive forces, to high cost of living and starvation."[75]

He did not further explore the idea of the movement of the colonial peoples against imperialism being a component of the world revolutionary movement in its own right. The colonial peoples appear as victims only in his book, the "backward countries" as loot to be fought over, but without their own agency in the struggle.[76] Bukharin's internationalism, typical of the time, extended as far as the workers of the world (mainly Europe in fact) but not to the colonial peoples, oppressed but non-proletarian as they were. Of course, he did not support national emancipation movements in Europe either, sharing his disdain for such survivals of a disappearing bourgeois epoch with Luxemburg amongst others. Lenin, as we shall shortly see, took strong exception to his views on this point.

Bukharin was therefore a prisoner of the fallacy, in Kiernan's words, "that all social relations everywhere were being transposed into one uniform pattern, a confrontation of capitalist and workman"[77] and that socialism in the more advanced areas of world economy was a precondition for social advance elsewhere, a view Lenin was to drastically modify.[78] He also appeared to endorse Hilferding's errors regarding the development of a universal state-capitalist organisation as a further stage of capitalism, seeing smaller nations as destined for elimination in the global evolution of one vast capitalist corporation. However, he shared Lenin's view that the emergence of a European Union would not be a step towards peace, but towards an intensified global struggle for markets.

As with the work of Hilferding and Kautsky and to a lesser extent Luxemburg, Lenin carried forward some of Bukharin's ideas while rejecting others, in a dialectic which defined the new basis for world revolution in a form which endured for most of the twentieth century. We will next turn to this process, which started in 1914 with the onset of war. This was the moment when imperialism – already a barbarous reality across Africa, Asia, the Middle East, and Latin America but a more abstract question for European socialists – became the most pressing issue for the latter too; the moment when the weapon of criticism beloved of the Second International leaders, was superseded by the criticism of weapons in the hands of the imperial general staffs. To the shame of the former, they speedily sought to subordinate themselves, for the greatest part, to the latter.

Notes

1. *The Junius Pamphlet* by Rosa Luxemburg (Colombo: 1992 [1916]) p 110
2. *Age of Empire* by Eric Hobsbawm (London:1987) p 60
3. See *Marx at the Margins* by Kevin B. Anderson (Chicago/London: 2010), the most comprehensive review of Marx's writings on colonial and non-capitalist peoples and countries, and Marx ahead of *Lenin: The current relevance of Marx's theory of imperialism*, a paper presented by Lucia Pradella to an IIPPE workshop in London, June 2016. Anderson's work is an essential guide to the question – his fifth chapter, on colonial and other international questions as reflected in Marx's economic writings, is particularly valuable.
4. Marx himself was particularly sceptical about the future of the Slav peoples, for example, for much of his life, before turning in his last years to the possibility of a path to communism in Russia that did not need to go through capitalism.
5. *The Philosophy of History* by G.F.W.Hegel (Mineola: 1956 [1830-1]) p 99. In the same passage Hegel argues for only the gradual abolition of slavery in Africa "since for this man must be matured"
6. *Ibid.* pp 142, 147
7. *Ibid.* p 158
8. Dispatches for the *New York Tribune* by Karl Marx (London:2007) pp218-9
9. *Ibid.* pp 221-225
10. See *Late Victorian Holocausts* by Mike Davis (London:2002), chapter one
11. *Marxism and Imperialism* by V.G. Kiernan (London:1974) p 201
12. *Orientalism* by Edward Said (London: 1995 [1978]) pp153-54
13. *Eurocentrism and the Communist Movement* by Robert Biel (London: 1986) p 30. The core of Biel's argument is that "during the nineteenth century, the formative period of socialist thought, there was also a period of expansion and consolidation of the colonial system, and a systematisation of its ideology, particularly in the pseudo-scientific race doctrine. There was a real struggle between European and non-European societies, which the racists theorised into a false doctrine (survival of the fittest etc). Serious bourgeois writers on political economy in Marx's day seem not to have had much to say about colonialism…Thus the field was left clear to the racists to draw their conclusions from the real conflict between nations. The function of socialist thought was to drag into the open the themes which the bourgeoisie suppressed, ask the embarrassing questions which **were** asked in the **domestic** sphere (who produces the wealth?) and thus challenge the racist monopoly in dealing with the really-existing black-white conflicts, to show that these were not a product of race but capitalism. This task was both political, because it meant entering into a necessary arena of struggle, and at the same time theoretical because a truly world-encompassing view of capitalism could thus be created, not the inevitably truncated view which would result in concentrating on the analysis of processes **within** the metropolitan

country. On the whole Marx failed to do these things." pp 22-23
14. *Marx/Engels Collected Works* vol 38, p 398
15. *Ibid.* vol 46 p 71
16. Cited in Biel (1986) p 39
17. *Marx/Engels Collected Works* volume 46, p 302
18. Biel (1986) again: "None of this detracts from the fact that the traditional structures cannot on their own create a new socialist mode of production without the intervention of the capitalist world-system. But the way capitalism creates these conditions is not as Marx and Engels tended to think by destroying an existing stagnation, but rather by itself creating stagnation in the place of an existing dynamism." And traditional society "…is prevented by world-capitalism from developing any further along its own lines" he argues in what is now a standard critique of the unilinear model of social development. pp 42-43
19. Pradella (2016) "Marx's positing a coincidence between the national and global levels, in fact, is a premise for conceptualising the world market, which includes both the internal and foreign markets of all nations participating in it…this abstraction makes it possible to include economic expansionism into the analysis of capital accumulation."
20. Anderson (2010) argues that this was modified in the French edition of *Capital*, prepared by Marx himself, in passages later largely omitted by Engels in editing the fourth German edition of 1890, used since as the definitive text. p 171 ff
21. *The Poverty of Philosophy* by Karl Marx (Moscow:1975 [1847]) p 140
22. Kiernan (1974) p 194
23. *Capital* volume three (London: 1981 [1894]) p 345
24. See *German Social-Democracy* by Carl E. Schorske (Cambridge, Mass: 1955) pp 59 ff and "Not One Man! Not One Penny!" by Gary P. Steenson (Pittsburgh:1981) pp 50-51
25. *Lenin's Struggle for a Revolutionary International* by John Riddell (ed.) (New York: 1984) pp 36-7
26. *Ibid.* pp 42-43. Quelch was among those who did not.
27. *Ibid* pp 43-44, 46-47
28. *Ibid.* pp 48-49
29. *Ibid* p 50 and *The History of the International* by Julius Braunthal volume 1 (New York: 1967) p. 319
30. *International Socialist Congress in Stuttgart* by V.I. Lenin in *Collected Works* volume 13 (Moscow: 1972) pp76-77. Lenin was also critical of the far left at the Congress, associated with the French anti-militarist Gustav Herve. This latter had attacked the German SPD in abusive terms: "you have become an electoral and accounting machine, a party of cash registers and parliamentary seats…the whole German social democracy has become bourgeois…the blind obedience of you German Social Democrats to 'Kaiser Bebel' is a deathlike discipline". This prescience did not suffice to prevent Herve himself becoming a supporter of French imperialism in 1914; Riddell (1984) pp 68-69.
31. "Only a conditional right of savages to the land occupied by them can be recognised," Bernstein wrote in his *Evolutionary Socialism* (New York: 2011 [1989]. "The higher civilisation ultimately can claim a higher right." Bernstein advocated Germany acquiring colonies, with only the most minimal regard given to the rights of their inhabitants. (p 145)
32. See for example Richard Day and Daniel Gaido in their introduction to *Discovering Imperialism* (Leiden/Boston: 2012) p. 61: "…the general argument of Kautsky's *Road to Power* treated imperialism as a consequence of the latest economic and political developments. Shortly thereafter, however, he began to argue that imperialism was a matter of policy – not an historical necessity – and that the policy might conceivably be changed to avoid a world war."
33. *The Road to Power* by Karl Kautsky (Alameda, CA: 2007 [1909]) p 68
34. *Ibid.* p 95
35. *Ibid.* pp 97-98
36. *Ibid.* p 99
37. Day and Gaido (2012) p 277. Day and Gaido's volume, *Discovering Imperialism*, is a work of surpassing scholarship, bringing together many otherwise unavailable writings from the socialist tradition, and is essential for anyone wishing to comprehend the development of

the debate on the left a century ago
38   *Ibid.* p 279
39   *Finance Capital* by Rudolf Hilferding (London: 1981 [1910]) p 225
40   See *Marxist Theories of Imperialism* by Anthony Brewer (London: 1980) p 98
41   Hilferding (1981) p 326
42   *Ibid.* pp 314-15
43   *ibid.* p 318
44   *Ibid.* p 319
45   *Ibid.* p 319
46   *Ibid.* pp 321-2
47   *Ibid.* p 313
48   *Ibid.* p 328
49   *Ibid.* pp 331-2
50   *Ibid.* p 335
51   *Ibid.* p 332
52   *Ibid.* p 366
53   *Ibid.* pp367,370
54   Brewer (1980) p 79
55   "British colonies could be sources of profit to Germany too," for example - see Kiernan (1974) p 26; or "…investment within the territory of another nation…would tend to decrease the importance of the division of the world market into different territories, rather than creating a motive for territorial expansion", Brewer (1980). p 92
56   Karl Radek described imperialism as "the policy of capitalism in the age of finance-capital" in 1912, to take one example from a well-known socialist publicist. Day and Gaido (2012) p 542. In the same year Paul Lensch wrote that "within scientific socialism…imperialism has always (my emphasis – *AM)* been described as the last and highest stage of capitalist society." *Ibid.* p 571
57   *Ibid.* p 65
58   *The Accumulation of Capital* by Rosa Luxemburg (London/New York: 2003[1913]) p 447
59   "The various branches of industry, which serve as markets for one another, do not develop evenly but outstrip one another, and the more developed industry seeks a foreign market. This does not mean at all 'the impossibility of a capitalist nation realising surplus value'…it merely indicates the lack of proportion in the development of the different industries" - *The Development of Capitalism in Russia* by V.I. Lenin, in *Collected Works* volume 3 p 66. For a straight-forward critique of Luxemburg's misunderstandings, see Ernest Mandel in his introduction to *Capital* volume two by Karl Marx (London: 1978) pp 62-69; or Anthony Brewer (1980) who writes that Luxemburg "…insists that the problem of realisation must be examined on the level of the aggregate social capital, but she then treats the aggregate capital as though it were an individual capital among many which has to sell its products in order to accumulate money with which to buy commodities. She seems unwilling to recognise the difference between a system and a component element within a system." p 67
60   Luxemburg (2003) p 343
61   *Ibid.* pp 446-47
62   Letter to L. Kamenev in *Collected Works* volume 35 p 94
63   As V.G Kiernan put it:"… she (like most Marxists) did not enquire how the surplus-value of the colonial world was being realized, or who, if not the ordinary man in Europe, was consuming the wealth extracted from it, largely in the form of consumer commodities." Kiernan (1974) p 21
64   "Her analysis remains weak, however, because the connections between competing capitals and competing states are not spelled out…", Brewer (1980) p 75
65   *Stalin* by Leon Trotsky (London: 2016 [1946]) p 335
66   *Socialism or Barbarism* by Rosa Luxemburg (London/New York: 2010) p. 140, 142; citing articles Luxemburg had written for the Polish socialist press in 1908-09.
67   Day and Gaido (2012) pp 692-3
68   Brewer (1980) p 76
69   The document known as Lenin's "testament", written shortly before his final illness

70.   rendered him effectively mute, he described Bukharin as a "valuable and major theorist" who, however "has never made a study of dialectics and, I think, never fully understood it." *Collected Works*, v 36 p 595
70. *Imperialism and World Economy* by N. Bukharin (London: 1972 [1917]) p 169. "Being a very large shareholder in the state capitalist trust, the modern state is the highest and all-embracing organisational culmination of the latter. Hence its colossal, almost monstrous power" p 129 and "Imperialist annexation is only a case of the general capitalist tendency towards centralisation of capital, a case of centralisation on that maximum scale which corresponds to the competition of state capitalist trusts" p 120
71. *Ibid.* p 73-4
72. *Ibid.* p 41. "Production is of a social nature; international division of labour turns the private 'national' economies into parts of a gigantic all-embracing labour process, which extends over almost the whole of humanity" p 106
73. *Ibid.* p 26
74. *Ibid.* pp 163-5
75. *Ibid.* p 167
76. "The stronger the process of industrialisation of the economic life and urbanisation of the country…the stronger is the competition between industrially-developed countries for the possession of backward countries, the more unavoidable becomes an open conflict between them." *Ibid.* p 95
77. Kiernan (1974) p 30
78. See Brewer (1980) p 80

Illustration overleaf
James Connolly

Chapter Three
Lenin, Kautsky, and Connolly (1914-18)

THE OUTBREAK of war did not come as a shock to Lenin, but the collapse of the Second International, and above all the decision of the German SPD to support the national war effort, did. Famously, it sent him into the libraries of Bern, where he was then residing in Swiss exile, to re-study Hegelian dialectics, the better to understand this cataclysm. This led him to his famous conclusion that, for want of serious engagement with Hegel, "...none of the Marxists for the past half-century has understood Marx."[1]

This is where what came to be called "Leninism" began, even if the propagandists of Bolshevism subsequently tried to give it an earlier birth. From the new positions staked out by Lenin in the months and years after August 1914 the twentieth-century communist movement emerged. Prior to 1914 Lenin's innovations had largely been in a context of trying to build a revolutionary socialist movement in the hard soil of Tsarist Russia, and had little international resonance. Lenin himself, moreover, scarcely conceived of himself as an international leader – he had operated within the mainstream left of the Second International, largely although not uncritically supportive of Kautskyite orthodoxy in the face of multiple revisionist challenges. This all changed with the start of the war and the apostasy of the main parties of the International – the old saw that "I have not left the Party, the Party has left me" seems entirely applicable to Lenin's case.

The war crisis appeared to Lenin to impose on him not just the task of orienting the Bolsheviks towards revolutionary defeatism directed against the Tsar's despotic regime, but of leading the reconstitution of international socialism, now in full collapse. In Kevin Anderson's words "...Lenin began for the first time to think of himself not only as a leader of Russian Marxism, but also as a crucial figure in the effort to rebuild international Marxism on the ruins of the old, discredited Second International."[2]

However, the new could not be imagined, still less called into existence, without a full reckoning with the reasons for the failure of the old. This in turn meant searching out the political roots of the degeneration of the leadership of social democracy in one country after another in the now-disappeared world of apparent peace and steady progress, and also establishing a fresh conception of world revolution suitable to the new times of blood and slaughter. This working out – the creation of "Leninism" – provided the basis for the eventual establishment of the Third International and its sections, including the Communist Party of Great Britain.

Studying Hegel undoubtedly reshaped Lenin's strategic vision, but it was hardly necessary for purposes of defining his attitude to the immediate question – where to stand on the war? There was never the slightest chance but that he would oppose the war policy of the Tsarist government. There would be no "sacred union" of classes and parties in the Russian Empire for the Bolsheviks, a position unique among the socialists of the European combatants with the exception of Serbia.

On the matter of war and imperialism, Lenin had always stood unequivocally on the left of the international movement. At the Stuttgart Congress of the International in 1907 he had endeavoured (unsuccessfully) to convene a left caucus in order to strengthen conference opposition to imperialism, and the next year he had explicitly rejected "defence of the fatherland".[3] By September 1914, Lenin had outlined his initial theses on the war,

which boiled down to four basic points:
1) The war is "bourgeois, imperialist and dynastic in character", a struggle among great powers to redivide the world.
2) The position of the International and the main Social Democratic parties is a "betrayal of socialism" and means the ideological collapse of the International.
3) The main task of the Russian Party is the struggle against Czarism, just as in peacetime.
4) Social-Democrats must break with the "petty-bourgeois opportunism" of the International and agitate to end the war by revolution.[4]

This assessment did not, however, sweep all before it – even in Lenin's own party initially. Some of those opposed to Tsarism and its war could not yet fully swallow the idea of ending the conflict through revolution. The word "imperialist" did not surface in RSDLP propaganda until November and "civil war" not until February 1915.[5]

Still less did Lenin's 1914 outlook find support internationally. The Bolshevik Party was more-or-less isolated among the socialists of the contending powers. Only the Serbian socialists joined Lenin in coming out unequivocally in opposition to their own rulers – ironically, since Serbia, facing Austro-Hungarian aggression, was the only combatant which, as even Lenin subsequently acknowledged, had a "national" case for defence in the conflict.[6] Yet Marcel Liebman has well expressed the dynamic of the moment. Despite its isolation, "Leninism and its founder acquired an *international* dimension. The breakdown of international relations in the European socialist movement and the retreat or realignment effected by the chief personages of the movement obliged those who would not accept the triumph of social-patriotism to come forward and take their place."[7] Lenin was foremost amongst these latter.

There were three closely connected aspects to Lenin's ideological work from 1914 to 1917, when his return to revolutionary Russia imposed new priorities on him. The first was the need for a complete rupture with the old socialism of the Second International and its panjandrums, exposing the sources of their opportunism. Second was the systematisation of a new theory of imperialism as the latest stage of a capitalism now massacring the youth of Europe in the trenches. Third was the development of a politics of national anti-imperialist democracy as the basis for a unity of the socialist working-class of Europe with the masses fighting for national liberation in the colonial and semi-colonial countries. Together, these formed the infrastructure of international revolutionary politics, of a new theory of world revolution, good for the next half a century at least.

Challenging opportunism

In all of these polemics, Lenin had one great target and one over-riding challenge – Karl Kautsky and the need to destroy his reputation and influence. This was not because Kautsky was the worst of the chauvinists and social-imperialists in the labour movement, but because his influence as the pre-war "Pope of Marxism" was the greatest. His equivocation as to the position of the working-class and its parties in the face of the conflict, his attempt to rationalise the national-unity tactics of the social-democrats, in Germany first of all, and his endeavour to pose solutions to the crisis other than revolution made him the figure who Lenin needed to bring down once and for all if a new working-class politics was indeed to emerge from the divisions in the international movement. When drawing the physiognomy of opportunism it was Kautsky's features which Lenin had in mind.

Kautsky was the principal theoretician of the Second International, and the man who had defended the integrity of Marxism from Bernstein's revisionism. He had retreated somewhat from revolutionary attitudes before the war, as Lenin and others, notably Rosa Luxemburg, had not failed to notice. He had temporised in the face of the developing hegemony of trade union officialdom and wait-and-see parliamentarism within the German SPD. Yet he had retained the profile of champion of orthodoxy, an orthodoxy which saw capitalism heading towards ultimate collapse and the socialist parties accreting strength ineluctably, until the point when a revolution could be declared. It was this plodding inevitability which events had confounded, and which imposed the requirement for a new Marxism.

Kautsky was invited to advise the SPD's parliamentary representatives on how to respond to the Kaiser's declaration of war, even though he was not an MP himself. His equivocal position – that the SPD should abstain on the vote on war credits, and that basically there was nothing to do except acquiesce in the war, wait out the conflict and reconstitute the International thereafter, while opposing annexationist aims on the part of the bourgeoisie, was a rationalisation for passivity and pusillanimity. Kautsky's view was in any event rejected by the SDP MPs in favour of the still worse decision to offer the Kaiser all-out support.

For Kautsky, the rights and wrongs of this position should be debated after the war, but no earlier. The International, he argued, could have done nothing other than it did, and to have expected more was unrealistic. Nothing need change in fundamental social democratic theory and practice. "The outbreak of the war signifies not the bankruptcy but on the contrary the confirmation of our theoretical conceptions…We have no regrets, nothing to revise. We feel decisively strengthened in the conceptions we upheld prior to the war."[8]

He wrote:

> "Although the world war has already meant a massive transformation and its consequences could bring still others, it need not change anything in the policy of Social Democracy….No policy of conquest but disarmament and democracy – these are the true foundations of Social-Democratic thought and will. We merely need to remain true to ourselves…."[9]

This is not to assert that Kautsky foresaw no change at all arising as a result of the war. It was merely that this would likely not be revolution or socialism, but rather the development of a new ultra-imperialist phase of capitalist development. Clinging to the idea that imperialism constituted a policy embraced by the capitalist class rather than a systemic development, he argued in September 1914 that "from the purely economic standpoint… there is nothing further to prevent this violent explosion from finally replacing imperialism by a holy alliance of the imperialists. The longer the War lasts, the more it exhausts all the participants and makes them recoil from an early repetition of the armed conflict, the nearer we come to this last solution…"[10]

This theory was essential to Kautskyism, to the politics of seeing the war not as the harbinger of revolutionary situations positing the end of capitalism but rather as a deplorable episode which could be superseded by a return to the peaceful development of capitalist society, on a new basis lying beyond imperialism. The bourgeoisie could recover from the disgrace of the war by initiating a system of international coordination, renouncing the policy of imperialism. While such a new phase would doubtless give rise to new depredations, nevertheless "...ultra-imperialism, like the Manchester capitalism of the 1850s and 1860s and the imperialism of the turn of the century, up to the international rise in prices, would initially usher in an era of new hopes and expectations within capitalism."[11] War would not lead to revolution, a return to peace would lead to evolution – the resumed advance of labour.

Rosa Luxemburg was among the first to attack this new perspective:

> "...it is ...astonishing to see Kautsky, amidst the lightning and thunder of the great world-historical catastrophe brought about by capitalism, finding occasion today...to sing his little song about 'disarmament', the 'national state', 'democratic development' and free trade as the nearest perspective for capitalism 'in its own interest'. A more upside-down historical perspective for orienting proletarians in the present war is hardly imaginable."

Kautsky made "imperialism...disappear in theoretical fumes." [12]

For Lenin, there was no more urgent political requirement than challenging these views of Kautsky's. This imperative informed Lenin's own *Imperialism* pamphlet, as we shall see. The immediate issue was to oppose Kautsky's acquiescence in the war. He contrasted Kautsky's significance with that of Britain's own miserable Henry Hyndman, the standard by which chauvinism-within-Marxism had to be judged.

> "...When, before the war, Hyndman turned towards a defence of imperialism, all respectable socialists considered him an unbalanced crank, of whom nobody spoke otherwise than in a tone of disdain. Today the most prominent Social-Democratic leaders of all countries have sunk entirely to Hyndman's position, differing from one another only in shades of opinion and in temperament. If you are convinced that Hyndman's chauvinism is false and destructive, does it not follow that you should direct your criticism and attacks against Kautsky, the more influential and more dangerous defender of such views?"[13]

That is what he did, bracketing Kautsky with his own erstwhile mentor in the Russian SDLP, Plekhanov, who was an even more bellicose supporter of the war. "All oppressing classes", Lenin wrote, "stand in need of two social functions to safeguard their rule: the function of the hangman and the function of the priest." He nominated Kautsky for the second role, for turning "Marxism into a most hideous and stupid counter-revolutionary theory, into the lowest kind of clericalism."[14] The vehemence of the vituperation which Lenin poured over Kautsky then and for the rest of his political life, frequently comparing him to religious functionaries inter alia, has been much remarked upon. Even allowing for Lenin's general tendency towards abusive polemics (one of his less benign bequests to the Communist movement), the passion directed against the dethroned "pope" is remarkable and can only be explained by the urgent requirement, as Lenin saw it, to wreck Kautsky's reputation and destroy his influence over the workers' movement. Perhaps there was also a note of personal betrayal and disillusionment. Kautsky's internationalism, Lenin argued, means that we must justify German workers firing at French workers, and French workers firing at German workers in the name of 'defence of the fatherland'". This was not unfair.[15]

The Collapse of the Second International, from which these quotations are taken, was written in May 1915 and was the first systematic exposition of Lenin's wartime views on the roots of the crisis in the socialist movement, and the measures that were needful to address it. We shall quote from it extensively. But as early as the preceding August he had started to set out the parameters of the combat. Surveying the ruin of the International he argued that "it is not socialism that has collapsed, in the shape of the present-day European International, but an insufficient socialism, i.e. opportunism and reformism. It is this 'tendency' – which exists everywhere...that has collapsed, for it has for years been teaching forgetfulness of the class struggle."[16]

And in November:

> "Advocacy of class collaboration; abandonment of the idea of socialist revolution and revolutionary methods of struggle; adaptation to bourgeois nationalism; losing sight of the fact that the borderlines of nationality and country are historically transient; making a fetish of bourgeois legality; renunciation of the class viewpoint and the class struggle, for fear of repelling the 'broad masses of the population' (meaning the petty bourgeoisie) – such, doubtlessly, are the ideological foundations of opportunism. And it is from such soil that the present chauvinistic and patriotic frame of mind of most Second International leaders has developed".[17]

Already Lenin was planning the creation of a new international to organise the "...revolutionary onslaught against the capitalist governments, for civil war against the bourgeoisie of all countries, for the capture of political power, for the triumph of socialism!"[18]

In *The Collapse of the Second International* Lenin elaborated on these fundamental insights. He asked the basic questions posed by the new situation:

> "Where did social-chauvinism spring from? What gave it strength? How must it be combatted?"[19] The rest of the European labour movement was shying away from this self-interrogation and was hoping for a swift return to business-as-usual on the basis of forgive-and-forget. Lenin's answer made the essential connection between the socialist leaders' behaviour in August 1914 and the preceding development of class-collaborationist ideas:

> "It is perfectly obvious that social-chauvinism's basic ideological and political content fully coincides with the foundations of opportunism. It is one and the same tendency. In the conditions of the war of 1914-15, opportunism leads to social-chauvinism. The idea of class collaboration is opportunism's main feature. The war has brought this idea to its logical conclusion, and has augmented its usual factors and stimuli with a number of extraordinary ones...

> "Opportunism means sacrificing the fundamental interests of the masses to the temporary interests of an insignificant minority of the workers or, in other words, an alliance between a section of the workers and the bourgeoisie...The war has made such an alliance particularly conspicuous and inescapable. Opportunism was engendered in the course of decades by the special features in the period of the development of

capitalism, when the comparatively peaceful and cultured life of a stratum of privileged workmen 'bourgeoisified' them, gave them crumbs from the table of their national capitalists, and isolated them from the suffering, misery and revolutionary temper of the impoverished and ruined masses. The imperialist war is the direct continuation and culmination of this state of affairs, because this is a war for the privileges of the Great-Power nations, for the repartition of colonies and domination over other nations. To defend and strengthen their privileged position as a petty-bourgeois 'upper stratum' or aristocracy (and bureaucracy) of the working class – such is the natural wartime continuation of petty-bourgeois opportunist hopes…such is the economic foundation of present-day social-imperialism."[20]

To those who sought to obscure the connection between the pre-war reformism and the war-time chauvinism, Lenin answered:

"Firstly, chauvinism and opportunism in the labour movement have the same economic base: the alliance between a numerically small upper stratum of the proletariat and the petty-bourgeoisie…secondly, the two trends have the same ideological and political content. Thirdly, the old division of socialists into an opportunist trend and a revolutionary, which was characteristic of the period of the Second International (1889-1914) corresponds, by and large, to the new division into chauvinists and internationalists…"[21]

"…it was the opportunist wing of European socialism that betrayed socialism and deserted to chauvinism. What is the source of its strength and its seeming omnipotence within the official parties?....The immense strength of the opportunists and the chauvinists stems from their alliance with the bourgeoisie, with the governments and the General Staffs…"[22]

"An entire social stratum, consisting of parliamentarians, journalists, labour officials, privileged office personnel, and certain strata of the proletariat, has sprung up and has become amalgamated with its own bourgeoisie…we can and must go fearlessly onward, from the preparatory legal working-class organisations, which are in the grip of opportunism, to revolutionary organisations that know how not to confine themselves to legality and are capable of safeguarding themselves against opportunist treachery, organisations of a proletariat that is beginning a 'struggle for power', a struggle for the overthrow of the bourgeoisie."[23]

In a pamphlet written with Zinoviev at the same time, Lenin had made the same point concisely:

"Opportunism and social-chauvinism stand on a common economic basis – the interests of a thin crust of privileged workers and of the petty bourgeoisie, who are defending their privileged position…opportunism and social-chauvinism have the same politico-ideological content – class collaboration instead of the class struggle, renunciation of revolutionary methods of struggle, helping one's 'own' government in its embarrassed situation, instead of taking advantage of those embarrassments so as to advance the revolution."[24]

The solution, set out in the *Collapse* pamphlet, was to reconstitute the movement on a new basis, completely separated from the opportunist leaders:

> "Social-chauvinism is an opportunism which has matured to such a degree, grown so strong and brazen during the long period of comparatively 'peaceful' capitalism, so definite in its political ideology, and so closely associated with the bourgeoisie and the governments, that the existence of such a trend within the Social-Democratic workers' parties cannot be tolerated."

The flimsy shoes of the old parties may have been good enough for walking in well-paved streets, but heavier boots were needed for walking through the hills post-1914, Lenin opined in a rare literary excursion into analogy.

> "In Europe socialism has emerged from a comparatively peaceful stage that is confined within narrow and national limits. With the outbreak of the war of 1914-15, it entered the stage of revolutionary action; there can be no doubt that the time has come for a complete break with opportunism, for its expulsion from the workers' parties." [25]

> "The epoch of imperialism cannot permit the existence, in a single party, of the revolutionary proletariat's *vanguard* and the semi-petty-bourgeois aristocracy of the working class, who enjoy morsels of the privileges of their 'own' nation's 'Great-Power' status. The old theory that opportunism is a 'legitimate shade' in a single party that knows no 'extremes' has now turned into a tremendous deception of the workers and a tremendous hindrance to the working-class movement."[26]

This pamphlet has been quoted at great length since it was the first and decisive rationalisation for the split in the international workers' movement which persisted, with variations from one country to another and with sundry ups and downs, for most of the twentieth century and indeed survives to this day to a more muted extent. Essentially, the leadership of the European socialist movement had betrayed the working-class because the former was already corrupted and class-collaborationist. Where revolutionaries saw opportunities to end capitalism during the war, the chauvinistic socialists saw only the need to ensure victory for their own country over its enemies, picking up the socialist thread at some later date. A new socialism, and a new international, had to arise from the crisis and the bloodshed. As Craig Nation put it, "what [Lenin] encouraged was not only an alternative strategy, but a new Marxism, liberated from the encrusted determinism of the Second International and aware that an epoch of struggle for socialism on a global scale had dawned."[27]

At the centre of this analysis stood imperialism – how the development of a global capitalist system resting on the power of a handful of great national centres had impacted on the labour movement by nurturing the opportunist trend within it. Here again Lenin broke new ground, and his focus was very much on Britain (or England as he often termed it) as the first country of industrial capitalism and the centre of the greatest Empire of all. As early as 1907 he had noted the link between this huge and ramified network of exploitation and the apparent backwardness, from a socialist point of view, of the British labour movement. Reporting on the Second International's Stuttgart Congress, he observed: "The British bourgeoisie...derives more profit from the many millions of the population of India and other colonies than from the British workers. In certain countries this provides the material and economic basis for infecting the proletariat with colonial chauvinism." [28]

Taking up this argument anew in his pamphlet *Imperialism and the Split in Socialism*, written towards the end of 1916, he asked "why does England's monopoly explain the (temporary) victory of opportunism in England?" before answering himself:

> "Because monopoly yields superprofits i.e. a surplus of profits over and above the capitalist profits that are normal and customary all over the world. The capitalists can devote a part (and not a small one at that!) of these superprofits to bribe their own workers, to create something like an alliance...between the workers of the given nation and their capitalists against the other countries. England's industrial monopoly was already destroyed by the end of the nineteenth century...Did all monopoly disappear?" Vast colonial holdings in fact remained.

> "A handful of wealthy countries – there are only four of them, if we mean independent, really gigantic, "modern" wealth: England, France, the United States and Germany – have developed monopoly to vast proportions, they obtain super-profits running into hundreds, if not thousands, of millions, they 'ride on the backs' of hundreds and hundreds of millions of people in other countries and fight among themselves for the division of the particularly rich, particularly fat and particularly easy spoils...

> "The bourgeoisie of an imperialist 'great' power can economically bribe the upper strata of 'its' workers by spending on this a hundred million or so francs a year, for its superprofits most likely amount to about a thousand million. And how this little sop is divided among the labour ministers, 'labour representatives'...labour members of war industries committees, labour officials, workers belonging to the narrow craft unions, office employees etc etc is a secondary question." [29]

Thus, the connection between the oppression of the colonial peoples and the crisis in international socialism was made explicit – perhaps crudely and with elements of a reductionism over-simplifying the mechanisms through which sections of the working-class were incorporated in the imperial system, but nevertheless decisively. It was further implicit that only on the basis of anti-imperialist politics could that crisis be overcome. That was an argument that Lenin did not hesitate to make. But before turning to that it is necessary to examine his own understanding of imperialism, and how it developed the thinking of Hobson, Hilferding, Luxemburg and Bukharin, authors we have already examined.

Imperialism

Lenin's pamphlet on imperialism is probably the most enduring and influential of all his works, and it still echoes in a world where the once-resonant polemics of *What is to be Done* and the utopianism of *State and Revolution* have shrivelled to more marginal significance. Probably only his *Left-Wing Communism* is now cited as often. Of course, *Imperialism's* canonical status has depended in part on Lenin's subsequent success in leading the October Revolution. Nevertheless, it also set out analytical parameters which have worn fairly well. If they are clearly dated in certain respects now, more than one hundred years later, this does not negate their resilience for much of a turbulent century.

It may be doubted that Lenin intended such reverence towards his pamphlet. Certainly, it has borne more political weight than he would have anticipated. Lenin was, his reputation notwithstanding, an alien to dogma. He wrote in *The Collapse of the Second International* that:

> "…a comprehensive scientific analysis of imperialism is one thing – that analysis is only under way and, in essence, is as infinite as science itself….Capitalism will never be completely and exhaustively studied in all the manifestations of its predatory nature, and in all the minute ramifications of its historical development and national features"[30] and, more generally, "…the very concept of purity indicates a certain narrowness, a one-sidedness of human cognition, which cannot embrace an object in all its totality and complexity."[31]

The full title of the work – *Imperialism, the Highest Stage of Capitalism* – perhaps made it sound more definitive than Lenin intended. According to Moira Donald, its original title was *Imperialism, the most recent stage of Capitalism*, and Lenin himself would have been happy to have seen it published as *Special Features of Recent Capitalism*, titles which would have made its conjunctural nature more apparent at the expense of the idea that it was a definitive analysis of capitalism's final phase, which it has proved not to be.[32] Lenin clearly did believe that imperialism was the last stage of capitalism in the sense that it represented the eve of revolution, and that it would be followed by socialism – indeed, monopoly capitalism prepared the way for socialism in many respects.

> "Capitalism in its imperialist stage leads right up to the most comprehensive socialisation of production; it, so to speak, drags the capitalists, against their will and consciousness, into some sort of a new social order, a transitional one from complete free competition to complete socialisation. Production becomes social, but appropriation remains private. The social means of production remain the private property of a few" he wrote, and "…the development of capitalism has arrived at a stage when, although commodity production still 'reigns' and continues to be regarded as the basis of economic life, it has in reality been undermined and the bulk of the profits go to the 'geniuses' of financial manipulation. At the basis of these manipulations and swindles lies socialised production; but the immense progress of mankind which achieved this socialisation, goes to benefit…the speculators."[33]

Lenin did not envisage the possibility of a further stage of capitalism, but that was a political judgement. The pamphlet, like all Lenin's writings in this period, can only be understood in the context of his polemics with Kautsky. While for Kautsky everything was to be deferred to another day, for Lenin everything was immediate and imminent, infused with the actuality of revolution. He wanted to refute Kautsky's ultra-imperialist theory, which offered the possibility of a return to the peaceful evolution of capitalism, to provide a statistical underpinning for his own projection of continuing conflict up to the point of revolution, and to supply a Marxist basis for his emerging theory of world revolution in contradistinction to the moribund official Marxism of the Second International. He was surely not looking to set up an all-time, all-weathers theory of a new stage of capitalism shorn of any political context.

His theory drew heavily on the work of Hilferding, as we have seen in the preceding chapter. He was reluctant to acknowledge the full extent of this debt, because Hilferding had stuck with Kautsky in the war crisis, and was therefore part of the problem in the international socialist movement. And Kautsky, whose theories were "sophistry and a dishonest defence of the worst opportunism", was of course the main target of Imperialism's polemical passages. "Kautsky's utterly meaningless talk about ultraimperialism encourages...that profoundly mistaken idea which only brings grist to the mill of the apologists of imperialism, viz., that the rule of finance capital lessens the unevenness and contradictions inherent in world economy, whereas in reality it increases them."[34]

This was the core of Lenin's position on the new stage of capitalism – that it intensified the various contradictions in the system, elevated them to a global level and therefore made revolution not just more likely, but unavoidable. In his introduction to Bukharin's *Imperialism and World Economy* Lenin had famously observed that:

> "there is no doubt that the development is going in the direction of a single world trust that will swallow up all enterprises and all states without exception. But the development in this direction is proceeding under such stress, with such a tempo, with such contradictions, conflicts and convulsions – not only economical, but also political, national etc, etc – that before a single world trust will be reached, before the respective national finance capitals will have formed a world union of 'ultra-imperialism', imperialism will inevitably explode, capitalism will turn into its opposite."[35]

So, Lenin did not challenge the general and very abstract direction of Kautsky's analysis, which is important to note in today's age of imperialist globalisation. He instead accused the SPD pontiff of ignoring the explosive ruptures which imperialism gave rise to, ruptures which must, Lenin believed, bring down the system as a whole. Indeed, the worst of the social democrats were not so much speculating upon the development of ultra-imperialism as actually promoting it. He cited a German social-democrat Gerhard Hildebrand as advocating a "United States of Western Europe" for the purpose of joint action against African Negroes and the "great Islamic movement", for the maintenance of a powerful army and navy against a Sino-Japanese coalition.[36] Reformulating the point he made in his introduction to Bukharin's book, Lenin again refuted Kautsky's assertion that from a "purely economic point of view" a new, "ultra-imperialist" phase of capitalism could be anticipated: "If by a purely economic point of view a 'pure' abstraction is meant, then all that can be said reduces itself to the following proposition: development is proceeding towards monopolies, hence, towards a single world monopoly, towards a single world trust. This is indisputable, but it is also as completely meaningless as is the statement that 'development is proceeding' towards the manufacture of foodstuffs in laboratories. In this sense the 'theory' of ultraimperialism is no less absurd than a 'theory of ultra-agriculture' would be." [37] A century on, of course, food is indeed being manufactured in laboratories (and the European Union exists as a quasi-imperialist bloc)!

Economically, Lenin saw the "deepest foundation" of imperialism as monopoly capital. "...We see the formation of a new type of monopoly: firstly, monopolist capitalist combines in all capitalistically developed countries; secondly, the monopolist position of a few very rich countries, in which the accumulation of capital has reached gigantic proportions."[38] He followed Hobson in seeing "the dominance of financial or investing over mercantile interests", while politically imperialism was "a striving towards violence and reaction." Summarising, Lenin listed the five criteria which became famous as the measuring sticks for imperialism. Some still strive to cram the contemporary world economy into these criteria. That is questionable, but there is no doubt that they corresponded to the bloody world of 1916. These were the concentration of production and capital to form monopolies; the creation of finance capital out of the merger of banking and industrial capital; the export of capital distinct from the export of commodities; the formation of international monopoly associations dividing the world between them; and the territorial division of the world among the great capitalist powers.[39]

So far, so Hilferding and Hobson. But Lenin broke new ground with his understanding of uneven development as the factor which made Kautsky's putative peace-and-harmony between great powers unsustainable. Lenin transferred Marx's understanding of the uneven and cyclical development between different sectors within a closed capitalist economy to the world scale, with disequilibrium at state level engendering war. While Kautsky acknowledged rivalry in the attempt by industrial nations to annexe agrarian areas for their raw material supplies, Lenin emphasised the struggle over outlets for capital export, and the fact that the development of industry in newer economic powers, like Germany, came up against the barriers erected by the older colonial empires of Britain and France above all.

> "Monopolies, oligarchy, the striving for domination instead of striving for liberty, the exploitation of an increasing number of small or weak nations by a handful of the richest or most powerful nations – all these have given birth to those distinctive characteristics which compel us to define it as parasitic or decaying capitalism. More and more prominently there emerges, as one of the tendencies of imperialism, the creation of the 'rentier state', the usurer state...it would be a mistake to believe that this tendency to decay precludes the rapid growth of capitalism. It does not....On the whole, capitalism is growing far more rapidly than before; but this growth is not only becoming more and more uneven in general, its unevenness also manifests itself, in particular, in the decay of the countries which are richest in capital (England)."[40]

So here was the basis for the final refutation of the theory of an impending peaceful convergence of the great powers: "...what means other than war could there be under capitalism of removing the disparity between the development of productive forces and the accumulation of capital on the one side, and the division of colonies and 'spheres of influence' for finance capital on the other?" he asked, evidently rhetorically.[41]

On the political impact of all this, Lenin effected a sort of synthesis between Hobson's theory of parasitism and the sketchy ideas of a corrupted Labour aristocracy which had germinated from Engels onwards, all of them living off the super-profits generated by imperialist exploitation.[42] For the roots of this process, which he saw as having emerged in Britain ahead of anywhere else on account of Britain's early and extensive imperial development, he relied on no less an authority than the colonial buccaneer Cecil Rhodes, whose own views on Empire he reproduced:

> "I became more than ever convinced of the importance of imperialism...My cherished idea is a solution of the social problem...in order to save the 40 million inhabitants of

the UK from a bloody civil war, we colonial statesmen must acquire new lands to settle the surplus population, to provide new markets for the goods produced in the factories and mines. The Empire, as I have always said, is a bread and butter question. If you want to avoid civil war, you must become imperialists."[43]

The analysis in Lenin's *Imperialism* has of course been the target of many criticisms, some well founded. The developments it described corresponded most closely to German monopoly capital – most of his statistical sources were German, and the debt to Hilferding has been noted. The finance capital fusion had not really occurred in the same way in the other powers. By the time of the First World War, the older imperial powers were mainly re-exporting old investment income, and a quarter of British overseas investment was in the USA, rather compromising the search-for-super-profit argument. As for Russia, "modern capitalist imperialism is enmeshed, so to speak, in a particularly close network of pre-capitalist relations," so in the Tsarist Empire it was not really the highest stage at all.[44] Kiernan also argues plausibly that Lenin's analysis, like that of all contemporary European socialists, did not fully transcend Eurocentrism. "Marxist theory took too little note of novel features [in the USA] or in Japan; it was too Eurocentric, its horizons failing to match those of an expanding world. One symptom of this was its preoccupation with export of capital from Europe, along with inadequate enquiry into the impact on particular regions outside."[45] Transcending those limitations was a contribution Lenin would himself make a little later on.

More generally, Lenin's stark choice for the workers of Europe – acquiesce in imperialism or make socialist revolution also proved problematic, as the history of the CPGB, amongst many others, tells us. He can, however, be forgiven his Manicheanism given the circumstances in which he was writing. Lenin was, moreover, shortly to suit deeds to his words.

National Liberation

Lenin's third innovation in revolutionary theory and practice was no less significant than the first two. He squarely faced the political consequences of imperialism in a global sense, notwithstanding Kiernan's point noted above. No other socialist had really done this hitherto, as we have seen. To run ahead of ourselves slightly, the most lucid expression of his thinking was made at the Second Congress of Communist organisations of the East, held in December 1919, two years after the speaker had been elevated to power:

"It is becoming quite clear that the socialist revolution which is impending for the whole world will not be merely the victory of the proletariat of each country over its own bourgeoisie. That would be possible if revolutions came easily and swiftly. We know that the imperialists will not allow this, that all countries are armed against their domestic Bolshevism and that their one thought is how to defeat Bolshevism at home. That is why in every country a civil war is brewing in which the old socialist compromisers are enlisted on the side of the bourgeoisie. Hence, the socialist revolution will not be solely, or chiefly, a struggle of the revolutionary proletarians in each country against their bourgeoisie – no, it will be a struggle of all the imperialist-oppressed colonies and countries, of all dependent countries, against international imperialism."
"We know that in the East the masses will rise as *independen*t (emphasis added) par-

ticipants, as builders of a new life, because hundreds of millions of the people belong to dependent, underprivileged nations, which until now had been the objects of international imperialist policy, and have only existed as material to fertilise capitalist culture and civilisation."[46]

More:

"…all the eastern peoples will participate in deciding the destiny of the whole world, so as not to be simply objects of the enrichment of others. The peoples of the East are becoming alive to the need for practical action, the need for every nation to take part in shaping the destiny of all mankind."[47]

The novelty of this was dramatic. For the first time, a socialist leader adumbrated a theory of revolution which gave equal place to the peoples of the colonial and semi-colonial world as compared to those of industrially-developed Europe and North America. The struggles in the one sphere and the other were interdependent and mutually-reinforcing. At a stroke, euro-centrism, and the patronising dismissal of the peasant were overcome, at least in principle. Here was a genuine programme of world revolution.

This was a remarkable, and yet at the same time natural, emanation from the understanding of imperialism then broadening in the labour movements through the forcing house of world war. And it was indeed during the war that Lenin had, through his usual favoured method of polemic, advanced the principles of national democracy as a necessary complement to "pure" proletarian revolution. Once again, he was challenging Marxist orthodoxy in the name of its revolutionary essence. His view, in Craig Nation's words, that "revolutionary transformation would occur 'in the course of an epoch' uniting 'civil war waged by the proletariat against the bourgeoisie of the leading nations with an *entire sequence* of democratic and revolutionary, to include national-liberation, movements in the underdeveloped, backward and oppressed nations" marked the single most important point of difference between the outlook of the Second International in even its best days and the Third International then gestating. [48]

Lenin set down the main lines of his thinking in a 1916 article *The Socialist Revolution and the Right to Self-Determination*. He argued that "Socialist parties which did not show by all their activity…that they would liberate the enslaved nations and build up relations with them on the basis of a free union – and free union is a false phrase without the right to secede – these parties would be betraying socialism" and that "the right of nations to self-determination implies exclusively the right to independence in the political sense, the right to free political separation from the oppressor nation." [49]

This was not an add-on to the basic socialist programme, but integral to the eventual achievement of a classless society. "In the same way as mankind can arrive at the abolition of classes only through a transition period of the dictatorship of the oppressed class, it can arrive at the inevitable integration of nations only through a transition period of the complete emancipation of all oppressed nations i.e.; their freedom to secede."

"The proletariat of the oppressor nations must not confine themselves to general, stereotyped phrases against annexation and in favour of the equality of nations in general…. The proletariat must struggle against the enforced retention of oppressed nations within the bounds of the given state, which means that they must fight for the right to self-determination."[50]

Going further, he urged the socialist movement to support the most advanced and revolutionary movements, even if they were "bourgeois democratic" seeking to liberate their nation from imperialist domination. "Socialists must not only demand the unconditional and immediate liberation of the colonies without compensation...they must also render determined support to the more revolutionary elements in the bourgeois-democratic movements for national liberation in these countries and assist their uprising – or revolutionary wars, in the event of one – against the imperialist powers that oppress them."[51]There were different views in the socialist movement on all of this, including on the revolutionary left. Luxemburg's views have been noted, and they were reflected within the Bolshevik party itself, including by Bukharin and Yuri Pyatakov. Lenin's 1916 pamphlets *The Nascent Trend of Imperialist Economism* and *A Caricature of Marxism and Imperialist Economism* challenged their outlook on the basis of democracy.

Lenin was careful to discriminate when it came to the politics of nationalism. "...not less than three different types of countries must be distinguished when dealing with self-determination...First type: the advanced countries of Western Europe (and America), where the national movement is a thing of the past. Second type: Eastern Europe, where it is a thing of the present. Third type: semi-colonies and colonies, where it is largely a thing of the future."[52]

In the advanced countries (by which he meant Britain, Germany, France etc), he argued "...the national problem was solved long ago...there are no 'general national tasks' to be accomplished. Hence, only in these countries is it possible now to 'blow up' national unity and establish class unity." However, "The undeveloped countries are a different matter. They embrace the whole of Eastern Europe and all the colonies and semi-colonies...In those areas, as a rule, there still exist oppressed and capitalistically undeveloped nations. Objectively, those nations still have general national tasks to accomplish, namely, democratic tasks, the tasks of overthrowing foreign oppression."[53]

Bukharin, Lenin asserted, did not understand the connection between democracy and revolution, linking his shortcomings with the earlier "Economists" in the Russian revolutionary movement who had soft-pedalled the struggle for democracy at the turn of the century. "...He cannot solve the problem of how to link the advent of imperialism with the struggles for reforms and democracy" just as "Economism" could not link advent of capitalism with struggle for democracy.[54] Lenin saw the fight for democratic freedoms as an essential pre-requisite for socialism, in this case through all-out support for the right of nations to self-determination, in contradistinction to those of his comrades who saw all forms of nationalism as outmoded relics of the past and superseded by a binary conflict between capitalists and workers. "All 'democracy' consists in the proclamation and realisation of 'rights' which under capitalism are realisable only to a very small degree and only relatively. But without the proclamation of these rights, without a struggle to introduce them now, immediately, without training the masses in the spirit of this struggle, socialism is impossible."

And, in words which still resonate today:

> "Socialism is impossible without democracy because: (1) the proletariat cannot perform the socialist revolution unless it prepares for it by the struggle for democracy; (2) victorious socialism cannot consolidate its victory and bring humanity to the withering away of the state without implementing full democracy. To claim that self-determina-

tion is superfluous under socialism is therefore just as nonsensical and just as hopelessly confusing as to claim that democracy is superfluous under socialism."[55]

In this matter as well as the others considered, Lenin was challenging the orthodoxy of the Marxism of the Second International which, as we have seen, paid scant attention to problems of nationalism and even less to those of colonial liberation. Circumstances in the Austro-Hungarian Empire, then disintegrating under the pressures of war, had compelled Austrian socialists led by Otto Bauer to consider the national question (in relation to the Empire's Czechs, Slovaks, Poles etc), but he remained an outlier. On the Marxist left, Luxemburg, Bukharin and Radek spoke for the conventional view – class was everything, national democracy nothing more than a waste of time and a clinging to the past. Considering the debate continues more than a hundred years on, it is clear that Lenin far better grasped the political implications of imperialism for revolutionary practice. The struggle of colonial and other oppressed peoples to free themselves from imperial domination constituted one of the main levers of world politics throughout the twentieth century. As Nation writes "More than any other socialist theorist of his generation…Lenin was also filled with a sense of the promise held out by the rise of revolutionary nationalism in the colonial world, regions containing, as he repeatedly noted, well more than half of the world's population."[56]

The originality and importance of Lenin's thinking, which was only amplified by his success in leading the socialist revolution in Russia, hopefully justifies the space given here to quoting his views directly. Even as he wrote them, they were being tested in life.

Easter 1916

Lenin was not entirely alone in grasping the significance of the national independence struggle for socialism in the time of imperialism. As he was pioneering the analysis of the question, James Connolly was giving his life for it in Dublin. Before his execution by the British Army for his leading role in the 1916 Easter Rising, aiming at the (partial) freedom of Ireland from British rule, Connolly remarked that "the Socialists will never understand why I am here."[57]

He was right to a very large extent. The same bemusement regarding nationalism which we have encountered in Luxemburg, Bukharin, and Pyatakov informed the response of the contemporary left in Britain towards this event, an abortive insurrection relatively easily suppressed but which became catalytic in securing the eventual freedom of the Irish people from British rule. The Easter Rising is memorialised to this day, in large part because of the brutal treatment of the rising's leaders, a politically heterogeneous group united mainly in their desire to liberate their country. The British Army embarked on a series of executions after they had surrendered, including of a wounded Connolly who had to be carried in a chair to be placed before the firing squad, until told to cease by the London government, concerned at international reaction. Connolly was himself a long-standing member of the Socialist Labour Party (he had been born in Scotland of Irish parentage and lived there for many years).

Connolly had long adopted a position on the relationship of national freedom to socialism that was very close to Lenin's. As early as 1896, when drafting a manifesto for the Irish Republican Socialist Party which he had helped to found, he wrote: "The struggle for Irish freedom has two aspects; it is national and it is social. Its national ideal can never be realised until Ireland stands forth before the world a nation free and independent. It is social and economic, because no matter what form of government may be, as long as one class owns as private property the land and instruments of labour from which all mankind derive their substance, that class will always have power to plunder and enslave the remainder of their fellow creatures...The party which would lead the Irish people from bondage to freedom must then recognise both aspects of the long-continued struggle of the Irish nation."[58]

Connolly expanded on these ideas in his major works, *Labour in Irish History* and *The Re-Conquest of Ireland*. In the latter he urged "...that the Labour Movement of Ireland must set itself the Re-Conquest of Ireland as its final aim, that the re-conquest involves taking possession of the entire country, all its power of wealth-production and all its natural resources, and organising these on a cooperative basis for the good of all."[59] Contrast this with Luxemburg's view that there was really no Polish national question at all.

Connolly also aligned with a revolutionary position from the start of the First World War. Within four days of the British Empire entering the war, dragging Ireland with it, he wrote in the *Irish Worker*: "Should the working class of Europe rather than slaughter each other for the benefit of Kings and Financiers, proceed tomorrow to erect barricades and destroy the transport services that war might be abolished, we should be perfectly justified in following such a glorious example and contributing our aid to the final dethronement of the vulture classes that Rule and Rob the world."[60]

This thinking was way in advance of the British labour movement, even its most forward sections. The SLP, whose general anti-parliamentary militancy we have already noted, maintained a public silence on the Easter Rising. It was unwilling to support a nationalist movement on principle, and was embarrassed that one of its own former organisers had involved himself in the business. The SLP newspaper did not even carry an obituary of Connolly until three years later! [61]

This was typical of the reaction to the rising on the British and international left. The founding father of general trade unionism in Britain, Ben Tillet, by this stage a leading labour chauvinist, told the TUC:

> "We are hoping that, instead of Sinn Fein or anything else trying to separate the working classes of Ireland from this country, the workers of Ireland will try to realise that they are in the same bondage as ourselves, and that the better wages and conditions they enjoy today are due to the work of the trade unionists in this country, and that the employers and farmers in Ireland are even more rapacious than our own employers."

A leading ILP newspaper proclaimed its perplexity, asserting that "a man must either be a nationalist or an internationalist."[62]

More surprisingly, elements on the international anti-war and anti-imperialist left misjudged events too. Karl Radek declared that "as something that could endanger Britain's international position, the Irish question is played out." Leon Trotsky wrote that "the historical basis for a national revolution has disappeared even in backward Ireland...the young Irish working class...had naturally wavered between syndicalism and nationalism...The experiment of an Irish national rebellion, in which Casement, with undoubted personal courage, represented obsolete hopes and out-dated methods, is over."[63]

There were stand-out exceptions in the British labour movement who supported the rising in Dublin, including among those who would be present in the emergence of the Communist Party. Sylvia Pankhurst, then organizing in London's East End, said that Socialists "…can make but one reply to the Irish rebellion, and that is to demand that Ireland should be allowed to govern itself" while T.A. Jackson organised a meeting in Leeds to protest Connolly's execution. John MacLean, then leading the developing movement against war on the Clyde claimed that "Britain's retention of Ireland is the world's most startling instance of a 'dictatorship by terrorists'" and wrote that "Britain rules Ireland against Irish wishes with policemen armed with bombs and a huge army."[64]

Lenin, of course, aligned with MacLean and Pankhurst and against the leftists who wrote off the significance of the Irish struggle for self-determination. In his article *The Discussion on Self-determination Summed-Up*, he noted that the Easter Rising "…must be the touchstone of our theoretical views." The opponents of self-determination say "that the vitality of small nations oppressed by imperialism has already been sapped…", the war "…has provided facts which refute such conclusions." Radek's argument, that the rising had been no more than a "putsch" without social support in a largely pacified agrarian country, was a "monstrously doctrinaire and pedantic assessment" which, moreover, coincided with the position of the liberal Cadet party in Russia.

The term "putsch…may be employed only when the attempt at insurrection has revealed nothing but a circle of conspirators or stupid maniacs, and has aroused no sympathy among the masses… Whoever calls such a rebellion a 'putsch' is either a hardened reactionary or a doctrinaire hopelessly incapable of envisaging a social revolution as a living phenomenon.

> "To imagine that social revolution is conceivable without revolts by small nations in the colonies and in Europe, without revolutionary outbursts by a section of the petty bourgeoisie with all its prejudices, without a movement of the politically non-conscious proletarian and semi-proletarian masses against oppression by the landowners, the church, and the monarchy, against national oppression, etc – to imagine all this is to *repudiate social revolution*. So one army lines up in one place and says 'we are for socialism' and another, somewhere else and says 'we are for imperialism' and that will be a social revolution! Only those who hold such a ridiculously pedantic view could vilify the Irish rebellion by calling it a 'putsch'. Whoever expects a 'pure' social revolution will never live to see it. Such a person pays lip-service to revolution without understanding what revolution is…"

> "It is the misfortune of the Irish that they rose prematurely, before the European revolt of the proletariat had had time to mature. Capitalism is not so harmoniously built that the various sources of rebellion can immediately merge of their own accord, without reverses and defeats."[65]

Here, once again, we see Lenin's broader political imagination at work, vaulting over the barriers of dogma which insisted that nothing revolutionary could come from an oppressed agrarian country, and that the only challenge to world capitalism must lie in the industrial working-class. This time applying his insights to a practical development he issued a challenge to the socialist movement to embrace what was dynamic and changing, and recognise national emancipation as a component part of the broader fight for social emancipation. Typically, he would allow no mealy-mouthed evasions, least of all among British socialists. "In the last issue of the English *Socialist Review*...organ of the opportunist Independent Labour Party we find...the resolution of the Party's Newcastle conference – refusal to support any war waged by *any* government even if 'nominally' it is a war of 'defence'. And in an editorial...of the same issue we read the following declaration: 'In no way do we approve of the Sinn Fein rebellion. We do not approve armed rebellion at all, any more than any other form of militarism and war.' Is there any need to prove that these 'anti-militarists', that such advocates of disarmament, not in a small, but in a big country, are the most pernicious opportunists?"[66]

The new left emerging in the heart of empire, reshaped in the heat of the barbarity of war and the hope of the October Revolution, started identifying itself with the struggle for freedom in the oppressed nations and began regarding their movements as essential allies for the labour movement "at home". The cause of Irish freedom, so vividly expressed in the Dublin insurrection, made the point inescapable, and drew a line of demarcation with the "pernicious opportunists".

Sylvia Pankhurst grasped it:

> "As Communists we stand for the self-determination of peoples and for the breaking up of Empires. In so far as the Irish Sinn Feiners weaken the power of British capitalist government we recognise that they are doing our work."

So too Fred Willis, Editor of the BSP's post-split journal *The Call*:

> "The Irish struggle for self-determination strikes a blow at the foundations of capitalism as embodied in British imperialism...the British Empire has become one of the strongest bulwarks of that capitalism we are out to destroy. So that, paradoxically as it may appear, every blow struck for Irish nationality is a blow struck also for that internationalism which is the very breath of our movement."

And finally John Maclean, speaking a little later, in 1920:

> "The Irish situation...is the most revolutionary that has ever arisen in British history, but unfortunately lads who fancy themselves the only revolutionaries are too stupid or too obsessed with some crochet to see with sufficient clarity the tight corner the Irish are placing the British in. The Irish Sinn Feiners, who make no profession of socialism or communism, are doing more to help Russia and the revolution than all the professed Marxian Bolsheviks in Britain."[67]

These insights reached, as we have seen, well beyond the mainstream understandings of pre-war British Marxism. International Marxism, however, had developed a stronger tradition which, taken to a different level by the war, intersected with the emerging "domestic" understanding to produce the conditions in which an anti-imperialist Communist Party could be formed in Britain in 1920.

October 1917

It is purely speculative to wonder how much purchase Lenin's new insights on revolutionary strategy might have gained in the international socialist movement had it not been for the ringing historical endorsement they received from the successful revolution in Russia of October 1917. It is, for sure, a fact that the victory of the Bolshevik Party set the seal on Lenin's emergence as an international leader, gave profound impetus to his demand for a formal split in the ranks of world socialism and the establishment of a new International and constituted a vindication for his denunciation of the opportunists and social-chauvinists in the socialist parties of Europe.

According to the latter, the taking of power by the Bolsheviks should not have happened – Russia should have been left to develop as a democratic bourgeois republic, the war notwithstanding – and Lenin's perspective of establishing socialism was purely fanciful. That could only be the task of the industrial workers in the more developed countries in central and western Europe. Lenin's nemesis Karl Kautsky, whose reputation and influence were on the cusp of a precipitate decline, had himself made his views plain as recently as February 1915. The Russian proletariat, he wrote, "...burdened with the traditions of serfdom, forcibly kept in ignorance by the state, barred from organising, and abandoned to overwork and alcoholism, is not even remotely capable of performing work such as that of the West European worker." Except, however, the work of revolution as it turned out![68]

Writing just a few months after Kautsky, Lenin had, in his pamphlet The Collapse of the Second International, understood things better. There he set out what was to become his famous guide to what constituted a revolutionary situation: "What, generally speaking are the symptoms of a revolutionary situation? We shall certainly not be mistaken if we indicate the following three major symptoms: (1) when it is impossible for the ruling classes to maintain their rule without any change; when there is a crisis, in one form or another, among the 'upper classes', a crisis in the policy of the ruling class, leading to a fissure through which the discontent and indignation of the oppressed classes burst forth. For a revolution to take place, it is usually insufficient for the 'lower classes" not to want' to live in the old way; it is also necessary that 'the upper classes should be unable' to live in the old way; (2) when the suffering and want of the oppressed classes have grown more acute than usual; (3) when, as a consequence of the above causes, there is a considerable increase in the activity of the masses, who uncomplainingly allow themselves to be robbed in 'peace time', but, in turbulent times, are drawn both by all the circumstances of the crisis and by the 'upper classes' themselves into independent historical action."[69]

Without these conditions, Lenin argued, a revolution would generally be impossible. But just three to four years after he wrote them out, those conditions were starting to pertain to one country after another across Europe – even in imperial Britain.

Notes

1. Lenin, *Collected Works* volume 38 (Moscow: 1972) p.180. This appears as a marginal note in 'Conspectus of Hegel's Science of Logic'.
2. 'Rediscovery and persistence of the Dialectic' by Kevin Anderson in *Lenin Reloaded* by SebasTan Budgen, Stathis Kouvelakis and Slavoj Zizek (eds) (Durham, NC: 2007) p 125. This essay is an excellent introduction to Lenin's wartime reconceptualisation of Hegel, representing a significant step away from the positivist strains in Second International Marxism, and towards a renewed dialectic of the subject and the object.
3. *War on War* by R. Craig Nation (Chicago: 2009 [1989]) pp 18-19
4. See 'The Tasks of Revolutionary Social-Democracy in the European War' in Lenin, *Collected Works* volume 21 pp 15-19
5. Nation, op. cit., pp 38-9
6. See Lenin, *Collected Works*, vol 21 p 235
7. *Leninism under Lenin* by Marcel Liebman (Pontypool: 2010 [1975]) p 114
8. Cited in K*arl Kautsky and the Socialist Revolution 1880-1938* by Massimo Salvadori (London: 1979) p 185
9. Day and Gaido (2012) p. 845
10. *Ibid.* p 774
11. Salvadori (1979) p 193. It may be argued that here Kautsky was not so much wrong as around eighty years premature, which still leaves the prognosticator useless as a guide to the actual situation and its remedies.
12. Day and Gaido (2012) p 856
13. Lenin, 'The Collapse of the Second International' in *Collected Works* vol 21 p 209
14. *Ibid.* pp 231-32
15. *Ibid.*p 220
16. Lenin. *Collected Works*, vol 21, p 21
17. *Ibid.* p 35
18. *Ibid.* p 40
19. From *'The Collapse of the Second International' Ibid.* p 242
20. *Ibid.* pp 242-43
21. *Ibid.* p 244
22. *Ibid.* p 246
23. *Ibid.* p 250
24. From 'Socialism and War' in Lenin, *Collected Works*, vol 21 p 310
25. From 'The Collapse of the Second International' *Ibid.* p 249
26. *Ibid.* p 257
27. Nation (2009) p 129
28. Lenin, *Collected Works*, vol 13 (Moscow: 1972) p 77. It is uncertain whether this assertion was actually accurate, or even whether such a computation could be realistically attempted, but the larger point stands.
29. Lenin, 'Imperialism and the Split in Socialism', *Collected Works*, vol 23 (Moscow: 1972) pp 114-15
30. Lenin *Collected Works* 21 p 212
31. *Ibid.* p 236
32. *Marxism and Revolution* by Moira Donald (New Haven: 1993) p 210
33. 'Imperialism the Highest Stage of Capitalism' in Lenin *Collected Works* volume 22 (Moscow: 1972) pp 205-06
34. *Ibid.* p 272
35. *Introduction to Imperialism and World Economy* by N. Bukharin (London: 1972 [1917]) p 14
36. Lenin, volume 22, p 281.
37. *Ibid.* p 271
38. *Ibid.* p 241
39. *Ibid.* p 266 ff
40. *Ibid.* p 300
41. *Ibid.* p 275-76

42 The relevant citations from Hobson, both of them rather prescient and with some resonance today are: "While the directors of this definitely parasitic policy are capitalists, the same motives appeal to special classes of the workers. In many towns, most important trades are dependent upon government employment or contracts; the imperialism of the metal and ship-building centres is attributed in no small degree to this fact" and "The greater part of Western Europe might then assume the appearance and character already exhibited by tracts of country in the South of England, in the Riviera, and in the tourist-ridden parts of Italy and Switzerland, little clusters of wealthy aristocrats drawing dividends and pensions from the Far East, with a somewhat larger group of professional retainers and tradesmen and a large body of personal servants and workers in the transport trade and in the final stages of production of the more perishable goods; all the main arterial industries would have disappeared, the staple foods and manufactures flowing in as tribute from Asia and Africa." See Lenin, *Collected Works* volume 22, pp 279-80
43 *Ibid*. p 256-57
44 *Ibid*. p 259
45 Victor Kiernan, *Marxism and Imperialism* (London: 1974) p 61. Kiernan adds however that Lenin's "belittlers have found no better interpretation", even though he "tried to draw out the consequences of capitalism too symmetrically." (*ibid*. p 67)
46 Lenin, volume 30, p 159
47 *Ibid*. p 160
48 "These conclusions moved Lenin away from the positivistic determinism of Kautsky and towards a reconceptualization of the fundamentals of Marxist theory." (Nation, 2009) p111.
49 Lenin, volume 22, pp 143, 146
50 *Ibid*. p 147
51 *Ibid*. pp 151-52
52 Lenin, volume 23, p.38
53 *Ibid*. p 59
54 *Ibid*. p 15
55 *Ibid*. p 74
56 Nation (2009) p 111
57 *A History of the Irish Working Class* by Peter Beresford Ellis (London: 1985 [1972]) p 232
58 *Collected Works of James Connolly* volume one (Dublin: 1987) p xiv
59 *The Re-Conquest of Ireland* by James Connolly (Dublin: 1934 [1913]) p 219
60 Connolly *Collected Works* vol 1, p xv
61 *Hesitant Comrades* by Geffrey Bell (London: 2016) p 20
62 Ellis (1985) pp 232-3
63 *Lenin's Struggle for a Revolutionary International*, by John Riddell (ed.) (London: 1984) pp 565, 562-4. The reference is to Roger Casement, a former civil servant who worked (including with Germany) in support of the rising, and was executed by the British state. Trotsky, not untypically, took a sharply different view a few years later, writing that "the British Socialist who fails to support by all possible means the uprisings in Ireland, Egypt and India against the London plutocracy – such a socialist deserves to be branded with infamy, if not with a bullet!" *Who's Afraid of the Easter Rising? 1916-2016* by James Heartfield and Kevin Rooney (Alresford: 2015) p 98
64 Heartfield/Rooney (2015). pp 90-93
65 Lenin, volume 22 p 353ff
66 Lenin, volume 23, p 104. Writing earlier, in 1915 and before the Easter Rising, he had stated with characteristic bluntness that "if Socialists of Britain do not recognise and uphold Ireland's right to secession…it is solely because they are in fact imperialists, not socialists." Bell, op. cit. p 157
67 Bell (2016) pp 171-73
68 Day and Gaido (2012) p 824

Illustration overleaf
International Women's Day march, Petrograd 1917

Chapter Four
Born Into Revolution
(1920-1926)

THE CPGB was formed in August 1920, the product of the efforts in Britain to give a political expression to the radical recomposition of the international working-class movement occasioned by the world war and the October Revolution. It represented the attempt to implant the new worldview articulated above all by Lenin and the Bolsheviks in the soil of Britain. Unique challenges were posed by this endeavour. The theory of world revolution adumbrated by Lenin posed special responsibilities for revolutionary socialists in Britain, at the heart of the most extensive Empire the world had ever endured. If the issues of defeating opportunism in the labour movement, of integrating proletarian struggle in a developed capitalist economy with the national liberation movement in the colonies and the semi-colonies and of rising to a new understanding of the tasks of proletarian internationalism were a central challenge anywhere, it was to be here. The problems facing British Communists in discharging these responsibilities were likewise imposing. Not the least of them was the fact that the new principles we have set out in the preceding chapters were only very dimly apprehended by those trying to introduce them.

Nevertheless, objective circumstances seemed as propitious as they would ever be. Three things militated in favour of the establishment of a viable Communist Party in Britain in the post-war world. First, there was the living example of the successful revolution in Russia, and its emanation, the Communist International, established to spread Bolshevik principles throughout Europe and the wider world. Second, British imperialism itself faced new crises, above all an upsurge of resistance in the nations it oppressed, but also insuperable obstacles obstructing the restoration of its pre-war economic potency. Third, there was a new mood of militancy amongst the working class, a mood which in significant respects passed beyond economic demands to a broader political challenge to the state. Little of this had been foreseen by those whose Marxism was shaped by the Kautskyism of the Second International which was, despite the storms of the wartime period, still the position of many socialists. These great changes formed the context within which the new CPGB embarked on the endeavour of overthrowing the most powerful capitalist class then existent, so we shall consider them in turn.

The Socialist State

Without the October Revolution in Russia, there would have been no CPGB, or it would have taken a dramatically different form. As noted, the left in Britain, as elsewhere, had already divided over attitudes towards the war, and this division would not easily have been repaired. However, without a strong external impulse, the tendency to settle back into old grooves, and to coalesce all political action around the Labour Party would most likely ultimately have prevailed. The Russian revolution was that impulse.

Harry Pollitt, later the CPGB's leader for many years, was a British Socialist Party activist in Lancashire at the time. Years later he described how he felt when the news came through from Petrograd:

"…Because I had been victimised from big factories and shipyards, I was working in a little shop in Swinton, Lancashire. I had read a little of Marx, but never anything of Lenin...but I know now what I felt then. 'The workers have done it at last.'...The thing that mattered to me was that lads like me had whacked the bosses and the landlords, had taken their factories, their lands and banks. I had never heard of the Dictatorship of the Proletariat or the expression Soviet Power. All I knew was the workers had conquered, were the top dogs somewhere in the world. That was enough for me. These were the lads and lasses I must support through thick and thin."[1]

And he did. Significantly, Pollitt added:

"I did not then fully understand the significance of the polemics between one section of social democracy and another. All I was concerned about was that power was in the hands of lads like me, and *whatever conception of politics had made that possible was the correct one for me* [emphasis added]."

In that last phrase we can see the basis for the hegemony the victorious Bolshevik Party of Russia was to secure in the international revolutionary movement and for the dominance of the ideas advocated by Lenin and his comrades. There were Pollitts in every land – many thousands of them, their ranks replenished in every generation over the next sixty years or so. And not just Pollitt's – the unfolding drama of the creation of a socialist society drew to Communism men and women of other classes who saw the future taking shape and wanted to make it their cause too.

The impact of the revolution in Britain was manifest on a far bigger stage than simply the creation of the CPGB. For a period, sympathy for the new government in Soviet Russia touched almost every corner of the working-class movement, at least to the extent of opposing British attempts to throttle the revolution in its cradle. Pollitt was famously involved in embargoing a boat load of munitions destined for Polish forces invading Soviet Russia, preventing them from leaving London docks. This was a mood that united class sympathy for the Soviet regime with profound opposition to any more war. It also gave birth to Councils of Action, proto-Soviets in their composition, uniting workers' organisations in support of direct action against the war threat. They made a brief appearance as new organs of class combat in the summer of 1920, as the CPGB was emerging, and were to reappear in the course of the General Strike.[2]

The October Revolution did not immediately produce a viable model of a socialist society – it was born amidst a poverty and violence which only worsened in the immediately ensuing years of civil war, famine, and economic collapse. It did, however, establish a viable example of working-class power, the first since the brief experience of the Paris Commune nearly fifty years earlier, when mass labour movements were in their infancy. The Bolsheviks had taken power in the name of soviets of workers and peasants, apparently at a stroke resolving the problems of power and transition which had so baffled Robert Blatchford and had boxed the far-cleverer Kautsky into a corner. Some saw Soviet Russia as a kind of utopia; others, more saliently, saw it as great leap for socialism away from the utopian and towards the practical and concrete. At any event, for the next seventy years the position a party, a movement, an ideology, or even an individual took in regard to the October Revolution and the regime it birthed remained an inescapable question across the socialist universe.

The CPGB, and the other Communist parties founded at around the same time, stood squarely on the side of emulation.

There were other views, of course. The stalwart social-imperialist Hyndman was among the unpersuaded. He held that the Bolsheviks and their methods were "likely to throw back the great conscious working-class movement for emancipation from slavery in all forms," he wrote.

> "That this untimely attempt in Russia, accompanied by the most fearful injustice and monstrous cruelty, has done much to hinder orderly transformation in other countries is already manifest...only by a miracle can the Bolshevik despotism, which has intensified the economic chaos already existing, be productive of good."[3]

There were more Hyndmans than Pollitts in the leadership of the labour movement, militant only in their aversion to revolution. Even these, however, drew the line at supporting Churchill's wars of intervention against the Soviet republic. In opposition to that, revolutionary and reformist were united, largely thanks to pressure from below. E.H. Carr noted the paradox: "Nowhere in Europe has Marxism so signally failed to penetrate the labour movement; nowhere was sympathy with Soviet Russia so keenly felt", a lesson in the fragmented forms class consciousness can take.[4]

The Russian October also put the ruling class on notice. Its franchise on social and economic power was not an immutable mandate of God or history. Communism thus begat anti-Communism, ferocious in proportion to the perceived threat to social privilege and hierarchy. Everywhere there was a working class or a national revolutionary movement – or even a democratic reform party - Bolshevism might lurk around the corner. And the British Empire by 1919 encompassed an awful lot of corners.

Empire under siege

British imperialism emerged from the First World War victorious but politically and financially weakened. If its victory was more than pyrrhic, it was still less than conclusive. Whatever problems had beset the Empire before 1914, they were greater still by 1919. The deterioration of its position was masked by the facts of a victory that allowed the inflation of the Empire to its maximum extent, adding Palestine, Iraq, and Tanzania amongst others to its territories, as Britain despoiled the holdings of its defeated German and Ottoman rivals - naturally without any regard to the opinions of the peoples living in those lands.

The latter, however, were making their feelings known regardless, from Ireland to India to Iraq. It is a myth that the subjected peoples had ever submitted meekly to their fate, but the world war brought discontent to boiling point across the King-Emperor's far-flung realms. Nearest to home, the Irish people, who might have once been content with the Home Rule they had been promised in 1914, now demanded full independence under the inspiration of the Easter Rising of 1916. This was reflected in a shift in electoral support from the constitutional nationalists to the republican movement Sinn Fein. The latter declared the country's independence on the basis of the 1918 election results, an act of self-determination which met with the support of both Soviet Russia and the Second International and the violent opposition of the British government. This led in turn to a colonial war of exceptional venom conducted against the Irish and the eventual partition of Ireland.

In India, Gandhi led a campaign of non-cooperation with the imperial authorities, who spoke of "reform" in the governance of the Raj but set their face firmly against Indian self-determination. For all his peculiarities of policy and method, Gandhi bought millions in India into action for independence. Nor was the imposition of British rule, under the thinnest of disguises as a League of Nations "mandate", any more welcomed in Iraq, where this exercise in neo-colonialism was in flagrant breach of the commitments made to the Arab peoples (or their rulers at least) by British diplomacy during the war. Here resistance was violent and sustained and was met by the deployment of the newly created Royal Air Force to attack recalcitrant villages, including with gas.

The attitude of labour towards these developments – and examples could be multiplied – was ambivalent. Unions which embargoed arms to Poland for use against the Soviet regime imposed no such restrictions on munitions to be used against the Irish people, despite political opposition to government policy. Nor were the Indian people given the unequivocal support they had a right to expect. Nevertheless, the crisis of British imperialism bore on the British working-class in other ways, which could not be so easily ignored.

The great conflict had undermined the economic basis on which the ramified imperial system rested. National debt soared from £706 million in 1914 to £7,349 million in 1919. Sterling was forced, temporarily at least, off the gold standard. By 1921 nearly all key indices of industrial production showed a sharp decline relative to the pre-war position.[5] The punitive imperialist peace imposed on the vanquished at Versailles also inhibited the restoration of international commerce. British exports suffered accordingly. New rivals, above all the United States, emerged to challenge Britain's hegemonic position in one part of the world after another. For the ruling class, this could mean nothing but an attack on working-class standards and organisation in order to exit the crisis with the essentials of the system unimpaired.

This was a situation, therefore, fruitful for the revolutionary perspectives championed by communism. Certainly, the conditions were propitious for a movement in Britain aimed at integrating the struggle for independence of the colonial peoples with the nearer-to-home battles which events were imposing on the British working class itself.

New horizons

Revolutionary fish need congenial water to swim in, of course. The impact of the war, the Russian revolution, and post-war conditions combined to create a fair-sized lake for British Communists. The mood of the workers varied of course from one region to another. But in many parts of the country a new political consciousness was brewing – the coalfields of South Wales and Scotland, "Red Clydeside" and the East End of London, most notably.

Here is one authoritative description of working-class attitudes in South Wales after the war:

> "The spirit of revolution was abroad in the coalfields where 'the whole existing order' and not only the private ownership of mines and minerals was being questioned. The miners, confronted directly by the British government, caught sight of new horizons: They began to have a heightened consciousness, beyond the ordinary reach of their trade union outlook, that theirs was a common struggle with the workers in every capitalist country and with subject peoples. There was an accession of international solidarity against the governments and the ruling circles of imperialism."[6]

An account by a miner from Fife in Scotland fills in details of the changed outlook and its concerns:

> "The Great War and the first year or two after it was a period of trade union and political ferment for me just as it was for so many other workers in Britain. There was our local activity in Fife. There was the Clydeside shop stewards' agitation and the rent strike, the Irish revolt, the impact of the Russian revolution, the crushing of the Spartakist revolt in Germany, the killing of Karl Liebknecht and Rosa Luxemburg, the returning soldiers, the serious discussions as to whether workers could achieve their emancipation by parliamentary or anti-parliamentary means. These things led to a tremendous fervour among the militants with whom I associated but also among the workers as a whole."[7]

The picture here is of sections of the working-class moving towards the sort of understanding of revolutionary internationalism set out by Lenin during the war, despite being in ignorance of the latter's writings (as opposed to his already-celebrated political accomplishments). This was not so surprising – we have already seen how figures like MacLean and Connolly had arrived at very similar positions. These views were not *in toto* those of the majority of the working class, but they reverberated throughout the movement nevertheless, affecting all organisations, up to and including the Labour Party. Even the Fabian grandees took note of the wind blowing from the east, and drafted a new constitution for the Party, including the famous Clause Four committing it to the attainment of some form of socialism.[8] As a Communist critic later noted:

> "Before the war the Party has obstinately refused, at conference after conference, to adopt any kind of programme whatever. Now it had been compelled by mass pressure to declare itself 'socialist' and to adopt the typical demagogic programme which was prepared by the Webbs and accepted by the Southport conference in 1919. This was the Labour Party's reply to the revolutionary movement's call for a revolutionary way out from the crisis of capitalism through the dictatorship of the proletariat and a Soviet socialist England."[9]

Whatever the intentions it is clear that, while debate on the purpose of the new formulation ranged for generations thereafter, Labour in office took only the most modest steps towards its translation into life.

Labour's shift to a nominal socialism and its gradual disentanglement organisationally and, more slowly, politically, from liberalism came as its share of the vote and parliamentary representation increased, to the point where it was to shortly supplant the Liberals, who had split in two over continued coalition with the Tories, as the second party in the country. This was merely the surface manifestation of the underlying social turbulence after the war. Red Clydeside exploded once more, with a battle in Glasgow's George Square as strikers confronted police, and the Red Flag being raised over the City Hall. A Triple Alliance of mining, railway and transport unions threatened united strike action to force an end to intervention in Russia, to military interference in industrial disputes and to conscription. Lloyd George's government conceded most demands, but the premier also called the unions' bluff, telling their leaders: "We are at your mercy…if you carry out your threat and strike, then you will defeat us. But if you do so…have you weighed the consequences…for if a force arises in the state which is stronger than the state itself, then it must be ready to take on the functions of the state, or it must withdraw and accept the authority of the state. Gentlemen, are you ready?"[10]

Rarely has the revolutionary question been so eloquently posed. The answer, of course, is that the leaders of the trade unions were far from ready to constitute their movement or themselves as the state power. They had neither perspective nor programme extending anything like so far. For the present, that did not prevent the securing of significant partial victories, but it was a shortcoming that was to prove decisive as the post-war crisis further unfolded – only one class was led by people willing to exercise state authority.

That did not mean that the capitalist class could rest easy at night. The fledgling MI5 monitored the situation amongst the working-class, and its newly enthused revolutionary element, closely. The head of the security service, Basil Thompson, reported to government the causes of revolutionary feeling in 1919, in what he held to be their order of significance – profiteering and high prices; bad housing; class hatred aggravated by the foolish and dangerous ostentation of the rich and "a government of profiteers"; education by Labour Colleges and the circulation of Marxist economic literature; the influence of extreme trade union leaders; unemployment; the working-class press; and external influences, including Russia, Ireland, Egypt, and India. On the other hand, as factors making for social stability, poor Thompson could only suggest the popularity of the Royal Family and sport.[11]

This was the world into which the CPGB was born – almost. In fact, the party was not founded until a year later, August 1920. It could be said that the supervening tragedy of the CPGB's history was that it missed the only bus that was to come along in its lifetime. It was a revolutionary party formed just *after* the conclusion of the only revolutionary situation which was to arise in the course of its seventy-year history. By the time the Party emerged blinking into the sunlight, the situation had stabilised somewhat as compared to 1919. The likelihood of the working-class being able to face down the government, as feared by Lloyd George, had shrivelled significantly. The capitalists and their state recovered their confidence and cohesion even as divisions widened in the working-class movement. The threat of a "workers' state" emerging in Britain receded, although it did not for several years disappear entirely.

The reasons for this failure were set out by Rajani Palme Dutt at the time, who unsurprisingly had a more nuanced view of the balance of forces than the panicked Basil Thompson. He identified the importance of "…strong non-revolutionary working-class institutions in the Labour Party and the trade unions" backed up by a "large middle class of undoubted White [i.e. not Red – AM] sympathies and…a large parasitic or loyalist proletariat."[12] Even when political militancy was at its fullest flood in the working-class, these were entrenched social obstacles that could not easily be overcome.[13]

Dutt's reservations were set out in a note boldly entitled "The Inapplicability of Third International Principles to Britain", not a position he was to maintain for very long. In fact, it was in 1919 that those principles would have found most fertile ground in Britain.

Birth of the Comintern
Internationally, that soil had been well tilled before the CPGB had even been founded. Two congresses of the Communist International (Comintern) had already been held, giving concrete shape to Lenin's determination to effect a rupture between revolutionaries and opportunists in the international labour movement, and powered by the struggles for class power which erupted in one European country after another once the world war had ended

in the November 1918 armistice. The story of the continent-wide revolution which the Bolsheviks had confidently anticipated would follow on their own seizure of power, and of its ultimate defeat in one country after another, most significantly in Germany, is well-known and lies outside the main thrust of this work. However, it will needs be recalled from time to time as forming the indispensable background for some of the judgements made and decisions taken by the Comintern, which powerfully influenced the British communist movement as it started to take shape. The world revolution was not a cut-and-dried process, and the perspectives of Leninism were tested in the most bitter battles, inevitably leading to their refinement.

The first congress of the new international, held in March 1919, was a scratch affair. It was assembled in haste by Lenin to catch the revolutionary wave then ascending. Outside his own Bolshevik party, represented by a distinguished delegation of Lenin, Stalin, Trotsky, Zinoviev, Bukharin and Chicherin, the organisations attending mostly lacked a firm representative base. A further ten of the 34 full delegates represented other, non-Russian, parts of what was to become the Soviet Union. The sole delegate from the Communist Party of Germany, then engaged in a revolutionary struggle, was mandated to oppose the creation of a new International as premature. He was persuaded otherwise by the course of the proceedings. The only British representative, Joseph Fineberg, was a consultative delegate from a transitory "British Communist Group" which was actually composed of British socialists, like Fineberg, resident in Russia. Fineberg had previously been a member of the BSP in London's East End, but his credentials as a representative of British revolutionaries at the Congress were certainly questionable. There were no full delegates from the colonial or semi-colonial world at the Congress, although representatives of Persia and China were to be found among the consultative delegates, who could contribute but not vote.

Despite Lenin's active presence, the proceedings of the Congress, while breathing a militant spirit, struggled to reach the levels Lenin's political thinking had ascended to during the war. While Bukharin, introducing the Comintern's platform, insisted that "we must examine the capitalist system…concretely in its character as *world* capitalism, and we should examine it as something that is a single entity, a single whole" he made no mention of the struggle in the colonies then unfolding.[14] This omission was challenged by consultative delegate S.J. Rutgers, who somehow contrived to be representing socialist propaganda groups in both the Netherlands and the USA. He urged that the International's colonial policy be expanded "to make quite clear to the colonial peoples that we seek to work actively with them, regardless of whether or not they have their own ideology or religion. We are prepared to go forward with them on the basis of opposition to imperialism, and if, for example, a rebellion were to erupt in India, that would be of enormous importance for us." Rutgers also challenged the formulation that the leading imperialist powers were only now "being exposed as international bandits" pointing out that such banditry had long been clear to the colonial peoples "who have been robbed and impressed for centuries, especially by Britain."[15]

There were more Eurocentric formulations in the *Manifesto of the Communist International*, drafted by Trotsky. It claimed, accurately enough, that "never has the problem of colonial slavery been posed more sharply than it is today. That is why there are open rebellions and revolutionary ferment in all the colonies," specifying Ireland and India among Britain's possessions. However, it then took a sharp wrong turn in a passage asserting that:

> "the liberation of the colonies is possible only together with the liberation of the work-

ing class in the imperialist centres. The workers and peasants, not only of Annam[16], Algeria and Bengal, but also of Persia and Armenia will gain the possibility of an independent existence only when the workers of Britain and France have toppled Lloyd George and Clemenceau and taken state power into their own hands….Socialist Europe will come to the aid of the liberated colonies with its technology, organisation and intellectual influence in order to facilitate the transition to a planned and organised socialist economy. Colonial slaves of Africa and Asia: the hour of proletarian dictatorship in Europe will also be the hour of your liberation!"[17]

As we have seen, such a presentation owed far more to Luxemburg than to Lenin, and reduced the colonial struggle from an equal partner in a united fight against imperialism to a consequence of European revolution. History has falsified such a perspective, although to be fair to Trotsky the European revolution did seem to be at hand in March 1919 and looked likely to precede any decisive uprisings in the colonial world. Fineberg did advance matters slightly when giving his report on the situation in Britain. While he made no reference to most colonial crises, he did acknowledge the revolutionary situation developing in Ireland and said that "the movement in Ireland will also contribute to revolutionising the working masses in Britain," describing Sinn Fein as "revolutionary nationalist."[18]

A better tone was struck by Bukharin in a short *Pravda* article on the International and the colonies published after the Congress had finished its work. Tying the development of bourgeois democracy with the horrors of colonial oppression he wrote "now that the proletariat has seen that its enemies are at home, it welcomes the uprising of the colonial peoples. The rebellion of the colonies hastens the collapse of imperialism. The movement in the colonies, therefore, although it may not be socialist at all, has joined the broad stream of the great liberation struggle that is shaking up the immense structure of world capitalism." He urged the unity of "revolutionary proletarian forces under capitalism with the efforts of colonial peoples who are liberating themselves."[19] This was nearer to Lenin's perspectives and to what actually was to happen.

The Comintern vs imperialism

Far greater attention was given to these questions, along with many others, at the Comintern's second congress, convened in Moscow in July and August 1920. This was a much larger event than its predecessor – in the intervening year communism had become a genuine mass movement across Europe, with large parties being formed in many countries, generally as a result of splits in the socialist parties of the Second International. This congress, under Lenin's intimate direction, not only gave the most penetrating consideration to the national liberation struggle in the colonial world but also to the tactical issues confronting British communists, in some cases unique in the international movement. The latter questions will be addressed in a subsequent section – here we shall look at how the Comintern sought to carry forward Lenin's insights on the world revolution and the enhanced role given to the struggles in the countries oppressed by imperialism, together constituting the great majority of humanity.

The Comintern congress got off to a good start in this respect by including thirty delegates from Asia and Latin America. Thus, the Indian revolutionary M. N. Roy could claim, with scant exaggeration that "for the first time, brown and yellow men met with white men who were not overbearing imperialists but friends and comrades."[20]

In an article previewing the Congress, Lenin had again asserted that "the revolutionary movement in the advanced countries would in fact be nothing but a sheer fraud if, in their struggle against capital, the workers of Europe and America were not closely and completely united with the hundreds upon hundreds of millions of 'colonial' slaves, who are oppressed by that capital." Yet in another sign that these perspectives had not been universally internalised, the report of the Comintern Executive to the Congress admitted that it has focussed its attention mainly on Europe and America while acknowledging that "the Eastern question would be of enormous importance in the near future."[21]

Lenin's report to the Congress built upon the insights of his *Imperialism* pamphlet and strove to turn them into workable political strategy for the new international communist movement. Again, he highlighted that "imperialism's economic relations constitute the core of the entire international situation as it now exists", and that these comprehended the oppression of more than a billion people by half-a-dozen capitalist powers, a regime of financial and economic dependency sustained by massacre.[22]

Returning to the connection between this regime and working-class politics, Lenin asked the congress how the persistence of "international Menshevism" in Europe was to be explained. "Why is this opportunism stronger in Western Europe than in our country? It is because the culture of the advanced countries has been, and still is, the result of their being able to live at the expense of a billion oppressed people." The billions of super-profit accruing from colonial exploitation formed "the economic basis of opportunism in the working-class movement", citing Britain, France, and the USA as countries where the resistance of labour movement leaders to communism was particularly strong.[23]

Lenin's manifesto was designed to strike terror into every ministry in London or Paris:

"At this Congress we see taking place a union between revolutionary proletarians of the capitalist, advanced countries, and the revolutionary masses of those countries where there is no or hardly any proletariat, that is, the oppressed masses of colonial, eastern countries. It is upon ourselves that the consolidation of unity depends, and I am sure we shall achieve it. World imperialism shall fall when the revolutionary onslaught of the exploited and oppressed workers in each country, overcoming resistance from petty-bourgeois elements and the influence of the small upper crust of labour aristocrats, merges with the revolutionary onslaught of hundreds of millions of people who have hitherto stood beyond the pale of history and have been regarded merely as the objects of history...

"The imperialist war has drawn the dependent peoples into world history. And one of the most important tasks now confronting us is to consider how the foundation stone of the organisation of the Soviet movement can be laid in the non-capitalist countries. Soviets are possible there; they will not be workers' soviets, but peasants' soviets, or soviets of working people."[24]

Little wonder that the armies of the great imperialist powers were even then invading Russia to overthrow the Bolsheviks and forestall any attempt to implement this programme. How this should be put into effect was a matter of controversy at the Congress, mainly between Lenin and Indian communist M.N. Roy. Lenin's original thesis stated that Communists should support bourgeois-democratic liberation movements in the oppressed countries. Roy argued that only authentically revolutionary movements of the masses should be supported and developed his own theses. In the ensuing debate both protagonists shifted their position somewhat, although the essence of Lenin's position was maintained, albeit with "bourgeois democratic" replaced by "national revolutionary" in defining those movements worthy of Communist backing, which Lenin acknowledged was a more precise formulation. Of course, this proved to be very far from the last word on the matter, which remained a practical question throughout the history of the world communist movement.

British delegates were obviously expected to address the issues which Lenin and the Comintern were raising. Lenin, in presenting his theses told delegates that "Comrade Quelch of the British Socialist Party spoke of this in our commission. He said that the rank-and-file British worker would consider it treasonable to help the enslaved nations in their uprisings against British rule."[25] This report drew a rejoinder from Karl Radek:

> "If Quelch only wants to point out that a strong imperialist current exists among British workers, that is a question of fact. But if this observation were to lead to our British comrades remaining passive during a colonial uprising, telling themselves that because of this mood they can do nothing more than adopt protest resolutions, then we would have to say that the Communist International has yet to teach its members the ABCs of communist politics. If the British workers, instead of confronting the bourgeois prejudices, support or passively tolerate British imperialism, then they are working for the suppression of every revolutionary movement in Britain itself...the fate of the British revolution will in large part depend on whether the peasants and workers of Ireland, India, Egypt and so forth will see the British workers as their defenders, or whether they will have grown accustomed to seeing the British working class as the accomplice of British imperialism."[26]

Radek added that the International would be monitoring the British comrades on this matter and would judge them not by the propaganda they produced but "by the number of comrades thrown into prison for agitating in the colonial countries." The CPGB was eventually to gain credit in this important respect, although Radek's other demand – that Communist MPs get themselves thrown out of the commons by the Speaker for raising colonial demands – remained unmet for want of Bolshevik parliamentarians.

Two British delegates contributed to the debate on the colonial question at the Congress. William McLaine, then a member of the BSP and an engineering worker, acknowledged that the British revolutionary movement was weak and had done little work in relation to the colonies. He endeavoured to explain Quelch's comments, emphasising that it was not being suggested that colonial work should be ignored, but that "we should recognise facts."[27] J.T. Murphy, later to become a prominent leader of the CPGB, told delegates that "today we have passed from the days of pious resolutions to that of revolutionary practice, and it is useless to say we sympathise with the subject peoples... unless such sympathy is translated into deeds." He demanded an end to complaints about "premature uprisings" in the colonies.[28]

This debate imposed an exacting mandate on the CPGB, shortly to be formed. The first hurdle was to be in securing deeper understanding of the connections between the struggle against British imperialism around the world with the tempestuous situation in Britain itself.

Proletarian jihad

An event of no lesser political significance, and even greater historical novelty, followed immediately on from the Comintern Congress. This was the first Congress of Representatives of the Peoples of the East, sponsored by the Comintern and held in Baku in precariously-Soviet Azerbaijan, a Muslim-majority territory.

Over two thousand delegates from what would now be called the Global South attended this unprecedented gathering, giving flesh-and-blood expression to the Communist unity of the proletarian struggle with the anti-imperialist fight of the masses in the colonial and semi-colonial world. About half were Communists, and many were from those parts of the former Tsarist lands once under the heel of Russian colonialism and where Soviet rule had now been established. However, numbers also attended from Turkey, Iran, India, Afghanistan, and China, answering a Comintern call signed by four British workers' representatives inter alia. Oddly, no colonial representatives served on the Congress's presiding committee.

Proceedings were opened by Zinoviev who declared that the Comintern's aim was "to put an end to the rule of capital everywhere in the world. And this will become possible only when we have lit the fire of revolution not merely in Europe and America, but throughout the world, and when behind us march the working people of Asia and Africa." But the "millions of peasants who live in Asia, our near and far east" were "the mighty mass of our reserves of infantry" – a patronising formulation indicating the continuing struggle within the European revolutionary breast on the subject, still privileging the struggle in Europe, although any insult was softened by a lyrical pledge that "...the sun of communism shines not only for the proletarians of the West but also for the working peasants of the whole world."[29]

In his main report to the Congress, the Comintern President could boast that the new international had "for the first time in the history of mankind" brought under one roof representatives of more than one-fifth of the peoples of the East....Even in its best days the Second International took the view that 'civilised' Europe can and must act as tutor to 'barbarous' Asia." Workers of Europe and working people of the East must conquer together or perish together.[30]

British imperialism was the main target of Zinoviev's oratory and, indeed, of the Congress as a whole, understandably so given its global extent. "Grasp this: every large-scale British capitalist forces to work for him not only tends and hundreds of British workers but also hundreds and thousands of peasants in Persia, Turkey and India and many other countries which are subject to British rule," Zinoviev said, before citing an unnamed Turkish liberal who said peasants understood "Bolshevik" as one "who wants to fight against Britain."[31]

Zinoviev concluded with a famous rhetorical synthesis of Marxism and Islam: "The real revolution will flare up only when we are joined by the 8000,000,000 people who live in Asia, when the African continent joins us...we are now faced with the task of kindling a real holy war against the British and French capitalists," repeating for emphasis that "we summon you to a holy war, in the first place against British imperialism." Thus, the Communist jihad was placed on the international political agenda – nearly a hundred years later the alliance of the socialist left and Muslims was still troubling the British elite at the time of the Iraq invasion.[32]

The main British contributor to proceedings in Baku was Harry Quelch. While not invoking holy war, he did optimistically assure the delegates that "the struggle of the British working class, which is advancing hand-in-hand with the working class of Russia and other countries, portends the downfall of British imperialism in the near future."

He further hoped that "the movement of the Eastern peoples will also contribute to the sweeping away of the British imperialists" and advised that "the organised workers in Britain have demanded and are demanding at their congresses that the right of self-determination be accorded to all peoples and nationalities."[33]

Concluding this exceptional event, Zinoviev pointed once more to its significance. The conference "went down in the history of mankind from the moment it began and when the enslaved oppressed, exploited peoples of the east assembled here...In this lies the great significance of our revolution. It has not only set fire to the West, but the East too is in conflagration before our eyes," he told delegates before they returned home.[34]

The British working-class movement was put on notice in the conference's appeal to the workers of Europe:

> "Workers of Britain...Hear the representatives of millions of toilers of the East! You have not heard our voice and no-one has told you of us, how we live, how we suffer under the rule of those who are also your masters."[35]

Taking the Comintern Congress and the Baku meeting together, it is clear that the international framework for British Communists was being reconstructed around them. They were being enjoined to shoulder responsibilities which no British socialists had hitherto needed to take particularly seriously in the areas of anti-imperialism, a perspective not informed by philanthropy of humanitarian solidarity but by the essentials of revolution in Britain itself.

A revolutionary fusion

While these excitements were unfolding in Moscow and Baku, the British left was striving to overcome its divisions and organise itself into a Communist Party. Unusually among the new Communist parties emerging across Europe at the time, the CPGB was the product of a process of fusion, bringing together existing and mostly very small Marxist groups, rather than of a split in an existing mass party. Indeed, the latter would have been extremely difficult, since the emerging mass party of the working-class in Britain, the Labour Party, mainly rested on affiliated trade unions unlikely to transfer their political engagements wholesale even if the CPGB had solicited such a move. Labour had only instituted the category of individual membership at the end of the war.

The parties mentioned in the preceding chapters – the British Socialist Party, the Socialist Labour Party, the Independent Labour Party – all either threw in their lot with the CPGB, or supplied a significant faction of their members to the new Party, which further attracted the support of still smaller anti-parliamentary socialist groups in South Wales and elsewhere. Two of the most charismatic anti-imperialist revolutionaries who had emerged during the war, John Maclean and Sylvia Pankhurst, did not however join the CPGB and instead pursued rival, and ephemeral, political enterprises. The absence of Maclean, who had acquired considerable international status and who had been named Consul in Glasgow for the new Soviet republic (an appointment which the British Foreign Office disdained to recognise), was a particular loss, notwithstanding that the decline in his physical and mental health, which would take him to an early grave, was already becoming apparent. According to one of his contemporaries "...he was unable to rise above personal antipathies and a limited national outlook...Had his health remained robust, he might well have learned (as many others of us did) from the experience of the revolutionary period following the war and have clarified his ideas in the course of international discussion."[36] His passionate anti-imperialism would be missed by the new party.

The process by which the majority of British Marxists came together in a united party under the umbrella of the new Communist International is described in detail in James Klugmann's initial volume of the CPGB's official history. His brief summation encapsulates the difficulties:

> "Those who set out to form a Communist Party in Britain found…in the revolutionary groups and organisations all sorts of differing approaches, differing tactics, differing weaknesses, left-wing and right-wing, reformist and sectarian."[37]

Klugmann offers this as an explanation as to why it took two years of negotiation to produce unity, but it would be wrong to infer that the time taken allowed the difficulties and divergences he identified to be more than superficially overcome. In fact, the CPGB was initially a very small and heterogeneous organisation called upon to implement principles of which it was practically ignorant to a very large extent. The largest single component was the British Socialist Party, linear descendant of Hyndman's SDF, which almost entirely went into the CPGB. It had some roots, but little grasp of Bolshevism. That did not diminish the international significance of the new party's formation. John Callaghan observes that "no section of the Comintern was more important than the tiny British party in the tasks of defending the Soviet Republic and promoting anti-imperialist struggle" since Great Britain was both the largest Empire extant and also the main promoter of anti-Soviet intervention by capitalist powers.[38]

The unifying points on which agreement was considered essential for entry into the new CPGB were very broad – support for communism against capitalism, "the Soviet idea as against parliamentary democracy" and the dictatorship of the proletariat. Opposition to colonialism and the need for a different type of party organisation were entirely omitted from the unity call.[39]

The Comintern had also adopted conditions for a Communist Party to be recognised as such, shortly to be described, which had no prior grounding for the most part in the traditions of British Marxism, still less the wider labour movement. The first period of the CPGB's history is therefore the story of its efforts to integrate these principles and the novel ways of working that accompanied them into its own practice of political leadership.

Labour and Parliament

At the outset, this focussed on two issues central to revolutionary strategy – the attitude to be taken towards participation in parliament, and whether Communists should seek affiliation to the Labour Party. The first issue was an international one, in that it arose in all the countries of capitalist democracy. The second was a more uniquely British conundrum, since the Labour Party had no exact parallels elsewhere in Europe. On both points, the guidance of Lenin proved decisive for the CPGB.

Lenin addressed these issues in his celebrated pamphlet *Left-Wing" Communism, an Infantile Disorder*, written in advance of the Comintern congress and distributed to delegates there. As a polemic on the tactics of Communist leadership, it is one of Lenin's works with the most enduring relevance.

It was here that he enunciated his famous requirements for a revolution.

"For a revolution to take place it is not enough for the exploited and oppressed masses to realise the impossibility of living in the old way, and demand changes; for a revolution to take place it is essential that the exploiters should not be able to live and rule in the old way. It is only when the 'lower classes' do not want to live in the old way and the 'upper classes' cannot carry on in the old way that the revolution can triumph."[40]

It was also where the notorious pledge "to support [Arthur] Henderson in the same way as the rope supports a hanged man" appeared, a phrase that has cast a long shadow over relations between British Communists and the Labour Party ever since.[41]

In fact, far more useful guidance was offered to the infant CPGB in a different passage, much less remarked upon. It is worth citing in full:

"We cannot tell – no-one can tell in advance – how soon a real proletarian revolution will flare up [in Britain], and what immediate cause will most serve to rouse, kindle, and impel into the struggle the very wide masses, who are still dormant. Hence, it is our duty to carry on all our preparatory work in such a way as to be 'well shod on all four feet'…It is possible that the breach will be forced, the ice broken, by a parliamentary crisis, or by a crisis arising from colonial and imperialist contradictions, which are hopelessly entangled and are becoming increasingly painful and acute, or perhaps by some third cause etc."[42]

The immediate point of interest here is Lenin's focus on the political sphere as the likely cause of a revolutionary situation arising in Britain – either in parliament or as a result of colonial crises. At this time and subsequently most socialists saw the industrial field as the one which would trigger such a development. There is something to be said for both perspectives in general. In 1920, in the wake of "Red Friday" and ahead of the General Strike, militant trade unionism must have seemed endowed with more possibilities than it actually possessed. At any event, this view haunted the CPGB well into the 1970s, by which time it had deteriorated into a spirited economism, detached from any plausible revolutionary outlook. But it is true that in the period before the General Strike, it was industrial struggles which initiated the widest working-class mobilisations. On the other hand, Lenin did not seem to expect such struggles to automatically lead to revolutionary confrontations. He saw the latter as the product of fissures in class relations at an explicitly political level – that is to say, around issues which exposed the unfitness and incapacity of the bourgeoisie to rule. Of course, he placed imperialism and its contradictions front and centre.

More generally, Lenin's argument was for flexibility and adaptability. In *Left-Wing Communism* he not only argued for the essential participation of Communists in parliament in order to use the opportunities for propaganda exposing the capitalist system and winning workers to the superiority of soviet democracy, he also insisted on the need to exploit any and every issue agitating all the classes in society, including the petty-bourgeoisie, as he had done all his political life, from *What Is To Be Done?* onwards. He offered no set path to revolution, nor cut-and-dried stages on the way there. In this again he differed from the later CPGB's increasingly dogmatic insistence on the "British Road to Socialism", leading through various intermediate forms from capitalism to socialism.

We are running ahead of ourselves here. In *Left-Wing Communism* Lenin's polemical targets in Britain were the Scottish militant Willie Gallacher and the charismatic East End agitator Sylvia Pankhurst, both of whom scorned any idea of Communist participation in parliament. The Bolshevik leader empathised with their revolutionary temperament but argued that such a quality was insufficient on its own. Gallacher had written that "our fight here is going to be a difficult one. One of the worst features of it will be the treachery of those whose personal ambition is a more impelling force than their regard for revolution. Any support given to parliamentarism is simply assisting to put power into the hands of our British Scheidemanns and Noskes.[43] Henderson, Clynes[44] and Co. are hopelessly reactionary. The official ILP is more and more coming under the control of middle-class Liberals…"[45]

Lenin responded that Gallacher had not asked "whether it is possible to bring about the Soviets' victory over parliament without getting pro-Soviet politicians into parliament, without disintegrating parliamentarism from within…" He acknowledged that the leaders of the Labour Party were "hopelessly reactionary" but that the revolution could still be advanced by giving them a measure of parliamentary support because "most British workers still follow the lead of the British Kerenskys and Scheidemanns and have not yet had experience of a government composed of these people."[46]

British Communists, he continued, "should unite their four parties and groups (all very weak, and some of them very, very weak) into a single Communist Party on the basis of the principles of the Third International and of obligatory participation in parliament",[47] going so far as to offer the Labour leadership a bloc against the Tories and Liberals, the bourgeois parties themselves increasingly uniting in defence of threatened private property. This was the way to secure a hearing from British Communists amongst the working-class, Lenin insisted, and it was in this context that the rope intended for Henderson's neck was introduced, alas. In *Left-Wing Communism* Lenin nevertheless reserved his opinion on the merits of Communist affiliation to the Labour Party. He was ready to take a position when the matter was debated at the Comintern Congress, however.

Gallacher, too, carried forward his position to the Congress. He dramatically warned delegates that the International was "on the way to becoming opportunist" and said that participating in parliament would lead to the working-class becoming adapted to democratic institutions. "The communist parties of the whole world have something better to do now than waste time on parliamentary elections."[48] He was opposed by J.T. Murphy, who argued that "the problem before us is not one of keeping ourselves spotless before the world but of carrying the revolutionary struggle not just into the institutions [49] of the working class but into the enemy camp as well…no important struggle of the workers against the employing class can take place outside parliament without having powerful repercussions inside parliament."

The Leninist theses, advocated by Bukharin on behalf of the Bolshevik Party received the overwhelming endorsement of the Congress. The theses approved detailed what revolutionary parliamentarism might entail. One formulation may particularly resonate today, in the light of debates over mandatory reselection of Labour MPs, and the means by which the labour movement might control its parliamentary representatives. This stated that:

"the organising of the parliamentary fraction must be completely in the hands of the Central Committee of the Communist parties…the Chairman and the executive committee of the Communist parliamentary fraction must be approved by the Central Committee. The Central Committee must have a permanent representative on the parliamentary fraction with veto, and on all important political questions the parliamentary fraction must request in advance instructions on its conduct from the party's Central Committee."[50]

This formula entirely reverses the flow of authority in the Labour Party (and other parliamentary socialist parties), wherein the parliamentary leadership dictates to the wider party, rather than serving its policies. Communist MPs were to be unequivocally subordinated to the party – and, ironically, no-one in Britain proved this more than Gallacher himself, who served as a Communist parliamentarian for fifteen years without becoming corrupted in the slightest.

When the Congress turned to debate the issue of Labour Party affiliation – an issue which, unlike parliamentary participation, was very specific to Britain alone – the British delegates were again divided, reflecting the differing views and histories of the organisations which were to come together to form the CPGB. Pankhurst said that affiliation would mean that "we are putting the fate of the proletarian revolution in Britain into the hands of the old trade unions" which were inimical to soviet power.[51] Gallacher enquired rhetorically how British Communists could "speak in the name of the very same party that Henderson represents?" Affiliation would, he said "deform the Communist Party's character… Leave us free to create a genuine Communist party on a really Communist basis, and let us find the ways and means to speak to the masses."[52]

McLaine, on the other hand, claimed that "the Labour Party is nothing other than the political expression of the workers organised in trade unions…workers organised in unions are turning to the left. We can see the union movement changing under the pressure of time and events. We cannot look upon the trade unions and their members as something set in stone." He supported affiliation if "other parties belonging to the Labour party keep their full freedom of action and criticism."[53]

Lenin weighed in on McLaine's side of the argument, while disagreeing with his claim that Labour was just the political expression of the unions:

"Whether or not a party is really a political party of the workers does not depend solely on whether its members are workers but also on who leads it and the content of its actions and political tactics. Only the latter really determines whether we have before us a political party of the proletariat. Regarded from this point of view, the only correct one, the Labour party is a thoroughly bourgeois party because, although made up of workers, it is led by reactionaries, and the worst kind of reactionaries at that, who act quite in the spirit of the bourgeoisie."

Labour, Lenin said, was "a highly original type of party, or rather, it is not at all a party in the ordinary sense of the word. Made up of members of all trade unions, it has at present a membership of about four million, and it allows sufficient freedom to all affiliated political parties" including, as of 1920, the British Socialist Party. He advocated testing by experience whether the advanced sections of the working-class were repelled from the Communists by affiliation to Labour.[54] The Comintern agreed with Lenin on this point too.

On both issues – taking part in parliamentary elections and affiliation to the Labour Party – the new CPGB accepted the Comintern position. This was certainly helped by the fact that Gallacher himself was swayed to Lenin's position after a meeting with the Russian premier. He returned from Moscow convinced of the Comintern's arguments, although Pankhurst remained unreconciled and, ultimately, marginalised.

The parliamentary debate was the more conclusive. Those opposing emphasised the corruption of working-class fighters sent to parliament and the belief, in Klugmann's summary, that "it was through industrial action and not through parliament that socialism would be achieved. Economic power was the issue and industrial action the road to it."[55] Such syndicalist views had more purchase then than for most of subsequent labour history, but they were insufficient against the authority of Lenin, and the recollection of the work of Communist parliamentarians like Liebknecht and Zetkin in Germany. The vote was 186 to 19. While the CPGB often debated the tactics of its electoral interventions since, as a matter of principle – utilising parliament for revolutionary purposes – the matter was never revisited.

The debate on affiliation to the Labour Party was much tighter. Many delegates argued that Labour was already discredited in the eyes of militant workers. Tom Bell urged "a Communist Party clear and distinct from any associations with reformism or the Labour Party" while others dilated on the difficulties of exposing the shortcomings of a party they would be affiliated to. Supporters of affiliation pointed to the diversity of groups, from the Fabians to the ILP and the BSP, already affiliated to Labour, and stressed the unique character of Labour as a federation of unions and political groups. A key point was made by J.F. Hodgson of the BSP who told the congress that "the mission of our Party is to be the vanguard of the revolutionary working class. You cannot be the vanguard unless you are going to march with the working class." Communists should be "in all of the working class movement, directing it, inspiring it, carrying it to ultimate victory." This position prevailed by 100 votes to 85.[56]

Nor was that the end of the matter – affiliation to Labour remained an issue for the CPGB, off and on, up until the end of the Second World War and the broader issue of Communist-Labour relations gnawed at the party until its final demise, although the matter had long since become one of indifference to Labour itself.

One earnest of the party's efforts to embed itself in the wider movement was the launching of *Labour Monthly* in 1921, shortly after the party itself. Although not officially a CPGB publication it functioned informally as the party's main magazine of theory and political discussion, and certainly gained far greater influence than those issued by the party itself, at least until the celebrity of *Marxism Today* in the 1980s. *Labour Monthly's* success was largely due to the editorship of Rajani Palme Dutt, who held the post from the outset until his death in 1974, including during his prolonged absence from Britain in the 1920s and 1930s and often alongside other positions in the party leadership (including stints as editor of the *Daily Worker* and as *de facto* general secretary of the party). He authored the Notes of the Month which opened each issue and which, despite their title, were an often-lengthy Marxist essay on contemporary events written from the perspective of CPGB policy and a deep understanding of the Marxist method. For decades these became one of the principal means of political orientation for activists throughout the labour movement and across the English-speaking world. Even in the depths of the CPGB's most intransigent phases, the magazine endeavoured to reach out to non-party authors and secure a wider audience than could be attained by an "official" theoretical journal, of which the CPGB had various from time to time.

As for Dutt himself, more perhaps than any other leading British Communist he both absorbed and represented the new insights of Leninism and its commitment to world revolution. We have noted how Pollitt was drawn to Communism by his powerful sense of class-consciousness and his identification of the October Revolution as an achievement of people of his class. Dutt, Oxford-educated, came to his Communism by a somewhat different route. In an unpublished memoir written decades later, he recalled an international meeting in December 1919 in Geneva as marking his conversion to the cause. Attending alongside later Labour minister Ellen Wilkinson, he became embroiled in an intense all-night discussion on tactics in the student movement.

> "The pros and cons were weighed; our organisation and line was analysed relentlessly like a body being dissected on a mortuary slab; at the end the decision was against us. As we came away in the cold air of the December night...Ellen Wilkinson said to me... 'This is the most ghastly, callous, inhuman machine I have ever witnessed'. I said to her 'at last I have found what I have been looking for: socialists who mean business.'"[57]

Dutt was to become as famous within the movement for his theoretical rigour and intransigence in his anti-imperialism as Pollitt was for his class militancy. They were as one in their loyalty to the USSR until the end of their lives.

The CPGB and the Colonies

The Party's official historian claimed, accurately enough, that fighting imperialism "was a new conception for the British working class. Before this there had existed amongst the advanced workers a deep-seated, more intuitive than scientific, sympathy for the oppressed colonial people." However, his subsequent assertion that "the CPGB was the first political party in Britain to recognise that the alliance of the British working class with the colonial people was the key to the victory of socialism in Britain" is to over-egg the pudding considerably. Bluntly, and without denying the step forward that the Party represented on this question, it recognised no such thing.[58] The struggle of the colonial peoples was to be supported, for sure, but it was not seen as intimately linked to the fight against capitalism in Britain itself, occasional articles in the Communist press notwithstanding.

Nevertheless, an anti-imperialist action policy for the new party was adopted by its Executive Committee as early as February 1921. This denounced the British Empire in uncompromising terms and pledged to "expose all the confusions about national equality and liberty which serve only as a cover for imperialism"; work closely with workers in subject countries "and cooperate with them in their struggle" and help the development of communist groups in those countries. Crucially, it also pledged to support broad national liberation movements in the colonies whether they were communist or (far more often in practice) not. "The oppressed masses must learn to feel that the CP of the home country is their friend."[59] An early article in *Communist Review*, the CPGB's journal, entitled 'Our Imperial Responsibilities' set out clearly that "the British Empire is the knot which socialism in this country will have to unravel if it is to succeed...the masses that are subject to the British Empire are not yet fully proletarian in character...But...their consciousness of economic misery is supplemented by their consciousness of national or racial subjugation." British workers enjoyed a relatively privileged position because of imperial exploitation, but were learning through hardship and war the reality of the need to end imperialism.[60] Here Lenin's ideas are starting to take root.

To some extent, the Party acted on these significant principles. Its two MPs at the time, Shapurji Saklatvala and J. Walton Newbold (both elected as Labour, with the latter not remaining associated with the CPGB for long) did indeed use the platform of the House of Commons to denounce British rule in India, the partition of Ireland and repression in Iraq; while the fledgling Young Communist League developed anti-militarist activity. Saklatvala and the Dutt brothers, Clemens and Rajani, all claiming Indian heritage and all playing a prominent part in the CPGB's work, itself a consequential point, also began to develop a Marxist political economy of India and to influence the first stirrings of a Communist movement in the sub-continent.

Saklatvala's parliamentary work was of great significance. Elected as Battersea North's MP until 1929 he "raised at every conceivable occasion the condition of India, to such an extent that the press referred to him as the 'Member for India'" and his very presence in the House of Commons at a time when non-white MPs were extremely rare sent a statement about the CPGB's internationalism and its opposition to racism.[61]

These beginnings did not over-impress the Comintern. Manuilsky stated at the Fifth Congress of the International in 1924 in summer 1924 that the CPGB had been passive on the colonial question and had failed to press unequivocally for the separation of the colonies from the Empire:

> "Do our British comrades think that the revolutionary process begins with the British proletariat liberating itself, and then in the capacity of a Messiah, carrying deliverance to the colonial peoples? ...Where is your fighting spirit, British comrades? Where is your readiness to carry a decisive struggle for freedom into the most far-flung corners of India?"

The Bolshevik official continued: "The Russian comrades are grateful to you for launching the slogan 'Hands Off Soviet Russia' at the time of the armed intervention. But the entire international would rejoice even more if you were now to launch another no less courageous call: 'Hands of the Colonies'." [62]

The same point was echoed by Roy, who told the conference, that "the British proletariat as a class as also the English interpretation of the theory of socialism is distorted and permeated thoroughly by the conscious or subconscious spirit of Imperialism."

One of the great figures of 20th century history joined in, Ho Chi Minh asking:

> "...what have our communist parties in England, Holland, Belgium, and other countries accomplished, which possess colonies...what have they done to educate the working class of their countries in the true spirit of real internationalism, in the spirit of reaching out to the masses of the colonies? All that our parties have done in this regard is more or less zero."[63]

In a sense, these strictures were not entirely fair. At the CPGB's own sixth congress, held a month before the Comintern gathering, a resolution had been passed underlining that it was of "the utmost importance that our struggle should be linked up with that of the workers in these colonies and Crown Dominions...the continued enslavement of the colonial peoples makes our own freedom in this country absolutely impossible...it is necessary in the interests of our own struggle that assistance should be rendered to the workers in the colonies."[64] At the next Congress it stated that "the trade union and political labour movements have been criminal in its neglect of the colonial masses, its fore most leaders actually sharing the prejudices and ideology of the British bourgeoisie on colonial exploitation and rule", pledging to take the fight forward against such "imperialist prejudices".[65]

Nor was the Comintern itself always above reproach on this matter - its strategies were not free of Eurocentric inclinations. For example, after the detailed debate on the national and colonial question by the Second Congress, at the third, held a year later, discussion on the matter was rushed and truncated, no new resolutions were adopted and no leader of the CPSU spoke in the session. Zinoviev devoted just three lines to the colonial struggle in a sixty-page report. E.H. Carr has suggested that this may have been due to Soviet diplomatic rapprochements with Britain, but true or not such treatment of the question could only send a negative signal to those parties already inclined to neglect or vacillate on their international responsibilities in this regard.[66]

By the time the fifth Comintern Congress came around the CPGB seemed to be wearying of the criticisms. Delegate E. Douglas addressed the reproaches:

> "Criticisms of the British Party have been plentiful, but not very reasonable. The British party is one of the weakest sections of the Communist International and it is confronted with one of the mightiest tasks which fall to any section...Manuilsky said that we had done nothing about the Bombay strike, and the Cawnpore trial, but if he had read *Workers' Weekly* he would have seen what steady propaganda we had carried on, showing that the workers were not only oppressed economically by imperialism, but were also refused the right to organise themselves in their defence. The British party defended the workers at the trial in Cawnpore and the Bombay strikers, and succeeded in rallying together a large movement among trade unions in its support."[67]

The Leninist understanding of the connections implicit in the idea of world revolution was making some headway in the CPGB's resolutions and also its practical action, harder work as the latter was. Later that year a colonial committee was established, but it neither lasted long nor achieved much.[68] The party's founding Chairman Arthur MacManus was appointed to lead colonial work, but he was to die before long. In early 1925 the Party dispatched Percy Glading to India to assist in the development of the Communist and working-class movements there – he was arrested and eventually deported.[69] Despite its inadequate performance, the CPGB was charged by Comintern with responsibility for overseeing the Indian Communists, a decision which did not meet with unqualified approval, not least amongst M.N. Roy and his supporters.

Glading was followed by George Allison, Phillip Spratt, and Ben Bradley to India, while Manchester Communist James Crossley was sent to Egypt. They all faced varying measures of repression, and should be remembered as being among the first British people to leave Britain for the colonies with honourable intentions. Here was a new tradition emerging, carried forward decades later in the London Recruits who went to South Africa to assist the anti-apartheid struggle at considerable personal hazard.

Dutt-Pollitt Report

Absorbing and acting upon the new understanding of world revolution was only one of the challenges facing the infant CPGB if it was to be regarded as a Bolshevik-type organisation. There was also the fact that the practices and procedures it had inherited from its constituent elements were a world away from the twenty-one conditions which the Comintern had specified as necessary for admission at its second congress.

These conditions, advanced by Lenin, imposed a formidable mandate on the new Communist Parties everywhere. They included the party press being under party control, the removal of reformists from all positions of leadership, the development of a parallel party structure to conduct work under conditions of illegality, agitation within the army (failure to do this would be 'betrayal'), a "particularly clear" attitude to colonial liberation in deeds as well as words and exposure of "their own" imperialists, the formation of cells in trade unions and a break with reformist trade unionism, subordination of parliamentary fractions to the wider party, periodical purges to remove petty-bourgeois elements from the party, an "iron" democratic centralism", unconditional support for socialist states and unequivocal subordination to decisions of the Communist International.[70] Here were the elements of what became known as "democratic centralism", the operating manual for Communist Parties worldwide, and which gave flesh to the sibling idea of a "vanguard party", the advanced section of the class as a whole, linked to and leading it.

The 21 conditions have been the subject of much controversy, starting from almost immediately after their adoption. Of course, they described an ideal Communist Party, which probably none have ever fully corresponded to. Nevertheless, they followed logically to a large extent from the political rupture and reorientation Lenin had been pursuing since 1914. They were the expression of the different type of organisation he believed was needed to advance the new strategy of world revolution he and others had developed. It was in part a blueprint born of revulsion at what had befallen the international workers' movement in 1914, led by reformist parliamentarians and union leaders into the arms of the warring capitalist classes; in part a reflection on the realisation that the roots of the chauvinist betrayal could be found in a pre-war opportunism diagnosed too late; and in part an attempt to learn from what had worked in Russia in terms of party organisation and from what hadn't in Germany above all. It was a form of working-class organisation suitable for a period of war, deep social crisis, and anticipation of imminent revolution, prioritising the international above the national and the party above its parliamentary representatives or union executives. It saw in the state an enemy to be disorganised and destroyed, not an instrument of social amelioration and it demanded the most resolute struggle against imperialism and colonialism, something which in itself demanded a rupture not just with the ruling class but with much of the leadership of the workers' movement.

Lenin later worried that his prescriptions were "too Russian". Certainly, implementing them across the movement drew the new line of demarcation between Communists and Social Democrats as far to the left as possible, and in the harshest possible manner. It has been argued that the intransigence of the Bolsheviks led to counter-productive outcomes through the imposition of a party model that was in some measure inappropriate for the more stable parliamentary democracies.

Of course, Lenin, with his eyes fixed on the world revolution, desired the creation of parties suitable for the challenges of the moment. The moment concerned saw the Red Army advancing into Poland, the German revolution still in the balance, ferment in Italy, and Soviet power on the agenda elsewhere. The 21 conditions spoke to that situation. Belief in the imminence of world revolution proved to be misplaced, but it was very far from an absurdity in 1920 – the bourgeoise feared it as much as Communists looked forward to it. Had it been foreseen that long years of struggle, either in a bourgeois-democratic framework or in resisting fascism, was the actual future ahead, perhaps some at least of the conditions might have been left by the wayside.

In any case, it took several years before the Comintern party model achieved any form of stability in most European countries, with Communism shedding supporters as the process of developing such organisations went along. Nevertheless, the 21 conditions were binding on all parties seeking to affiliate to the Comintern and, through it, identify themselves as standing militant on the side of the October Revolution and the Soviet Union.

To put it mildly, these theses were not in the least a description of the actual practice of the infant CPGB. Broadly, the party was federalised rather than centralised, based in localities rather than workplaces, indifferent to the rigours of Marxist political education and propagandist rather than immersed in working-class life and struggle. Membership came with few expectations placed upon it in terms of individual activity. Local branches were often inactive and isolated from the central leadership of the party and the struggles of the people alike.

To address this, a commission was established in 1922 to investigate the CPGB's organisation and make recommendations to improve it. This was chaired by Palme Dutt, with Harry Pollitt and Harold Inkpin as members, the latter being the brother of the party's first general secretary.[71] Its report was thus largely the work of the two men who were to play the most decisive part in the party's history over the next forty years and more. It was, in the words of John Mahon, "animated by a central idea, the transformation of a loose association of socialist-minded people into a leading political party of the working class, capable of giving leadership in all aspects of the struggle against the capitalists and their state machine."[72] A tall order for a party only a few thousand strong, concentrated in just five areas of the country, to be sure.[73]

The report itself was unsparing in describing the problems: "in these two years, with all these opportunities, and with the tireless activities and energy of individual workers, the Party has made no real progress either numerically or in terms of influence….we make pronouncements on current events, and we call upon the workers to do this and to do that, without our Party being organised to make our pronouncements to be taken seriously…Our efforts are spasmodic and chaotic in character; and there has been no central direction that would combine effectively the activities of the Party."[74]

The principal recommendations of the commission, adopted at the party's fifth congress, included:

- that every party member should be an activist, breaking with the old social-democratic style of work,
- that the central committee should lead the work of the districts and branches,
- that the party's activities should be directed to the trade unions and the workshops with "fractions" of Communists being formed to direct work in the former and "cells" based in the latter to give Communist leadership to the workers at the point of exploitation. "The factory or workshop… is the real unit of the working class, and should be the main field of our activity."[75]

- that the party's paper should be changed so that it appealed to factory workers rather than being a "small magazine of miscellaneous articles of Communist bias",
- and that a system of political education of the membership should be established "to make of every recruit a useful member of the party."[76]

All this was, of course, novel, and while the commission's recommendations were adopted much of the party leadership either had doubts about their feasibility or simply did not know how to advance them. As the report noted "the principles of Communist organisation represent a complete revolutionary break with the old socialist traditions of ineffectiveness in this country."[77] The focus on the factory required a rupture with the existing branch structure, and the emphasis on leadership at all levels revolutionised the understanding of what a party member was, and what his/her relationship should be to the party as a collective. The implementation of the Dutt-Pollitt report was thus slow and piecemeal, despite its authors being incorporated into the central leadership of the CPGB, while a number of the intellectuals who had adhered at the party's foundation now fell away.[78] It was not perhaps until 1929 that the work was undertaken in earnest.

The Commission was concerned to emphasise, however, that all the organisational changes in the world were insignificant compared to the development of the party's political line. "Organisation is only important as a means of achieving a certain policy: otherwise it is dead. Its value, therefore, depends on the value of the policy calling for it."[79] That too continued to pose challenges.

The First Labour Government

The evolution of the Labour Party's own position on imperialism was scarcely positive. Its manifesto for the first post-war general election, held at the end of 1918, demanded the "immediate withdrawal of the Allied forces from Russia" and also pledged that "Freedom for Ireland and India it claims as democratic rights, and it will extend to all subject peoples the right of self-determination within the British Commonwealth of Free Nations." By 1922 this had become "the recognition of the real independence of Egypt and self-government for India". In 1923, for the election that brought the first minority Labour government to office, the manifesto dropped all mention of the Empire, India, or colonies. Even the ILP, soul of Labour's left, while railing against imperialist exploitation, advanced a policy the City could well live with, warning that it would tell the colonial peoples "We will lend you our capital, and as long as the world continues the practice of paying interest, you shall pay the current rate of interest. We will bring you our technical skill and our engineering and managerial capacity, and you shall pay for them at proper rates."[80] Thus MacDonald entered Downing Street in 1924 as unencumbered by commitments as he was by conscience on the matter.[81]

This effacing of any anti-imperialist commitment went hand-in-hand with changes to Labour's federal working-class structure. First, the door was barred to the affiliation of the Communist Party (unlike the BSP before it) on grounds of its opposition to parliamentarism and its affiliation to the Communist International. Yet the same door was flung open to individual members for the first time, allowing many middle-class refugees from the declining Liberal Party to join, despite a complete lack of socialist commitment. Communists, however, were not allowed to join as individuals any more than their Party could join collectively. Later still, trade unions were prohibited from sending Communists as their representatives to Labour committees and conferences, national or local. This substantially infringed on the rights of the unions themselves, and curbed the democratic basis of their affiliation to Labour. Its passage was a measure of the desperation of Labour's leaders to exclude any communist influence from the Party and was obviously part and parcel of offering themselves as fit and proper custodians of the Empire when called upon.

These circumstances made it challenging for the CPGB to operate the Comintern's turn to united front politics, agreed at its Fourth Congress in 1922. This called for unity between Communists and Social Democrats at the base, in joint struggle for immediate demands, and if possible by agreement at the top. The latter was utterly precluded in Britain, since the officialdom at Transport House[82] would have nothing whatever to do with Communism. However, many Communists were also individual members of the Labour Party until their exclusion was rigorously enforced, so a form of de facto unity persisted. The CPGB explored novel ways to develop a unified political left, but these had little or no impact on the performance of the first Labour government to hold office, an event which had its historic significance, but corresponded to none of the scenarios for the formation of a "workers' government" which the Comintern had sketched.

In fact, the Fifth Congress of the Comintern was not wide of the mark when it described MacDonald's government as "a government of the imperialist bourgeoisie" and "the faithful servant of his majesty the king of the empire of capitalists."[83] The first Labour administration was servile to the capitalist state, and intransigent in its defence of empire. Under considerable mass pressure, it did extend diplomatic recognition to Soviet Russia. But its tone was set by the new Colonial Secretary, right-wing railway workers' union leader Jimmy Thomas, who declared that he and his colleagues "were proud and jealous of, and were prepared to maintain the Empire", doing nothing to "weaken the position and prestige" of their imperial inheritance.[84]

Suiting deeds to their words, Labour intensified colonial repression. In the course of its nine months in office, Indian revolutionaries were put on trial at Cawnpore, Iraqi villages were bombed, new military commitments made in Egypt, a cruiser dispatched to Sudan and nationalists arrested in Burma.

The Communist Party was too small to materially affect the course of the first Labour government, although not so small that Labour's hierarchy had neglected to ensure its effective exclusion from the party's counsels. However, it played a signal, albeit indirect, part in MacDonald's downfall. Firstly, the indulgence of the Liberal party, which had sustained the minority Labour administration in office, was withdrawn after the government declined to prosecute J.R. Campbell, editor of the party's *Workers Weekly* newspaper[85], for sedition after he had run an article calling on soldiers not to turn their guns against their fellow workers. This decision precipitated a general election which, at its conclusion, was marked by the publication of the notorious "Zinoviev Letter". This was a document, sensationally reported in the *Daily Mail* and other right-wing newspapers, which purported to be instructions from the President of the Comintern to the CPGB, inciting the latter to all means of unconstitutional political disruption. The "letter" was in fact a complete forgery, laundered by MI6, the secret intelligence service, into the public domain. By conjuring the spectre of Bolshevik insurrection, it was credited with ensuring the defeat of a Labour government which had recognised the Soviet state.

Indeed, the fear of Communism in the ruling class, anxious for their Empire and fretful at the changed mood among the workers at home, somewhat outran the Party's actual capacities. The establishment took no chances, however. The British section of the world revolutionary movement had made itself a perceived menace and, as the post-war social disequilibrium persisted and moved to its climactic moment, it was to be treated as such.

General Strike and its impact

In spring 1925 the Comintern Executive heard from its President, Zinoviev (he of the non-existent letter), that "the centre of gravity of the further development of world revolution may gradually begin to move to England."[86] There was no sharper sign of this than the policies adopted by the 1925 meeting of the TUC, certainly the most militant to date. A great majority of delegates agreed their "complete opposition to imperialism" and "the domination of non-British peoples by the British government." This was a high water mark of anti-imperialism in the British labour movement, and it was not coincidental that it was reached as the decisive class battle of the General Strike was coming into view. It was this coalescence of rising industrial militancy with deepening political consciousness that gave the strike the revolutionary colouring which so alarmed the capitalist class at the time, even though Lenin's pre-requisites for a revolutionary situation as set out in Left-Wing Communism were missing, at least to the degree of maturity which a revolution would have required. For one thing, the Labour Party conference in 1925 at Liverpool exhibited none of the TUC's progressive character. It took further measures to exclude Communists from any part in the party's proceedings and was, in the CPGB's estimation "a blow for the working class...the purely Liberal resolutions adopted, the repudiation of the fight against imperialism and the Dawes Plan, which are degrading our fellow workers abroad, and thereby striking at British conditions, the failure to face the capitalist attack on wages and hours, were intended to please the capitalists. The TUC has frightened them. The decisions at Liverpool have reassured them."[87]

For another thing, the Communist Party's influence was weak, outside of a few areas. As mandated by the Dutt-Pollitt report, and indeed as imposed by the whole crisis of post-war British capitalism, the party had devoted considerable efforts to building up its position in the trade unions and the factories. The most important manifestation of this had been the development of the National Minority Movement, which aimed to unite left-wing and militant forces within the trade unions on a common platform of struggle, out with the control of the right-wing leaders of the major unions. Pollitt himself was its national secretary, and veteran international labour agitator (and CP member) Tom Mann its Chairman. The NMM did not seek to split trade unions or establish "red" alternatives to the official structures, recognising that to do so would be to take the road to isolation – however, Pollitt later conceded that "it tended to create the impression that it was a separate and rival body to the trade unions and to the Trades Union Congress, although this was never its true aim".[88] The NMM built a considerable base in the coalfields of Scotland and Wales, and among engineering workers and had affiliated trade union organisations with a membership of over a million, a considerable section of total trade union membership at the time. In the words of Arthur Horner, a Communist militant from the South Wales coalfield, "the aims we put forward could not but command the support of any genuine trade unionist" and the "violent opposition" of the right-wing of the labour movement.[89]

Parallel to this, a National Unemployed Workers Movement was initiated, to organise the millions of those who could no longer find work in the depressed post-war economy. These workers were effectively ignored by the official movement, despite mass unemployment constituting an Achilles heel for organised labour. Many of the unemployed (two million in total in 1920) were ex-servicemen or workers from the war industries. The NUWM adopted the principle of "work or full maintenance at trade union rates of wages." Communist Wal Hannington became the first national organiser of the new movement, which was soon at the forefront of struggles against central and local authorities, despite the indifference of the Labour Party hierarchy.[90]

Through these organisations, the CPGB established an influence in the working-class movement, despite its small numbers. It had 161 of its own factory cells on the eve of the general strike, albeit with fewer than 1,000 members in total.[91] The impact the CPGB had on the labour movement of the time was summed up by J.T. Murphy, then a member of the party leadership: "It helped the unemployed workers to organise as never before...it saw the workers leaving the trade unions and raised the cry 'Back to the Unions'...It saw the significance of the collapse of the Trade Union International and participated in the formation of the Red International of Labour Unions. It took up the cudgels on behalf of international working-class solidarity...it led the way in organising the discontent within the unions and helped the creation and development of the Minority Movement. It saw the potentialities of the existing Trades Councils and directed the awakening forces within them...It saw the weaknesses of the trade unions and their lack of central leadership and raised the demand for power to be invested in the General Council..." On all of these issues, Murphy argued, the leadership of the unions had followed the Party's lead eventually and in some measure. "It cannot be gainsaid that the victories and achievements of the labour movement in all these crises have corresponded to the degree to which it has approximated the measures indicated by the Communist Party..."[92]

Despite this growing influence, the party was barely implanted in many working-class areas of the country, and was in a position to give an effective lead, outside of and if needs be against the official movement hierarchy, in very few indeed. As evidence of this weakness the party's seventh congress, held in 1925 and two years after the publication of the Dutt-Pollitt report, found many of its recommendations still unimplemented, as evidenced by renewed calls for the formation of factory cells and more political education of the membership.

The story of the strike has oft been told – indeed the second volume of the official history of the CPGB is devoted almost entirely to the issue. The general strike itself was the product of the post-war crisis of British imperialism, and the culmination of the aggravated class relations which had been developing since 1918. It was precipitated by the decision of the Conservative Chancellor, Winston Churchill, to do the City's bidding and return the pound to the gold standard as an earnest of the drive to re-establish British imperialism's pre-war position, a savagely deflationary move which hit workers in export industries particularly hard, and which he subsequently regretted. The coal owners, despite having made nearly £100 million in profits since the war,[93] determined that the adjustments must be borne by the miners, in terms of a pay cut of at least 13% and an added hour a day at the coalface - a comprehensive attempt to increase the rate of surplus value in a decisive industry without any fresh investment. The Miners Federation of Great Britain (MFGB) then the largest union in the country, rejected these attacks on its members. An initial attempt at imposition of these draconian deteriorations by the coal-owners was met by a threatened general strike in summer 1925, whereupon the government backed down and agreed to subsidise the industry for a period, alongside establishing a commission to enquire into its reorganisation and economics. This Tory retreat was known as "Red Friday" as a signal day of victory for the working class. However, such victories under capitalism can only ever be temporary or vulnerable, in this case very much so. The capitalist state was in 1925 unready for the showdown, but spent the next nine months preparing for it, while the trade unions did not, despite insistent prompting from the Communist Party. Among the measures taken by the ruling class was the establishment of a strike-breaking force, the civil-military Organisation for the Maintenance of Supplies, which the Party dubbed "the most definite step towards organised fascism yet made in this country."[94] Klugmann was right to point out that, in contradistinction to the dogmas of reformism, "Baldwin, Churchill and the Government took it for granted that the state was their state, the state of British capitalism, and proceeded to mobilise and use it for their aims". [emphases in original][95]

The supervening problem was that the leaders of the labour movement either regarded that state as theirs too or were at least quite unwilling to challenge its authority. The General Council shuffled with the utmost reluctance into the strike, ostentatiously declining to make any preparations adequate to ensure its success and clinging until well past the eleventh hour to hopes of the miners being induced to accept some form of compromise. The political leadership were still worse, being overtly opposed to the whole idea of a general strike. Ramsay MacDonald wrote once the stoppage was underway that "I don't like General Strikes. I haven't changed my opinion. I have said so in the House of Commons."[96] Indeed he had – in a speech that miners' leader A.J. Cook called one of the most "sickening" in parliamentary history, he described the MFGB's resistance to wage cuts and longer hours as a "dogma" and added "with the discussion of general strikes and Bolshevism and all that kind of thing, I have nothing to do at all."[97] Jimmy Thomas, leader of the railway workers and staunch imperialist on Labour's front bench as well, avowed mid-strike that he had "never disguised that I did not favour the principle of a General Strike."[98] Dragged into a confrontation beyond their political conceptions, ensnared by their acceptance of Prime Minister Baldwin's definition of the terms of the strike – "it is not wages that are imperilled; it is the freedom of our very constitution"[99] – the leadership of the labour movement had been defeated in their heads before the strike actually began on May 3. One side was led by men fully understanding that they were engaged in a political confrontation, as Baldwin's words prove, while the other was led by those desperate to keep the issues strictly within industrial bounds and then even on that basis to terminate it on whatever terms were to be had or, in finality, no terms at all. They were far more alarmed at the consequences of winning than of losing.

More than one and a half million organised workers supported the strike call, in addition to more than one million miners locked out by the owners. The response was solid throughout, bringing transport across the country to a halt immediately, and the number of works on strike only increased as the struggle unfolded. While Churchill was urging military action – vetoed by the calmer Baldwin – the TUC was advising strikers to avoid idleness by playing sports or staging entertainments.

Eventually, the TUC, turning over every stone in search of a way out, as Klugmann put it, found Herbert Samuel under one of them.[100] Samuel was a Liberal politician who had led the official commission looking into the mining industry, and who had also served as High Commissioner in Britain's new mandate of Palestine. He came back from an Italian sojourn to write a memorandum, without government sanction, setting out a basis for new negotiations but committing no-one to anything. That was enough for the General Council. The ineffable Thomas challenged Cook: "…will you not accept the word of a British gentleman who has been Governor of Palestine," a challenge almost lyrical in its expression of the worldview of British imperialist reformism.[101] The leaders of the TUC went to Downing Street to surrender in person to Baldwin, who made no commitments whatsoever in response.

The mass of the workers on strike were stupefied – they had been anticipating more trades being called out, not total capitulation. However, dressed up, it was a defeat, and one rejected by the MFGB itself, whose members remained locked out in support of their existing wages and hours. Cook was scathing about the General Council's performance: "A few days longer and the government and the capitalist class, financiers, parasites and exploiters, would have been compelled to make peace with the miners…They threw away the chance of a victory greater than British labour has ever won."[102] That judgement still stands.

A revolution missed?

How revolutionary was the strike? A quarter of a century later, Willie Gallacher insisted that "for nine days, there existed in Britain two governments. The bourgeoisie and their hangers-on looked to and took their orders from the Baldwin government. The organised working class fought the Baldwin government, ignored its orders, looked to and took its orders from its own government – the General Council, and proceeded to set up its own administrative machinery throughout the country – Councils of Action."[103] This would seem to be something of an overstatement – the Councils of Action did indeed contain the beginnings of a system of dual power, but only in a few places did they actually reach that potential, above all in the coalfields of the North-East. And as Gallacher acknowledged, the leaders of the General Council in no way saw themselves as an alternative government and were as frightened as the ruling class by any suggestion of dual power.

Klugmann's more measured judgement allowed that "where strike committees or Councils of Action were most effective, where they really embodied the unity of the local working class, really developed efficient organisational methods, carried out mass picketing, issued permits for transport etc, there began to develop an embryo alternative centre of government, something like a type of 'dual power'."[104] Klugmann could have added control of food distribution and the formation of workers' defence units in some communities to his list of functions the Councils of Action discharged. In places, the Councils formed country associations, but such power as they exercised was never more than local, it was not national or even regional. Any development in that direction would have required in fact the overturning of the existing leadership of the General Council, a project which would have encountered a number of obstacles, including that prevalence of constitutional ideas in the mass of the working class to which Klugmann also drew attention.

Solomon Lozovsky, the Soviet leader of the Red International of Labour Unions claimed at the time that a "sort of dual power" existed during the strike, but noted the lack of political slogans in an event which he held to be greater than the Russian revolution of 1905. Karl Radek, on the other hand, told a visitor that the strike was "not a revolutionary movement…simply a wage dispute."[105] The reality would seem to lie somewhere between these judgements. "Dual power" could have evolved, and might have done so had the strike been prolonged, or had government military action escalated the confrontation, but things never reached that pitch. The state – the first power – was not seriously threatened in its functions, while the second power – the working-class leadership - had for the most part no desire at all to establish itself as an alternative source of authority.

The confrontation occurred when the moment of greatest potential for revolutionary change in the post-war period had already passed, as we have seen. Earlier threated general strikes could have had greater revolutionary impact, but on those occasions the ruling class had backed down or compromised, doubtless in recognition of the peril. By 1926 reformism had consolidated its hold on the leadership of the working-class movement, and the outcome of the strike was only to solidify this position. The election of a Labour government in 1924, however brief its tenure and nugatory its achievements, served to strengthen the tendency to look to parliamentarism as the best, and proper, way to seek social advance. "The revolutionary years of 1918, 1919 and 1920 were past and gone," Page Arnot wrote in 1926.[106] More than forty years later, Arnot's comrade James Klugmann made the same point more fully:

> "The British working class was still in the 1920s paying the price of living in the historic centre of imperialism...The reformism that goes with imperialism was still exercising a strong influence over the great majority of the British working class, including some of the most militant organised workers. The British working-class movement was still strongly empirical; it fought hard in a class sense and in a class way for its rights and standards within the capitalist system, but still, through the influence of reformism, in the main accepted the existence of the system, or at least, if it wanted to change it, accepted to work within it, accepted the capitalist state."[107]

Klugmann can only be faulted for the implication that in the 1960s, when he was writing, the working class had substantially different attitudes for the most part – in fact, as in the 1920s, so in the 2020s.

Notwithstanding, the establishment was unrelaxed about a revolutionary alternative leadership emerging. As part of its extensive preparations for the looming struggle, the government arrested and prosecuted a dozen leaders of the CPGB. All were imprisoned for up to a year, beheading the party at a critical moment. The judge offered leniency to those who were prepared to renounce their Communist convictions but found no takers.[108] He also unilaterally declared the CPGB to be an illegal organisation.[109] A shadow executive, headed by Dundee Communist Bob Stewart, took over.

The CPGB still managed to acquit itself heroically, and its political judgements were broadly correct throughout the crisis as even the Comintern, sparing in praising its sections as it was, acknowledged. In January 1926 it had started urging serious preparations on the TUC, raising the demand of empowering the General Council to lead the whole trade union movement in the coming struggle. That may now seem like a mistake in the light of the General Council's wretched performance. However, it must be borne in mind that the General Council was a relatively new institution, having only been established in 1920 to supersede the TUC's Parliamentary Committee. It was the only body with the potential authority to lead the movement as a whole and its conduct in 1925 had been resolute enough. It was also empowered by the militant spirit of the 1925 Congress itself. In the end, the CPGB's proposal was adopted in April, as the only means available of directing a General Strike. Other unions would have been unwilling to subordinate themselves to the MFGB alone, and the CPGB itself and the Minority Movement it led absolutely lacked the purchase to call a general strike unilaterally. As Murphy put it:

> "It may be asked why the Minority Movement and the Communist Party did not set up a new leadership. The answer is a simple one. Both are in a minority, and whilst the influence of both organisations is...growing...neither have a sufficient organic

control, that is have not yet sufficient leading positions in the unions to be able to control the unions even in the crisis…"[110] The January manifesto also urged practical measures like an agreement with the Co-Op on provisioning strikers, the formation of Workers' Defence Corps "to protect trade union liberties against the fascists" and uniting with the unemployed to "counter…the capitalist attempt to force the unemployed into black-legging".[111]

As the strike began in May, the Party made it clear that victory meant simply acceptance of the MFGB's demands on wages, hours and national agreements, albeit sustained by the creation of Councils of Action based on the Trades Councils and backed by Workers' Defence Corps. It made no stronger demands, although on the second day of the strike it issued additional slogans- "all together behind the miners…nationalisation of the mines, the resignation of Baldwin and the formation of a Labour government"- which were hardly revolutionary either.[112] It did not raise the demand of soviet power or the formation of a revolutionary government at any time. As argued, this was realistic.

During the strike itself, the Party's Covent Garden HQ was raided by police three times, and 135 Communists ended up in prison.[113] 1,200 Communists in all were arrested in the course of the strike, nearly one-quarter of the party's total membership.[114] The Party, under these blows of state repression, nevertheless managed to produce a regular Workers Bulletin supplying news of the strike and taking a far more militant stand than the TUC's official *British Worker*. It endeavoured to give the lead required. When the impending betrayal was consummated, it railed against the General Council's treachery and, perhaps belatedly, noted that its left-wing had "tolerated defeatist agitation and not protested against this treacherous decision". It urged workers to now "take things into their own hands"[115] which, outside the coalfields, did not happen as a slow return to work commenced and unions in each industry and company negotiated the best surrender terms they could, endeavouring, far from always successfully, to minimise victimisation of militants.

The Comintern in Moscow approved of the British party's endeavours through the strike. Lozovsky declared that it had acted as "a real Bolshevik party" and Stalin said that it was "one of the best sections of the Comintern" with "completely correct" policies during the strike, handicapped mainly by its weak following among the workers.[116] Trotsky, then still a member, albeit an oppositional one, of the Russian party leadership, took a different view. He insisted that the substitution of a proletarian for a bourgeois state had been on the agenda, and that the strike would "at least greatly hasten its approach", both points which were incorrect. He subsequently wrote that "the whole present 'superstructure' of the British working class – in all its shades and groupings without exception – is an apparatus for putting the brake on revolution", a semi-anarchist formulation that was widely understood to be a denunciation of the CPGB *inter alia*. He was consequently forced to tell the CPSU Politbureau that it was untrue, that he considered the British party "a reactionary organisation, an obstacle in the path of the working class."[117]

The Comintern Executive pronounced that "by and large the CPGB passed the test of its political maturity. The attempt to present it as a 'brake on the revolution' is beneath criticism…the CPGB gave a correct appraisal of the liquidation of the strike as 'the greatest treachery'". It added, correctly, that "the strike was called off because it was spreading, for the leaders feared nothing so much as its extension" into a more acute class struggle. "The tactics of the government and the bourgeoisie were the tactics of vigorous and calculated offensive. The tactics of the trade union leaders were the tactics of betrayal and surrender." However, it saw only a diminishing basis for "traditional English liberalism" going forward as imperialist super-profits declined.[118]

The polemics in Moscow were entwined with a controversy over the Anglo-Russian Trade Union Committee, which had brought together representatives of the two trade union centres for the purpose, in the Russian view at least, of helping block the way to imperialist war against the USSR. Trotsky and Zinoviev argued that persisting in this union committee risked giving credibility to the reformist leaders in Britain and demanded a public rupture. Stalin accused them at the CPSU Central Committee of "trying to get us to overthrow the General Council from Moscow, without the British trade union masses." He added:

> "Is it difficult to understand that in the event of a rupture we lose contact with the British trade-union movement…and we delight the hearts of the Churchills and the Thomases, without getting anything in return except discomfiture? Trotsky takes as the starting point of his policy of theatrical gestures, not concrete human beings, not the concrete workers of flesh and blood who are living and struggling in Britain, but some sort of ideal and ethereal beings who are revolutionary from head to foot."[119]
> In fact, the unity committee did not survive much longer as Communist criticism of the British union leaders mounted, and its activities had little or no impact on the course of the strike. The General Council rejected a large cash donation from the Soviet trade unions, the MFGB did not.[120]

The CPGB's resilient support for the miners and the evident acuity of their condemnation of the movement's leadership earned it growing respect and support. By the end of 1926 its membership had doubled, to more than 10,000 for the first time. Most of the new recruits were in the coalfields, particularly in Durham and South Wales, where resistance to the colliery owners' lockout was at its strongest. It was a challenge to integrate these new members into the party's often precarious organisations, and many were lost again before long. At its eighth congress later in the year, the Party summed up the lessons for itself: "The Party must explain to the workers on the basis of their experience the impossibility of maintaining even their present conditions without the overthrow of capitalism. It must draw upon the strike experience to expose the real nature of the capitalist dictatorship, and on the basis of this, to dispel all illusions regarding the possibility of realising socialism through the mechanism of the present state machine."[121]

With the defeat of the General Strike the period of post-war crisis for British imperialism, already over the worst, definitively passed. New crises lay ahead of course, and before long. But they did not embody such volatile and unstable class relations as the 1919-26 period. It would be more than two generations before industrial militancy reached a similar pitch (and when a general strike was very briefly mooted once more) and by then the political make-up of the British labour movement had to a considerable extent, calcified. Orienting British Communism under these circumstances was to present a range of new challenges.

Notes

1. *Looking Ahead* by Harry Follitt (London: 1947) pp 41-42
2. See *The Councils of Action 1920 and the Britsh Labour Movement's Defence of Soviet Russia* by John Foster (London: 2017) for a detailed analysis of the Councils and their importance.
3. *Evolution of Revolution* by H.M. Hyndman (London: 1920) pp 388-9
4. *The Bolshevik Revolution* vol. 3 by E.H. Carr (Harmondsworth: 1953) p 417
5. *The Class Struggle in Britain in the epoch of Imperialism*, Part II by Ralph Fox (London: 1933) pp 54-5.
6. *South Wales Miners 1914-26* by Robin Page Arnot (Cardiff: 1975) p 161
7. John McArthur in *Militant Miners* by Ian MacDougall (ed.) (Edinburgh: 1975) p 17
8. The Clause read: "To secure for the producers by hand or by brain the full fruits of their industry, and the most equitable distribution thereof that may be possible, upon the basis of the common ownership of the means of production and the best obtainable system of popular administration and control of each industry or service." This remained in Labour's Rule Book until 1995, when Tony Blair secured its deletion.
9. Fox (1933) pp 67-8
10. *The Making of the Transport and General Workers' Union* by Ken Coates and Tony Topham (Oxford: 1991) p 716. 11 *Ibid.* p 720.
12. *Class or Nation* by Neil Redfern (London: 2005) p 63
13. Communist journalist Ralph Fox later put the emphasis instead on "the weaknesses of the English Communists themselves", in particular "the heritage of opportunism...the complete ignorance and under-estimation of illegal work and anti-militarist activity, the failure to expose the vicious and counter-revolutionary pacifism of the ILP...the strong anti-parliamentarism and syndicalist tendencies..." Fox (1933) pp 52-53. Fox is identifying some of the political expressions of the social forces which Dutt directed attention to.
14. *Founding the Communist International* by John Riddell (ed.) (New York: 1987) p 173.
15. *Ibid.* pp 187-8
16. A contemporary name for Vietnam.
17. *Ibid.* pp 317-8.
18. *Ibid.* p 159
19. *Ibid* pp 424-5
20. *Workers of the World and Oppressed People's Unite – Proceedings and Documents of the Second Congress, 1920* by John Riddell (ed.) (New York: 1991) p 39
21. *Ibid.* pp 66, 92.
22. *Ibid.* pp 108-9
23. *Ibid.* pp 121-2
24. *Ibid.* pp 123-4
25. *Ibid.* p 216
26. *Ibid.* p 231-2. Quelch had form. He once referred to black labourers at London docks as "jolly coons" and raised the racist trope about black men being a sexual threat to white women. He was rebuked for this racism by the visiting Bolshevik Georgi Chicherin, but not by his own comrades. See *Rajani Palme Dutt* by John Callaghan (London: 1993) p 95.
27. Riddell (1991) p 262. McLaine became a member of the CPGB's first Central Commttee, but left the Party in 1929 and subsequently became anti-communist.
28. *Ibid.* p 270 29 Baku Congress of the Feoples of the East (London:1977) p.12-13
30. *Ibid.* pp 24-27
31. *Ibid.* pp 29-33
32. *Ibid.* p 34-36. Karl Radek also used the "holy war" motif in his speech to the Congress.
33. *Ibid.* pp 17, 72.
34. *Ibid.* pp 155-60
35. *Ibid.* p 174ff. Other points of interest from the Baku Congress, peripheral to this work, include Bela Kun's claim that in the countries of the east Soviet power "will be the expression of the dictatorship of the poorest peasantry" (p. 124) and concerns, vigorously expressed, by delegates from Muslim areas of Soviet Russia concerning the boorish anti-religious behaviour of some Bolshevik cadres,

who were thus provoking counter-revolutionary feelings among the toilers (pp 59-64).
36 *John Maclean* by Tom Bell (Glasgow: 1944) pp152-3. A more recent biography, *John Maclean* by Henry Bell (London: 2018) goes into greater detail as to his politics and his health in his later years. He died in 1923 at the age of 44, and his funeral remains the largest Glasgow has seen to this day.
37 *History of the Communist Party of Great Britain* volume 1 by James Klugmann (London: 1968) p 15.
38 'The Communists and the Colonies: Anti-imperialism Between the Wars' by John Callaghan in *Opening the Books* by Geoff Andrews, Nina Fishman and Kevin Morgan (eds.) (London: 1995) p 5
39 Klugmann (1968) pp 36-37
40 *Collected Works*, volume 31, V.I. Lenin, pp 84-5.
41 *Ibid*, p 88
42 *Ibid*. p 97
43 Leaders of the German SPD who had participated in the suppression of the Spartacists in 1919.
44 J.R. Clynes was a trade unionist and Labour MP who later became leader of the Labour Party. A supporter of British imperialism in the First World War.
45 Lenin vol 31 p 79
46 *Ibid* pp 80-84
47 *Ibid*. p 86
48 Riddell (1991) vol 1 p 44
49 *Ibid*. p 453
50 *Ibid*. p 477
51 Riddell (1991) vol 2 p 942
52 *Ibid*. pp 946-7
53 *Ibid*. pp 944-5
54 *Ibid*. pp 948-53
55 Klugmann (1968) p 42-3
56 *Ibid*. pp 44-48
57 Callaghan (1993) p 34 58 *Ibid* p 157 ff
59 *Ibid*. p 160
60 *British Communism : A documentary history* by John Callaghan and Ben Harker (eds) (Manchester: 2011) p 86
61 *Saklatvala* by Mike Squires (London: 1990) p 118
62 First Congress of the Communist InternaJonal – abridged report (London: 1924) p 193
63 *Comintern and the Destiny of Communism in India 1919-1943* by Sobhanlal Datta Gupta (Kolkata: 2006) pp107-8
64 Klugmann (1968) p 302
65 Squires (1990) p 143
66 Carr (1953) p. 385
67 *Fifth Congress* p 205
68 The CPGB did not actually employ a full-time official to deal with colonial issues unti 1949! Andrews et al (1995) p 9.
69 In 1938 Glading was imprisoned for having passed on documents relating to the Royal Arsenal to Soviet intelligence. He remained a Communist until his death in 1970.
70 The 21 conditions are fully set out in Riddell (1991) vol 2 pp 979-87
71 Arthur Inkpin was the CPGB's General Secretary until 1929, but the post did not then carry the expectation of political leadership of the Party that it was to acquire under Pollitt and subsequently.
72 *Harry Pollitt* by John Mahon (London: 1976) p 86
73 London, Lancashire, Glasgow, Fife and South Wales together accounted for over eighty per cent of the membership in 1922.
74 *Report on Organisation*, CPGB, (London: 1922) p 10
75 *Ibid*. p 38
76 *Ibid*. p 53
77 *Ibid*. p 15
78 However, a recommendation by Dutt that Pollitt should be appointed the party's general secretary immediately was not agreed by Comintern. *HarryPollitt* by Kevin Morgan (Manchester:1993)p 32.
79 CPGB (1922) p 6
80 *How to End War* by Fenner Brockway (London: 1923) p 10. This is essentially the programme of

neo-colonialism, thirty years ahead of time.
81 *British General Election Manifestos 1900-1974* by F.W.S. Craig (London: 1975) pp 31, 38, 47-49.
82 From the mid-1920s the HQ of not just its owner, the Transport and General Workers Union, but the TUC and the Labour Party as well.
83 *Socialism in One Country* vol 3 by E. H. Carr (Harmondsworth: 1964) p 134
84 Klugmann (1968) p 301
85 The paper had been renamed and relaunched, changing its name from its predecessor *The Communist* as part of the attempt to implement the Dutt-Pollitt report's recommendations.
86 Carr (1964) p 352
87 *History of the Communist Party of Great Britain* volume 2 by James Klugmann (London: 1969) p 88
88 *Serving My Time* by Harry Pollitt (London: 1940) p 168
89 *Incorrigible Rebel* by Arthur Horner (London: 1960) p 67
90 See *Unemployed Struggles 1919-1936* by Wal Hannington (London: 1977[1936]) for the story of the movement.
91 *The British Communist Party and Moscow 1920-1943* by Andrew Thorpe (Manchester: 2000) p 92
92 *The Political Meaning of the Great Strike* by J.T. Murphy (London: 1926) p 17.
93 Murphy (1926) p 35.
94 *The General Strike May 1926: Its Origins and History* by Robin Page Arnot (London: 1926) pp 48, 52.
95 Klugmann (1969) p 172
96 Arnot (1926) p 173.
97 *The Nine Days* by A.J. Cook (London: 1926) p 15
98 Arnot (1926) p 201
99 *Ibid.* p 166
100 Klugmann (1969) p 125
101 Cook (1926) p 20
102 *Ibid.* p 23
103 Willie Gallacher foreword in *The General Strike of 1926* by John Murray (London: 1951) p 9.
104 Klugmann (1969) p 159.
105 *Foundations of a Planned Economy* vol 3 part II by E.H. Carr (Basingstoke:1976) pp 317-8 106 Arnot (1926) p 73
107 Klugmann (1969) p 188.
108 The imprisoned leaders were Tom Bell, J.R Campbell, Ernie Cant, Willie Gallacher, Wal Hannington, Albert Inkpin, Arthur MacManus, J.T. Murphy, Robin Page Arnot, Harry Pollitt, Bill Rust and Tom Wintringham. Palme Dutt escaped detention because he was resident in Brussels at the time and facing a charge, later dropped, of conspiring against the King of the Belgians, which trumped the presence of a Special Branch detective from London seeking his extradition.
109 Klugmann (1969) p 78. In fact, while the Communist Party was heavily harassed, its rights curtailed and some of its publications suppressed, it was never actually declared illegal.
110 Murphy (1926) p 113
111 Arnot (1926), pp70-2
112 *Ibid.* pp 163, 177
113 Thorpe (2000) p 94
114 *The International Working-Class Movement* vol 5 by S.S. Salychev (editor) (Moscow: 1985) p 172
115 Arnot (1926) p 212
116 Carr (1976) pp 320, 325. 117 *Ibid.* p 322-3
118 *The Communist International 1919-43 Documents* vol 2 by Jane Degras (editor) (London: 1971) pp 303-6
119 *On the Opposition* by J.V. Stalin (Moscow: 1928) pp 353, 360-1
120 The Soviet unions condemned the TUC for its "treachery", which the CPGB regarded as undiplomatically sharp, although it did not seem to go beyond what the party itself had said. Stalin called the leaders of the TUC and the Labour Party "downright traitors or spineless fellow-travellers of these traitors." Degras (1971) p 301.
121 Klugmann (1969) p 224

Illustration overleaf The National Unemployed Workers Movement

Chapter Five
The Challenges of Bolshevisation
(1926-1929)

THE YEARS from the end of the First World War to the defeat of the General Strike were not only replete with struggles of enduring significance, their outcome set the framework for working-class politics for years to come. They were years when class power in Britain was to some extent moot, when British imperialism was trying every manoeuvre to recover its preeminent position in the world and when the labour movement was ascending to new power and responsibilities. The Communist Party was formed and came of age in those years, equipped with a theory of world revolution which it but dimly comprehended and which was largely shaped in its implementation by the Communist International. The Comintern was itself centred on Russian Bolshevism which remained, as of 1926, victorious if somewhat precariously placed. Its own perspectives were clouded by the New Economic Policy introduced by . to stabilise the workers' state's relations with its overwhelmingly peasant population and permit the economy to recover from the devastating depredations of war and civil war.

By 1926 the glorious perspectives of a swift triumph of the revolution across Europe had abated. In one country after another the revolutionary working-class had been defeated, most significantly in Germany. The expected relief of Soviet Russia through the establishment of socialism in more developed countries had not arrived and was no longer imminently anticipated. The Comintern had first addressed this deficiency at its Fourth Congress in 1922, which advanced the demand for a united front of workers' parties, trying to overcome on a practical plane at least the consequences of the split in the international workers' movement. It raised the slogan of forming workers' governments, a capacious formulation which in theory extended from the Labour-Liberal administration in Britain[1] through to Communist-led governments in still-bourgeois states. This approach helped the new Communist parties strengthen their positions in the labour movement, but it did not lead to any larger political breakthroughs. Rather, the fascist takeover in Italy and the subsequent destruction of the workers' parties by the renegade socialist Mussolini more portended the future. Nor was the world revolution necessarily doing better in the colonial and semi-colonial world. The Communist Party of China, by far the most significant Comintern affiliate in such countries, was to suffer a shattering blow in 1927 when its allies in the nationalist Kuomintang turned on it, massacring tens of thousands of workers as it did so. Indeed, the whole idea of world revolution was being incrementally recalibrated to cover a prolonged historical process rather than a more-or-less simultaneous event in the main capitalist powers.

The CPGB had to take its bearings in the aftermath of the defeat of 1926. As with many such defeats (and victories) its import was not immediately clear — was it a setback or a rout? Was reformist leadership now discredited or entrenched? How long would the period of retreat go on for? How should the Party now seek to express its leading role? Above all, how should it address the fact that its position in the labour movement was by now quite different from the fluid arrangements that had existed at the time of its birth, six years earlier, when there had been few institutional barriers to the full participation of Communists in the political and industrial organisations of the movement alike?

The salient facts seemed to be these: The leadership of the labour movement had comprehensively betrayed the interests of the working class and the principles of the movement, on the political field in 1924 and industrially in 1926, and proved itself supporters of imperialism and the bourgeois state; the left-wing outside the Communist Party had been vacillating and pusillanimous, quite incapable of providing a real alternative to the right; the Labour Party had agreed to bar Communists from its ranks at every potential point of entry, thereby limiting dramatically the CPGB's capacity for political intervention; the Communist Party itself was very weakly-implanted in the movement, even if its influence considerably outstripped its feeble membership figures, meaning it could not plausibly constitute itself as an alternative centre of leadership, at least with any significant following.

There were assets too, of course. The Party was building up an experienced cadre, tested in class battles. Its capacity to issue clear responses to the unfolding situation was growing, as shown during the General Strike. The Soviet Union continued to enjoy widespread sympathy in the working class. And while there was no route to formal engagement within the Labour Party, Communists had myriad connections with left-wing forces in and around the party. Nevertheless, a new strategy was needed and as ever it was to emerge from the interplay of domestic and international factors, with the Comintern, the summit of the world Communist party, ultimately having the decisive say. This dialectic led to the adoption of the "class against class" or "third period" (the post-war crisis and the subsequent capitalist stabilisation being the first two) strategy by the CPGB, as for Communist parties everywhere. It would be wrong to ignore, however, the indigenous roots of this shift as well as the conclusive international pressure, nor to neglect its achievements alongside its evident and considerable shortcomings, the latter lying in the direction of extreme sectarianism. That is the story of this chapter, a further unfolding of the relationship between a putative revolution in Britian and a world revolutionary process not proceeding as anticipated.

Strike lessons

Not many months elapsed before the CPGB's conduct during the General Strike, hitherto assessed favourably both in Britain and in Moscow, came under more critical scrutiny. Two members of the CPGB leadership, J.T. Murphy and Robin Page Arnot, wrote an article for the Comintern press asserting that the party had erred by not sufficiently exposing the role of the left-wing union leaders during the strike – a right deviation.[2] This judgement was an error, since the main problems besetting the conduct of the strike had been, firstly, the role of the capitalist state and, secondly, the dominant right-wing on the General Council. The role of the union left-wing had been dispiriting but not decisive.

Nevertheless, the importance of the sally was that it raised for the first time the charge that the CPGB was insufficiently militant. Other seeds of the "class against class" approach were also being sown. R. Palme Dutt, in his pamphlet on the strike, proclaimed its defeat as the start of "a new era, the era of mass struggle, which can only culminate in open revolutionary struggle." The strike was "the first stage of the revolutionary struggle of the masses for power; but this struggle was endeavouring to find expression through an obsolete apparatus of liberal trade unionism and parliamentarism which was wholly unsuited for it and could only betray it."[3] This apocalyptic scenario was not to be borne out by events, and indicated the extent to which the defeat suffered by the workers was under-estimated. Dutt's "most important" task, "the fight for the mass Communist party as the sole means to establish the new revolutionary leadership" was unlikely to gain much traction while based on such a misreading of the situation.[4]

At the same time, Comintern economists were starting to predict the end of the stabilisation of capitalism, forecasting the outbreak of a new economic crisis. Yet the TUC leadership was moving into a period of more committed class collaboration in the wake of the strike defeat, a retreat headed by Ernie Bevin, the powerful leader of the Transport & General Workers' Union now emerging as a dominating force in trade unionism and the wider movement, who became ever more anti-communist with the passing of the years. His strategic vision was of the integration of the working-class movement into the state, as a recognised force in the community. The Tories, of course, had other ideas, and used their victory in the General Strike to pass anti-union legislation, outlawing solidarity action and mass picketing, banning civil service unions from affiliating to the TUC, removing trade union immunities and changing the basis of the political levy to one of "opting in", which meant members had to positively decide to pay the levy, rather than it being an automatic obligation of membership which one would have to proactively opt out of. This last measure was aimed at defunding the Labour Party.

The response of the unions was to offer cooperation to the employers. Dismissing a policy of class struggle as "futile, certain to fail, and sure to lead to bloodshed and misery", the General Council, over the lone opposition of A.J. Cook of the miners, agreed to what became known Mondism, after the Chairman of the chemical giant ICI, who agreed to lead the employers' side of an industrial council looking at reorganising industry and arbitrating disputes in a bargain which saw union recognition traded off against a commitment to peace in the workshops. As Allen Hutt observed: "The meaning of Mondism was not long in making itself clear. Throughout industry conditions worsened, with extensive speeding up, breaking of piece rates, violating of agreements" and wage cuts, particularly savage in the coalfields.[5]

Parallel to this, several unions altered their rules to exclude Communists from holding any office as part of measures to isolate the Minority Movement and prevent it ever becoming a majority. These circumstances combined with more parochial issues to lead to the creation of the only breakaway "red union" of any significance in Britain – the United Mineworkers of Scotland.[6] This was led by Communists, primarily in the Fife coalfield, after undemocratic maneouvres by the right-wing forced a split. In other European countries, dividing trade unionism along political lines became normal, but in Britain it came up against the entrenched desire for unity which had made trade unionism, rather than socialism, the mainspring of working-class expression. Even in the depths of the "class against class" period the Comintern hesitated to push the CPGB in the direction of "red" breakaways in any concerted fashion, sometimes curbing its sister organisation the Red International of Labour Unions in its enthusiasm to spread the Scottish mining split across the whole country. Disputes over the conduct of the party's industrial work remained frequent and acute, however, as we shall see.

Bolshevisation

As the CPGB sought to negotiate this new landscape, it did so in a changed international setting. The Communist International, parallel to its pursuit of a united front strategy in the workers' movement, had also raised the slogan of the "bolshevisation" of the Communist Parties. The meaning of this was simple – all Communists must learn from the experience of the Russian Bolsheviks, and seek to emulate its principles and practices (or the received view as to what these were) in their own work. This was unsurprsing – the failure of the revolution in Europe in the post-war years shone the spotlight ever more exclusively on the one party which had established working-class power and a socialist regime: the Soviet. Its example was irresistible and doubts about its transferability to very different conditions were swept aside.

Comintern President Zinoviev was the main progenitor of this argument in the world movement, initially using the "bolshevisation" slogan as a stick to belabour the dissident Trotsky, with his long history of opposition to Bolshevism – Zinoviev was himself to be on the losing side of renewed inner-party struggle in the CPSU(B) against Stalin and Bukharin before long. He told the 14th Russian party congress that "Bolshevisation of the Communist parties means utilising the experience of the Bolshevik party in three revolutions (and the experience of the best Comintern sections) in its application to the concrete situation of the given country."[7] The fifth congress of Comintern had given a more expansive definition of this project. Bolshevisation meant that "The party must be really a mass party maintaining the closest and unseverable ties with the mass of the workers both in legal and illegal conditions and serve as the expression of their needs and aspirations; The party must follow a flexible tactic free from dogmatism or sectarianism…it must essentially be a revolutionary, Marxist party, undeviatingly and under all circumstances working towards its main goal, that of bringing nearer the victory of the proletariat over the bourgeoisie; It must be a centralised party with a strict discipline that is not merely mechanical, but expresses the unity of party will and party action."[8]

Even this last description leaned towards the very general. It fell to the fifth plenum of the Comintern executive in April 1925 to dot 'i's and cross 't's, the meeting at which, as we have seen, Zinoviev was particularly bullish about revolutionary prospects in Britain. Here the Finnish Comintern leader Kuusinen explained that the slogan was "directed against opportunist tendencies, but not at all in favour of sectarian tendencies", navigating the perpetual Scylla and Charybdis of Communist politics. It mandated recruiting new workers from the factories and creating a "new revolutionary type of party worker-official." Firm discipline was to be allied to "the democratic method within the party," another desirable synthesis to be often invoked but more rarely obtained.[9] The immediate priority turned out to be "iron discipline" in pursuit of reliable Marxist-Leninist parties. As Carr notes, given that "bolshevisation" was associated with a period of capitalist stabilisation, in which imminent revolutionary upsurges in Europe were not to be anticipated, the slogan easily became associated with the unconditional defence of the USSR.[10] These two features have led Trotskyist historians to see the process as a turning point in the history of the Comintern, with "bolshevisation" nothing more than "a stop inflicted on parties which still had the pretension to think for themselves… a disciplinary regime imposed by the Moscow bureaucracy…"[11] This entirely neglects the reality of the failures and complexities the Communist parties were grappling with, and the endemic factionalism which paralysed their capacity to do so (the CPGB was getting off lightly in this respect as of 1925).

An enormous resolution adopted by the plenum touched on what bolshevisation meant in almost every aspect of work. As far as the CPGB was concerned, it spelt out that: "the central task of bolshevisation consists in 1. Work in the trade unions. Particular attention to the Minority Movement…2. Agitation against the imperialist sentiments of the English labour aristocracy…3. The creation of a firmly centralised party organisation and liquidation of dilettante methods of work. 4. Systematic application of united front tactics."[12]

Notably, the first point in this programme of Bolshevisation – activity in trade unions – was very soon to be called into question.

The CPGB has barely begun to absorb the implications of all this before it was plunged into the vortex of the General Strike, with the associated police repression of the party. This exacerbated the weaknesses the party had in meeting the demands of bolshevisation – a lack of factory cells being one and the lack even of a central organisation department another. The issue of bolshevisation therefore framed the party's development over a much longer period, and the controversies over "class against class" lay at least in part in the party's continuing struggle to meet the expectations which the Comintern and some of its own cadre placed upon it – creating a revolutionary organisation able to emulate the outstanding victories of the CPSU. The Party's seventh congress agreed on its "transformation into a mass organisation, saturated with the ideas of Marxism and Leninism, and capable of utilising them in the most varying circumstances and in most varied ways." So much was only on paper, of course. Klugmann acknowledges that the change was not assisted by the term "bolshevisation", which was alien to British ears. It "would have been better… presented in terms more proper and comprehensible to the British working-class movement, for there was nothing alien in the ideas."[13] The same point might be made in relation to "democratic centralism", an imposing term describing concept which is only an extension of regular working-class practice. Workers may, for example, oppose a decision to go on strike but, if in a minority, are expected to abide by the majority decision.

Ideology, the ILP and India
In the aftermath of the General Strike, all trends on the socialist left in Britain were floundering, the semi-bolshevised-at-best CPGB not excluded. The largest socialist organisation, and the CPGB's principal rival on the left within the working class movement, was the Independent Labour Party. While it still claimed the membership of Ramsay MacDonald and Philip Snowdon their affiliation was increasingly nominal and more a matter of historic sentiment than anything else. In practice, the ILP was moving to the left (MacDonald and Snowden were not), and to a sharper critique of capitalism, although not to a revolutionary point of view. Searching for a distinctive agenda to advance, in 1926 the ILP adopted a living wage policy, originally advanced by John Strachey (later a Communist fellow traveller, later still an imperialist cabinet minister) and Oswald Moseley (later Britain's leading fascist) and then developed by a commission including H.N. Brailsford and J.A. Hobson, the author of *Imperialism* many years earlier.

The policy, broadly a proto-Keynesian project aimed at expanding the home market, included measures of demand management, social welfare and nationalisation of industry and land, was intended as a programmatic guide for the next Labour government, although MacDonald was opposed from the outset at what he saw as trespassing on the prerogatives of parliamentarians.[14] In practice it played no part in Labour's policy at the time, but it is of relevance here in that it prompted the most comprehensive statement of views in this period by the CPGB in Palme Dutt's polemical response, *Socialism and the Living Wage*. Dutt's pamphlet represents one of the first Marxist critiques of Keynesian economics, and repays study on those grounds alone.

Straight from the start, Dutt indicated that the Party was now taking a far harsher approach to the non-Communist left: "The ILP ideology gathers into itself all the confusion, relics, middle-class illusions, veiled imperialism, pacifist make-believe, constitutionalism, utopianism and defeatism, which still shackle the advance of the working class in Britain. Only by the consequent smashing of this ideology can the working class free its path forward..." This set the tone for the next several years of Communist propaganda.[15]

Dutt postulated that there was a growing gap between the discredited reformist leaders and "the *vanguard* of the workers" fighting wage cuts and capitalist reorganisation. The ILP programme he saw as attempting to bridge that gap: "This utopian 'living wage' is to be achieved by a series of legal and administrative changes within capitalist society, reviving trade by the development of the home market, ensuring larger profits than ever to the capitalists, etc. Thus, the propaganda is a propaganda of capitalist reconstruction" holding out the illusion of fresh progress within capitalism.[16]

He built his argument on an analysis cutting to the heart of Britain's world role. "The British capitalist class is today maintaining its wealth by means which are not primarily based on the expansion and advance of British industry, but are in fact directly hostile to the interests of British industry and to the livelihood of the mass of the population in Britain...All these will be found to turn on the imperialist position of Britain."[17] Here was the position that imperialism not only exploited the peoples of the oppressed world, but also tended to impoverish the workers of Britain itself, strengthening the basis for international unity against the British bourgeoisie. It marked a significant advance in British Communist thinking. Dutt identified the main problems as "the restriction of production, and exaction of monopoly prices on a limited production...the increasing role of Britain as a financial rather than as a manufacturing centre" and "the development of foreign and imperial industrial production, largely on the basis of enslaved labour in Asia and Africa". The last point was to become controversial, as we shall shortly see, but the first anticipated a line of argument heard in the labour movement to this day, developed generations before anyone had invented the term "financialisation".[18] In a curious alignment, Dutt first outlined this concern in the same era as his class adversary Winston Churchill, then Chancellor of the Exchequer, was claiming that he "would rather see finance less proud and industry more content," not a policy his decision to return Britain to the gold standard actually promoted.[19]

Flowing from this, Dutt developed a political position which was to recur in different forms over the years: "In the period of capitalist decline a reformist leadership and party has no longer any basis, and can only maintain itself for a while by acting more and more openly as the decoy agent of the capitalist class in the task of repression and stabilisation on the backs of the workers..."[20]

This exemplified a tendency to read a correct economic assessment straight over into definitive political conclusions, down-playing mediating factors, subjective elements and so forth which would (and did) retard such developments. Dutt's view does, however, again indicate that a home-grown flowering of the "class against class" line was advancing, well ahead of any Comintern dictation. The ILP was, Dutt held, guilty of a "centrism" which served no purpose beyond ensuring that workers disillusioned with MacDonald and company did not reach "the alternative of communism or revolutionary class struggle" and remained instead attached to the "old bureaucratic machine" of the labour movement.[21] Where the ILP placed reforms at the centre of their perspectives, Dutt placed class struggle, wherein he highlighted the ILP's "hypocritical betrayal of the workers' struggle" during the General Strike.[22]

This was only one of the extensions of Marxist analysis that emerged in this period within the CPGB. The other, again from the pen of Dutt, was the publication of *Modern India*, a pioneering political economy of Britain's relationship to the largest colony in the world. It marked a major step in the attempt to integrate the class struggle in Britian with that unfolding across the Empire oppressed by British capitalism. "The subjection of India is one of the strongest bases of English capitalism," Dutt wrote. "Of the 450 millions of the British Empire, 320 millions are Indian. Historically, the plunder of India during the seventeenth and eighteenth centuries was one of the principal sources of primitive accumulation which made the development of capitalism in Britian and the industrial revolution possible...British investments in India are estimated at one thousand million pounds, or more than the total in all the Dominions put together. The role of India in British capitalist economy is relatively increasing...The control of India is the keystone of British Imperialism."[23]

As Dutt pointed out, this made the importance of the Indian national struggle "in the world fight against imperialism sufficiently obvious...in the present epoch the international working class cannot free itself by purely local struggles without at the same time overthrowing the imperialist domination of subject nations which is today the strongest basis of modern capitalism."[24] The connection between the interests of the British working class and Indian emancipation were getting closer he argued, as the period when "the subjection and poverty of the Indian masses was one of the concealed bases of the higher standards of the British workers"[25] was succeeded by a new phase wherein British industries and, hence, jobs were being exported to India were rates of exploitation could be still higher. The Dundee jute industry was instanced. This was to be countered by the Comintern a little later, most controversially.

Dutt detailed the political economy of India's exploitation and outlined the development of the movement for national independence, and of the working-class of India within it. His conclusion highlighted the extent to which the precepts of Leninism were beginning to take hold. "Modern imperialism is based on the subjection of two social forces, which together are destined to overthrow it – the working class at home and the subject nations abroad. It is obvious that the struggle of these two elements against imperialism is a common struggle, and their interest a common interest. Imperialism, which is a world force, cannot be fought effectively on the basis of a single country. This is a lesson which is being learnt today both by the working class in the imperialist countries and by the national movement in the subject countries. It is a lesson which carries very important political consequences for both."[26] He added that "of all the obstacles that have stood in the way of an effective alliance of the Indian national struggle and the British working class, the heaviest is the record of the Labour Party, in office and in opposition, and this obstacle must be frankly recognised and faced, before any real progress can be made."[27]

In this, the ILP was no reliable ally. Its own report on imperialist issues dripped with patronising condescension. It made clear that in Africa "self-government...is not immediately attainable" for want of education, and stressed that the role of socialists in Britain was "to prepare the Asiatic and African subjects of the Empire for self-government", assistance which the colonial peoples were not soliciting.[28] The editor of the ILP's main journal *Forward*, published in its Glasgow stronghold, Thomas Johnstone, was also an early advocate of Empire Socialism, denouncing the idea that the Empire was "an engine of grab and oppression and that it is and can be nothing more". He urged instead imperial development "under a Socialist inspiration."[29]

Dutt therefore probably did not have the ILP, or its leadership at least, in mind when he identified the new forces in the British working-class movement which "are committed to a definite anti-imperialist policy and to full support of the subject peoples in their struggle against British rule" – these were the Minority Movement in the trade unions, "the organised Left-Wing in the Labour Party" and the Communist Party. This larger Communist-oriented left-wing, which understood that "the British working class can only achieve its own freedom in conjunction with all the peoples who are subject to the British bourgeois yoke", is the subject to which we should next turn.[30]

The Left-Wing

Dutt's strategic political insights remained of limited import if the Party could not overcome the growing gap between its own small organisation and the great body of the labour movement, a gap which Labour and TUC officialdom was working to widen day in, day out.

The CPGB's endeavours to overcome this incipient isolation focussed on building a left-wing alternative to the prevailing reformism, a campaign still framed, as of 1927, by the Comintern's adherence to a united front strategy. In terms of any agreement between the CPGB and the leaderships of the Labour Party or the TUC, the united front was an entirely dead letter. As far as Labour was concerned, the barriers to Communist participation now included barring affiliated unions from sending Communists as their delegates to Labour bodies. Constituencies and committees which refused to go along with these draconian limitations on democracy were summarily suspended or dissolved by the leadership, a plan of coercion still being vigorously pursued by Sir Keir Starmer a century later. In 1925 Dutt had written that the Labour left "however strong separately and locally, have not yet been able to unite in a common bloc or on a common programme. The various groups, tendencies, movements…are all dispersed. They have no common programme, and not the most rudimentary form of common organisation. In consequence the right wing is able to maintain its power."[31] That, too, still resonates.

To address this weakness the Party initiated the National Left-Wing Movement to bring together sanctioned Labour organisations and their supporters with the Communists in a united front, posing an alternative to the reformist twins of MacDonaldism and Mondism. The NLWM aimed to win Labour for "a militant socialist policy in place of its present policy of compromise with capitalism."[32] At the time of the General Strike, there were still nearly 1,500 CPGB members holding Labour Party cards so united work was not an impossibility.[33] Notwithstanding, from at least 1927 on there were some in the CPGB leadership who doubted that the desired shift in Labour's policy was any longer attainable. As a united front the NLWM got off to a shaky beginning when all its national officers proved to be CPGB members, a position modified somewhat after non-Communists expressed discontent.[34]

In 1927 the NLWM claimed an affiliated membership of 150,000, but this number began to decline under pressure from the implacable Labour bureaucracy. Its network of disaffiliated Labour organisations was weak outside London and Lancashire for the most part (the NLWM had been initiated by Bethnal Green Labour Party). It did however benefit from a weekly newspaper, the *Sunday Worker*, backed by the CPGB, to amplify its message. Ultimately the NLWM was doomed because of the ambiguity in its purpose, standing between a Labour Party deaf to its appeals and a Communist Party increasingly confident in its own Leninist leadership and seeking to win the working masses directly to its banner. The NLWM suffered from the classic problems of "half-way houses". The CPGB certainly did not want to see it develop as a third party in its own right, although leading Communist

J.T. Murphy flirted with this idea. Increasingly strident in its critique of left-wing social democracy as it moved towards the "class against class" policy, the CPGB had little to offer the disaffiliated Labour left and wanted little from it beyond a full and complete transition to Bolshevism. Stuck in a no-man's land, the constituencies and branches disaffiliated from the Labour Party had no prospect beyond gradual disintegration.

The challenges of any form of left unity were highlighted by the launch in 1928 of the Cook-Maxton manifesto. A.J. Cook was of course leader of the Miners Federation and an ally of the CPGB, while James Maxton was a charismatic leader of the ILP and an MP from Glasgow. The Manifesto – *Our Case for a Socialist Revival* – was an explicit challenge to the MacDonald leadership on the basis of the class war and the overthrow of capitalism. It denounced Mondism and Labour's timorous policy as "an enlightened liberal programme" rather than socialism. Significantly, it went further in demanding the abolition of the monarchy and the House of Lords and the complete self-determination of the peoples of the Empire.[35] Its demands were closely aligned with the programme of the NLWM, and Willie Gallacher had played a part in the discussions leading to the campaign.

This initiative aroused considerable enthusiasm across the left but became bogged down almost immediately within the ILP, upset at its chairman having launched the campaign without any discussion within the party at all. Opinion in the CPGB was also initially divided, with some of those involved in the NLWM welcoming it, while others felt it continued to propagate illusions in the likelihood of the Labour Party transforming itself and tending to lead to the creation of "a pseudo-left opposition in the parliamentary Labour Party and the trade union bureaucracy, resulting in diverting the workers from the real struggle."[36] In the event, the manifesto campaign sputtered out amidst squabbling and reproach, which the CPGB could only take as further vindication of its increasingly intransigent insistence on its independent Leninist leadership of the working-class movement, meagre resources notwithstanding.

As the Party moved definitively into the third period, the NLWM became an anachronism – by then all-but moribund, it was closed down in 1929 after some hesitation, and the *Sunday Worker* went with it, to be replaced by a daily, as we shall see. The NLWM's own secretary supported its closure, which was agreed by the Party Congress over the reservations of the central committee, which wanted it to limp on for a little longer.[37] As an exercise in united front politics it had little to show for itself, beyond establishing that the Party could build bridges with the Labour left if it felt there was a struggle worth winning in the mainstream organisations of the labour movement. This of course is an issue which was to recur throughout the Party's history, and nearly always in the context of right-wing domination of those institutions.

Comintern and colonialism

The Sixth World Congress of the Comintern, held in Moscow in July 1928 was mainly devoted to the impending economic crisis and the need for sharper and more confrontational tactics by the Communist parties in response. Its principal work was preparing for the shift to "class against class" tactics and the adoption of the Comintern's Programme.

Nevertheless, it also featured a rather extraordinary humiliation for the CPGB, whose delegates found themselves alone in voting against the theses on the national and colonial question presented to the Congress, an unenviable position for the Communists at the heart of the world's largest empire. The point at issue was the question of "decolonisation".

Stated simply this view held that the colonies, and above all India as the greatest colony of all, were in the throes of speeded up industrialisation carried through by the native bourgeoise in alliance with the imperial power, and were therefore starting to develop an autonomous economic base. As we have seen, Dutt held to the view of increased industrialisation in his *Modern India*. The Comintern, however, maintained that there was little evidence of such a development in India, let alone anywhere else, and that colonial oppression was actually intensifying. The debate at the Congress pitted the whole British delegation (with the exception of J.T. Murphy), including those deeply divided on the new line within the labour movement, against the rest of the world party.

The report to Congress on the colonial question was given by Otto Kuusinen, the Finnish Communist leader. As far as decolonisation went, he mildly remarked that, while India's industrialisation was progressing "some British comrades have gone too far in seeing a new course in this."[38] The subsequent debate showed less moderation, doubtless in part reflecting the frustration many felt at the CPGB's slow progress in grappling with its anti-imperialist responsibilities. Indian delegate Sukander Sur (Shaukat Usmani) claimed that the theory of decolonisation was harming the Indian revolutionary movement and could only have been concocted by "those who are sitting far away and have lost all contact with India." He added that British imperialism was allying itself with the landed power in India, rather than the national bourgeoisie.

Carney, a delegate from Ireland, said that "the Communist Party of Britain is of the opinion that in any action directly connected with the colonies and the Empire the initiative and responsibility rests in the main upon the colonial parties", going on to demand that the CPGB campaign for the withdrawal of British trade unions from Ireland. Roux, representing the South African Communist Party, did not attack the CPGB but did make the telling observation that "the British working class stands in the relation of an aristocracy of labour to the oppressed colonial workers and peasants in the colonies and in the countries dominated by British capital.

> "Are we to say that the Welsh miner is an aristocrat of labour and a parasite? Of course, that is ridiculous. And yet, the unemployed Welsh miner who gets unemployment benefit has a higher income than an employed Indian miner…if the British bourgeoisie had no colonial empire to exploit, they would be unable to pay unemployment benefit to the miners."

There is a wealth of understanding in these formulations, the implications of which are powerfully felt in the global political economy a century later.

But the CPGB was not having any. Its position was initially put by the Comintern delegate to Britain Max Petrovsky (Bennett), who shared the party's position on the matter. He categorically declared that "everyone who speaks about any shadow of a possibility of the national bourgeoisie playing any positive active part in the national revolution was spreading illusions" which were disarming the Indian workers. This was a position which was to prove categorically wrong. Andrew Rothstein told the congress that it was erroneous to describe the colonies as agrarian any longer and Idris Cox said the Comintern line was ignoring the facts on the ground. The debate only got sharper. A German delegate, armed with facts from the Comintern's statistical bureau relating to Indian industrial production accused the CPGB of "indiscriminate re-echoing of the high priests of the League of Nations" in claiming there was widespread industrial development, and the lone dissident in the CPGB delegation, Murphy, denounced his comrades for drawing ultra-left conclusions from a "Menshevik picture of the colonial problem."

Robin Page Arnot, for the CPGB, made a somewhat unfortunate attempt to retrieve the position by asserting that the reason for the low use of coal in India – one of the facts produced earlier in the debate to argue against industrialisation – was the Indian's preference for burning cow dung. He compounded this misjudgement by asserting that official British government documents had committed to industrial development, rhetorically inquiring "would they lie?". A now clearly enraged Sukander Sur rejoined "let Arnot throw his cow dung on Buckingham Palace, but let him not entertain the delegates with it. Arnot surpassed all when he brought quotations that in such-and-such a report imperialism had promised the industrialisation of India. In support of his absurd assertion he vehemently asked: do these governments tell lies? Yes, comrades, the imperialist governments tell lies – thousands of times more than we could dream of. In conclusion I would say that these arguments of comrade Arnot and other comrades are nothing more than an open defence of imperialism."

Replying to the debate Kuusinen indicated that Palme Dutt, who was not present at the Congress, had "partly revised his former point of view" on the issue and was moving towards the Comintern position.[39] He chided the CPGB for doing too little to expose imperialism's pretension that it would peacefully develop the colonies. His parting shot to Congress, amid general merriment, was: "Yes, industrial development is taking place in the colonies but very, very slowly. In fact, just as slowly as the Bolshevisation of the British party under the leadership of comrade Petrovsky."[40] The British delegation was entirely isolated in the subsequent vote, which endorsed Kuusinen's view that imperialism was holding back economic development in the colonies. Unamused, the delegation protested against Kuusinen's "polemical methods" and returned to Britian feeling rather hard done by.[41]

Were they? In asserting that the Indian national bourgeoisie had formed a bloc with British imperialism the CPGB was wrong. Through its leadership of the Congress Party, the bourgeoisie in India headed up the drive for national independence, with all vacillations and compromises allowed for. The Comintern theses adopted at the Congress were right to assert that while part of the bourgeoisie upholds the interests of imperialism "the other parts of the native bourgeoisie, especially the portion reflecting the interests of native industry, support the national movement and represent a special vacillating compromising tendency which may be designated as national reformism."[42] Communists in India would only end up isolated if they ignored this, particularly in view of said national reformism's strong hold over the peasant masses. As to whether India was industrialising, the only issue in the statistical exchange was the degree at which it was doing so. The main point was that imperialism overall retarded and warped the economic development of the colonies by subordinating it to the requirements of the accumulation of metropolitan capital and the production of super-profit.

In the words of the theses: "…colonial exploitation presupposes some encouragement of colonial production, this is directed on such lines and promoted only in such a degree as correspond to the interests of the metropolis and, in particular, to the interests of the preservation of its colonial monopoly….the export of capital to the colonies accelerates the development of capitalist relations there. The part which is invested in production does to some extent accelerate its industrial development; but this is not done in ways which promote independence; the intention is rather to strengthen the dependence of the colonial economy on the finance-capital of the imperialist country…'"'"[43]

Certainly, it was tone deaf of the CPGB to sail blithely into this polemic without realising how it would be seen by the rest of the movement. The central role which history ascribed to revolutionaries in the heart of the biggest empire in the world, in the new context of a world-revolutionary process, still sat heavy on the CPGB's shoulders.

Towards Class Against Class

So too, and not coincidentally, did the expectations of the Comintern. These were to provoke the first general political crisis in the CPGB's history as the political line of the world movement changed. The shift to the "class against class" agenda is now almost friendless in the historiography of international communism. This is not unjustified – the abandonment of the policy of the united front did not lead to revolutionary success anywhere, rather to the serious weakening of the influence of the Communist parties; and it contributed to the rise of Nazism in Germany and hence to the outbreak of war, although its impact in this respect is sometimes exaggerated.

Nevertheless, there needs to be more scope for nuance in assessing the "third period" which broadly ran from 1929 through to 1934. The CPGB's membership declined rapidly initially, but then grew again. It emerged from the period with a stable and tested leadership for the first time, which endured for the next quarter of a century, and with a daily newspaper. The basis for further advance was certainly laid. It must also be acknowledged that while ultimately the changes in policy were driven by the Comintern, this was not without considerable encouragement and enthusiasm from the CPGB's membership as well, particularly amongst the youth.

Neither internationally nor in Britain was the new line simply sucked out of thin air, nor was it merely an extension of the tensions within the leadership of the CPSU then gearing up for the wrenching social transformations of collectivisation and rapid industrialisation. We have already noted the changed position in the British labour movement coming out of the General Strike, including the effective exclusion of Communists from the Labour Party and increasingly aggressive right-wing leadership in the trade unions, alongside the negative experience of the first Labour government and the windy posturing of the Independent Labour Party. These were one side of a coin, the other face of which was the overall unity of the labour movement and its established institutions and the great weakness of a free-standing CPGB outside of a few mining districts.

Internationally, the new line rested on several interconnected assumptions. The first was the impending end of capitalist stabilisation and the likely advent of a fresh economic crisis – on this the Comintern was accurate while the professors of the bourgeoisie and social democracy were not. The second was the growing reactionary role of social democracy, for which abundant evidence could be adduced, and not merely from Britain. And the third was that the combination of the first two circumstances would lead to a radicalisation of the working class, a turn to the revolutionary leadership of communism, and revolutionary crises. This last assumption was clearly deeply flawed and rested on that mechanistic translation of economic conditions into political action which we have already identified in Dutt's response to the General Strike. The experience of capitalist crisis and workers' struggles over the last century has now clarified beyond argument the erroneous basis of such politics and indeed tends to point to the reverse – growing demoralisation and decay in the working class movement at times of slump, to the advantage of conservative forces within the movement and right-wing, even far right, politics without it. Reading back that experience into the debates of 1928 and 1929 would be, of course, misleading – the slump of 1929 represented the first great crash of the post-1917 world order and the first on that scale since the development of the modern workers' movement. The Comintern's political judgements were wrong, but not in their time absurd.

The sectarian weaknesses of the "class against class" approach were not slow in becoming apparent, not least the absence of the anticipated radicalisation of the working-class under the impact of the slump, but the Comintern was tardy in modifying or abandoning it. In part this was because its failure was not so apparent in the case of the two most important Communist parties outside the Soviet Union – the German (KPD) and the Chinese (CPC). The former saw its electoral strength and membership grow (albeit largely amongst the unemployed after the great crash) throughout the period of the most violent attacks on social democracy, all the way up until 1932. The brittle nature of such achievements was brutally exposed after the Nazi conquest of power, but the nature of Nazism was itself misunderstood. The Comintern seemed to continue to believe in the possibility of revolution in Germany until 1934, by which time the KPD underground network had been largely destroyed by the Gestapo – today that can be seen of course to be an amazing misjudgement and that the prospects of revolution in Germany had ended in 1923 at the latest. In China the CPC recovered from the disaster of its split with the nationalist Kuomintang in 1927 to the extent of being able, at the price of a large measure of isolation from China's great cities and its working class, to establish a Soviet government in central areas leading millions of working people. That too proved unsustainable – the point however is that, surveyed from Moscow, the "third period" did not present an unvarying picture of setbacks and weakening of the movement.

The imposition of the new line was a protracted and controversial process in many countries, and often brought new leaders to the fore in the Comintern's affiliates. In Britain the change was more bitterly fought than in much of the rest of Europe, and the change in the party's leadership most extensive. In the late 1920s the Comintern was yet to become the quasi-monolith (in public at least) that it later developed into. Debate and division could be public and unsparing. Yet there was no doubt that in finality the judgement of the international leadership in Moscow was always going to prevail. The failure of the revolutionary movement in the west meant that the international leadership was itself in turn dominated by the leaders of the Bolshevik Party, who had the enhanced status of heading the only victorious party. Nevertheless, dissent was permissible and argument was not avoided. That makes it possible to trace the change of line and the contending positions relatively easily.

The critical issue was Communists' relationship to the Labour Party and indeed the whole assessment to be made of the latter. Was the united front policy still appropriate, and did Lenin's advice in relationship to Labour still provide a viable strategy for advance?

We have noted how the main arguments for a new line had emerged in embryo in the course of the varying assessments of the General Strike. However, the argument really began to erupt at the end of 1927.[44] The Comintern sent the CPGB a telegram calling for a "struggle against the bourgeois leadership of the Labour Party", which struggle would include the Party "preparing to take its stand in the forthcoming elections as an independent party with its own platform and its own candidates, even in cases where so-called official candidates of the Labour Party will be put up against the candidates of the CP." According to Robin Page Arnot, this injunction did not reach the CPGB in time for its ninth congress, taking place at the end of the year, because of a "technical mishap." As a result the congress did not discuss the party's electoral tactics at all, leaving the existing policy of support for Labour in most constituencies unchanged.[45]

When the Comintern's view did reach London, it met nearly united resistance from the CPGB central committee.[46] The committee stood pat on the existing position that the Labour Party had not been fully converted into a classical social democratic party and that, as per Lenin, a further period in government was necessary before workers shed all their illusions in it. This presupposed limited Communist electoral contests against Labour, since the possibility of Communists standing for Labour was now precluded. The controversy then moved back to Moscow, and the Comintern Executive. Different opinions were now emerging. Arnot and Dutt had written to the Comintern urging a "direct fight for independent political leadership against the official Labour leadership", a very big ask for a party no more than a few thousand in number. Their position was that Labour candidates could only be supported if they endorsed Communist policy, that workers should continue paying the political fund in their unions but should fight for it to be handed over to the CPGB, that one further application for affiliation to Labour be made for form's sake, and the issue then abandoned. The official policy of the party leadership was more equivocal: "The leaders of the Labour Party have…taken serious steps in the direction of…forestalling the development of the Labour Party into a class organisation and in transforming it into a bourgeois party, a third party of the capitalist class."[47] This fell short of the Comintern position, while moving somewhat closer to it.

The Executive's position as finally formulated had an air of unreality: it demanded that the CPGB cease campaigning for the election of a Labour government – a "revolutionary workers' government" was preferred – yet proposed continuing to try to affiliate, obviously contradictory demands. For the rest of 1928 the party veered this way and that, gradually toughening its line against Labour yet trimming as it found the demands of "independent leadership" beyond it. For example, a decision to stand an independent workers' candidate in a by-election in Stoke-on-Trent foundered on the near non-existence of the CPGB in that proletarian city, with a consequence that it ended up recommending a Labour vote anyway, to the anger of Dutt, who was increasingly reforging his alliance of 1922 with Pollitt in the campaign for the new line.[48]

Their views appeared to have wide support among the party membership which, if anything, wanted a still more decisive shift towards aggressive opposition to Labour, the result doubtless of their treatment by Labour's bureaucracy. While the leadership vacillated, party aggregate meetings across the country voted either unanimously or overwhelmingly in support of the Comintern position, sometimes accompanied by demands to go further still.[49] They were to have their wish.

1929 – Year of Crisis

The debates of 1929 knitted together a range of strategic questions – whether it was possible to support Labour candidates, whether the trade union political levy should be paid and to whom, should affiliation to Labour still be sought, the attitude towards the non-Communist left – with a dissatisfaction at the state of the party's own work, a sense that it was lagging in almost every department. Initially, at least, alignments retained a degree of fluidity, but Dutt, Pollitt and Murphy emerged as partisans of the new line, which was also strongly championed by YCL leaders like Bill Rust and Walter Tapsell, who constituted the far left of the party. In the other corner was most of the leadership of the 1920s, including Andrew Rothstein, general secretary Arthur Inkpin, Tom Bell, and J.R. Campbell.

It was also a debate in the British labour movement strongly framed in an international context. Such debates had, of course, occurred before the first world war but here the balance was entirely different. It was couched in terms of an overriding loyalty to a world revolutionary process which the CPGB saw itself as a part of, and to an international which was the guiding instrument of that process. That there was a continuing dialogue between the national and international, Britain and Moscow, throughout the year, in itself marked out the Communist Party as something entirely new in Britain's labour movement.

As the year began, opinion in the Party was starting to polarise between supporters of the new line, generally backed by the Comintern, and opponents who sought to at least mitigate the effects of its application in Britain. Pollitt now argued that Labour had developed into a "third capitalist party" alongside the Tories and Liberals, while Campbell took the view that the changes had not been sufficient to justify breaking with Lenin's position that revolutionaries should endeavour to work wherever the workers are to be found, which clearly included the Labour Party, constitutionally still the party of the trade unions.[50] Murphy wanted to campaign for trade unionists to stop paying the political levy, which Campbell denounced as "a helpless, hopeless, sectarian policy."[51] Dutt pursued his argument for a broad electoral challenge to Labour by the Communist Party in order to give effect to its strategy of independent leadership, with a Labour vote being recommended only where that party's candidate was prepared to support the united front demands of the CPGB.[52]

The Party's tenth congress was supposed to finally resolve these disputes. This it did not do, even though the official report asserted that it "succeeded in settling many of the questions arising" out of the application of the new line.[53] Campbell opened the Congress by asserting that the party had held a "sharp, vigorous and on the whole good humoured discussion". As Noreen Branson notes "the good humour wore thin" as the congress proceeded.[54] Indeed, a delegate from Portsmouth denounced Campbell's report as being more appropriate to an assembly of the Salvation Army. The Congress approved a resolution from Pollitt, in the teeth of opposition from Murphy, that payment of the political levy be maintained, but as already noted overturned a proposal from the central committee to keep the National Left-Wing Movement going a while longer, with the NLWM's own secretary advocating its dissolution. This was seen as a vote of no confidence in the existing leadership.[55]

The resolutions of the Congress sounded unequivocal enough. "The entire Social Democratic leadership, including the British Labour Party leaders, are today the open defenders of imperialism, supporting by the policy of Mondism and class collaboration the capitalist offensive and the war preparations of the imperialists." The position had changed from 1920 when Lenin gave his famous advice.

> "The central task of the Communist Party is to come out boldly and clearly as an independent political party, make clear its attitude towards the Labour Party, establish its direct independent leadership of the masses in the teeth of the opposition of the reformist bureaucracy, and of the bourgeoisie, and to bring into the forefront of its whole political activity, the slogan of a revolutionary workers government…This general change in tactics determines also the election tactic of the Party. The Party will enter the General Election against all other parties as an independent party, with its own programme…"[56]

As for the ILP, the party's task was "to differentiate between the honest workers who follow the ILP and the petty bourgeois leadership which is playing the double game of posing as 'independents' while actually supporting the policy of MacDonaldism and the Labour Party", striving to win over the former.[57]

Having apparently embraced the new line, the Congress nevertheless clung to the old leadership, including the unrepentant Rothstein. Moreover, it failed to elect to the new central committee two of the strongest champions of the Comintern, Robin Page Arnot and Bill Rust, the latter then the CPGB representative on the Executive of the International. Arnot was eventually included but Rust was not, and this circumstance alone would have been sufficient to ensure the prolongation of the internal conflict in the party.

As discussion resumed within the Party – as much over the leadership's conduct and capacity to lead a true bolshevisation of the CPGB as over the policies required for independent leadership – the new line encountered its initial test in the May 1929 general election, the first since the General Strike. The Labour Party again ignored the Empire and imperialism entirely in its election manifesto, as if for all the world securing government office in Britain did not also mean ruling over hundreds of millions in a worldwide Empire, whose views were of course not solicited. It did however find room to assure the voters that "the Labour Party is neither Bolshevik or Communist. It is opposed to force, revolution and confiscation as means of establishing the New Social order. It believes in ordered progress and in democratic methods." What ordered progress and democratic methods meant in practice was shortly to become apparent.[58] The Communist Party fielded 25 candidates of its own, fighting for a "revolutionary workers government".

A move in the central committee to urge support for Labour in other constituencies was heavily defeated. The party's candidates included Shaukat Usmani, sharp critic of the CPGB at the 6th Comintern Congress, in the Yorkshire textile seat of Spen Valley, campaigning from an Indian prison where he had been incarcerated in preparation for the Meerut trial.[59] The election special of the *Workers Life* was headlined "Against the Empire of Exploitation". The party's election manifesto, *Class Against Class* stated that "it is now no longer possible for the Communist Party or the trade unions to bring pressure to bear on the Labour Party from within. It is a completely disciplined capitalist party...Class is against class. The Labour Party has chosen the capitalist class. The Communist Party is the party of the working class."

The proposed revolutionary government would implement a 16-point programme including the establishment of revolutionary workers' armed forces, the repudiation of the National Debt, widespread nationalisation of banks, industry, trade and farms, confiscation of all housing property, disestablishment of the Church of England, a free medical service, a seven-hour working day and a raising of the school age to 16. There would be a "declaration of independence of every country hitherto ruled and controlled by British imperialism" and unity with the USSR, while the League of Nations was to be repudiated as "a capitalist and imperialist institution."[60]

The working class did not for the most part embrace these prospects (some of which later came to pass). The 25 candidates polled in total around 50,000 votes. Saklatvala, opposed by official Labour for the first time, lost his seat in Battersea North, leaving the party without parliamentary representation. Arthur Horner in Rhondda East polled 15% and Willie Gallacher in Fife West over 20% – these were the party's best performances, both in militant mining districts. MacDonald's Labour Party, however, polled 37% of the national vote and gained 136 more seats, becoming the largest party in the Commons for the first time, albeit still dependent on Liberal acquiescence to form a government. The working class remained decisively attached to its existing organisations, leaders and all, and spurned the offer of "independent leadership" from the Communist Party. The results of the election, and the whole situation in the British party, was submitted to scrutiny at a meeting of the Comintern executive in July. This meeting marked the culmination of the Comintern's leftward shift and the advent of the notorious concept of "social fascism" as applied to all reformists.

Speaker after speaker at the meeting, including the future German Democratic Republic head of state Walter Ulbricht, attributed the party's political failings to its leadership, which they insisted must be changed. The British delegation was bitterly divided with Pollitt and Rust joining in the attack on the party's leadership while Bell, Campbell, and Horner tried to mount a defence. Manuilsky wound up the proceedings by accusing the party of "complacency" and of possessing only two correct theoreticians – Dutt and Arnot. The final resolution enjoined the CPGB to "root out all survivals of right opportunist deviations in its ranks."[61]

This pressure on the leadership from above was complemented by pressure from below. A resolution from the party's Tyneside district demanded the convocation of a special congress to elect a new leadership. It observed that Communists were becoming "more and more isolated from the masses" had "no organised roots in the factories" and found their "influence in the trade unions rapidly waning." The Young Communist League, in the van of this movement, urged a purge of "right-wingers" and a London aggregate voted by 206 to 13 to call for a new congress. All these resolutions criticised the absence of work to launch a daily paper, the lack of self-criticism at the top and failures to organise in the factories and trade unions.[62] In August the leadership finally threw in the towel, producing an extremely long resolution analysing its own mistakes, summoning a special congress for November and finally removing three supporters of the "old line", including Andrew Rothstein, from the political bureau while appointing Harry Pollitt as the party's general secretary.[63]

For much of the party, this was just the start. It became clear that the Comintern was by no means forcing changes upon an unwilling membership. The Tyneside district complained that the Politbureau was still dominated by such "right-wing comrades as Campbell, Horner and Pollitt" while the West Wales local insisted that the new central committee should be composed of at least 50% industrial workers, a proportion rising to 80% on the Politbureau.[64] Elements of hysteria appeared to creep in. One contribution from a Tyneside member warning of "heresy hunting" was followed the next week by one from his local leadership announcing his expulsion. When Dutt took public issue with the description of Pollitt, now general secretary with full Comintern backing, as a "right-winger" he was in turn denounced as a "conciliationist" for "trying to exculpate Pollitt and for not wanting to completely clear out the old leadership."[65]

The Pollitt-Dutt duo themselves, set to become the leading, if sometimes conflicted, force within the party over the next twenty-seven years, set out their own analysis of the problems in articles in *Communist Review*. Dutt warned, in line with orthodoxy, that the "right danger" was the main problem facing the CPGB, and located it in Britian's strong traditions of bourgeois parliamentarism, in the lack of an equivalent tradition of revolutionary Marxism, the consequent relative strength of social democracy vis a vis communism and the party's lack of firm roots in the factories. The manifestations of the right danger included over-estimating the prospects for stable capitalist development, scepticism about the "independent" line of the party (opposition to Labour), illusions in left-wing social democrats, "legalism" in trade union matters, passivity over launching a daily paper and a lack of self-criticism together with a reluctance to renew the party leadership.[66] Pollitt for his part wrote that the party's problems, including the feeble vote in the general election, were "the result of a long period in which the political line of the party had not been clear and in which a whole series of mistakes and vacillations had taken place", faults he blamed on the old leadership of the party. His own reasons for the CPGB's lack of progress included "no daily paper; the weakness of factory groups; the neglect of recruitment; a sectarian and rigid approach to forms of united front work; no explanation of the party's fundamental aims." In case anyone was still in doubt, he concluded that "the party congress will have as one of its most important tasks a real political discussion on the composition of the central committee."[67] Or, as Dutt put it privately, "we must set ourselves to exterminate every sign of weakness, hesitation and scepticism in the party leadership."[68]

It is noteworthy that by this stage Pollitt and Dutt were not mainly animated by arguments over the "new line" of all-out opposition to the Labour Party and the leadership of the labour movement, pitting the CPGB's aspiration for "independent leadership" of the working class against these powerful and entrenched forces. That matter was regarded as settled, bar details of implementation. Instead they were, as in their organisation report of seven years earlier, confronting the problems of the CPGB's inheritance from its constituent organisations and, more generally, the weaknesses of the pre-Leninist Marxist tradition in Britain, a tradition which had largely stood aloof from trade unionism and the day-to-day class struggle, was amateurish in its approach to propaganda and party discipline, paid little attention to Marxist education, was vacillating in its attitude to parliamentarianism, had no conception of the centrality of anti-colonial and anti-imperialist work and was suffused with a legalism towards the state. The leaders they sought to replace were mainly the products of that tradition, albeit they had struggled hard to adapt themselves to the new world and to the rigours of Comintern internationalism; the forces they sought to lead were primarily among the younger communist workers, impatient with the pre-war legacy and full of confidence to confront the old at every turn, absolutely unafraid of the charge of sectarianism.[69] The party these new forces shaped was to endure in its essentials long after the excrescences of the "new line" had been discarded.

As the agonised reorientation reached its culmination, the CPGB had at least addressed one criticism satisfactorily. At the Comintern Executive meeting Manuilsky had accused the party leadership of being "too polite" and behaving as if the CPGB was a "society of friends" within which a "little breach" was necessary. By the end of 1929, that charge could no longer be laid.[70] With a final encouraging nudge from the Comintern to shed its "typically social democratic organisation" and its habit of adopting resolutions and then doing nothing about them, the party proceeded to its second congress of the year.

The congress was, according to Pollitt's later recollection, "the most difficult congress I have ever attended. I made a political report that was received in stony silence."[71] Nevertheless, it resoundingly endorsed all the positions associated with the new line, to the extent of condemning the "fascisation of the trade union apparatus" as well as denouncing any programme which suggested "the possibility of reforming the Labour Party" or "the possibility of carrying out a Left Socialist programme through parliament".[72] It demanded the speedy launch of the *Daily Worker* and directed all leading comrades to work in factory cells, whether or not employed there, in order to overcome the party's industrial isolation.

It also finally acted decisively to change the leadership, with Walter Ulbricht superintending on behalf of the Comintern. More than half the outgoing central committee was not re-elected, including some, like Arthur Horner, who would later return to play central roles. Even those whose eviction from the leadership proved permanent, like Andrew Rothstein and Tommy Jackson, nevertheless played significant parts in the party's future work.[73] J.R. Campbell survived the cull in spite of his resistance to the new line, doubtless because his political abilities outweighed other considerations, and Wal Hannington was elected to the central committee in the teeth of resistance from the platform. A new secretariat was formed to lead the party's daily work consisting of general secretary Pollitt, Gallacher, Rust, Walter Tapsell, and Idris Cox. They were joined on the new Politbureau by Dutt (still in Brussels), Murphy, Arnot, Jimmy Shields and R.W. Robson.[74] The party was now, as Rust told the congress, in a phase of reconstruction, not just criticism, which must have come as a relief, although as we shall see criticism was far from abandoned. Tapsell introduced the official report of the Congress with the warning that "the fight against the Right danger is not ended...opportunism and passivity and sectarianism must be rooted out on the basis of intense activity and planned work..." The activity, the work, and the understandings which guided them, will be considered next.[75]

Notes

1. The first Labour government, formed by Ramsay MacDonald in 1924, was the most proletarian in its social composition of any in British history to date, a quality which had little bearing on its conduct of course but may have brought it within the Comintern definitions of a 'workers' government'.
2. Klugmann (1969) p 287
3. *The Meaning of the General Strike* by R. Palme Dutt (London: 1926 a) pp 3, 5
4. *Ibid*. p 36
5. *British Trade Unionism* by Allen Hutt (London: 1975) pp 115-121
6. *The Scottish Miners* by Robin Page Arnot (London: 1955) pp 190-196. The split was more the work of the right-wing, headed by William Adamson MP, than of the CPGB and was eventually healed in 1936, shortly after Adamson had been defeated in the parliamentary election in West Fife by Willie Gallacher. There was also a small breakaway union sustained for a time in the garment trade.
7. *The Communist International 1919-43 Documents* volume two by Jane Degras (ed.) (London: 1971) p 188.
8. *Outline History of the Communist International* by A.I. Sobolev et al. (Moscow: 1971) p 216.
9. *Socialism in One Country* volume three by E.H. Carr (Harmondsworth: 1964) pp 305-6
10. *Ibid*. pp 311-12.
11. *Histoire de L'Internationale Communiste* by Pierre Broue (Paris: 1997) p 367.
12. Degras (1971) p 195.
13. Klugmann (1969) pp 334-35.
14. *Under Siege* by Ian Bullock (Edmonton, Canada: 2017) pp 99-124
15. *Socialism and the Living Wage* by R. Palme Dutt (London: 1927) p 9
16. *Ibid*. p 17
17. *Ibid*. p 43
18. *Ibid*. pp 43-45
19. Cited in *The Economist* 29 November 2007.
20. Dutt (1927) p 75
21. *Ibid*. p 79
22. *Ibid*. p 235.
23. *Modern India* by R. P. Dutt (London: 1926 b) pp 9-10
24. *Ibid*. p 10
25. *Ibid*. p 10
26. *Ibid*. p 164

27 *Ibid.* p 171
28 *Socialism and the Empire*, report of the ILP Empire Policy Committee (London: 1926) pp 16, 18.
29 *Imperialism and the British Labour Movement in the 1920s* by Stuart Macintyre (London: 1975) p 16.
30 Dutt (1926 b) p 174
31 *Communists and Labour – The National Left-Wing Movement 1925-29* by Lawrence Parker (2018) p 27.
32 History of the Communist Party of Great Britain 1927-41 by Noreen Branson (London: 1985) p 7.
33 *Class Against Class* by Matthew Worley (London: 2002) p 29.
34 *The British Communist Party and Moscow 1920-43* by Andrew Thorpe (Manchester: 2000) p 107.
35 Parker (2018) pp 56-7.
36 Branson (1985) p 33.
37 *Ibid.* p 35.
38 This and all other quotes from the debate are from *Inprecorr* 4 October 1928 and subsequent, which is the stenographic record of the Congress.
39 Dutt's view was indeed somewhat different. He asserted that India was industrialising, as it surely was, but insisted that this was being done under British control and in British interests. He was certainly no advocate of imperial "decolonisation." See *Rajani Palme Dutt* by John Callaghan (London: 1993) pp 123-4.
40 This last passage is not in the verbatim record of the debate. It is to be found, *inter alia*, in *Black Bolshevik* by Harry Haywood (Chicago: 1978) p 275. Haywood was an African-American member of the CPUSA who attended the Congress. He speculates that the remark was left out of the offcial record to spare the CPGB's blushes (and Petrovsky's). Remarkably, the whole debate does not merit a line in Noreen Branson's official history of the CPGB.
41 Thorpe (2000) p 133.
42 Degras (1971) p 538.
43 *Ibid.* p 534-5.
44 The most detailed descriptions of the 1927-29 controversies can be found in Worley (2002), Branson (1985) and Thorpe (2000).
45 *Foundations of a Planned Economy* volume 3 part 2 by E.H. Carr (London: 1978) p 359
46 The minority included Pollitt, Saklatvala and Percy Glading. Thorpe (2000) p 122.
47 Carr (1978) pp 361, 363.
48 Thorpe (2000) p 128. Dutt himself remained in Brussels for reasons that have never been entirely explained – they range from his health, that of his wife Salme's, to Salme's legal status (she was a Finnish national) to the wishes of the Comintern. In a party biography submitted to the Comintern in 1935 he wrote of a "severe breakdown in 1924 [which] compelled me to work under conditions of medical treatment and semi-isolation until the present year." (Dutt papers, British Library)
49 See Worley (2002) p 102, Thorpe (200) p 129. The largest minority in these meetings – 44 out of 106 attending – was in London, but this was to the *left* of the new offcial line.
50 *Labour Monthly* November 1928.
51 *Communist Review*, January 1929 pp 40-50
52 *Ibid.* pp 21-35
53 *The New Line*, CPGB (London: 1929) p 5
54 Branson (1985) p 34.
55 *Inprecorr* nos 5, 6 & 8 1929.
56 *New Line* pp 57-59
57 *Ibid.* p 75
58 *British General Election Manifestos 1900-1974* by F.W.S. Craig (ed) (London: 1975) pp81-82
59 Usmani secured 242 votes, or 0.6 per cent of the poll.
60 *Class Against Class*, CPGB (London: 1929)
61 Carr (1978) pp 390-92
62 *Communist International* 1 October 1929; *Workers Life* 26 July 1929 and 9 August 1929.
63 *Communist Review* September 1929 pp 560-567
64 *Workers Life* 20 September 1929.
65 *Workers Life* 29 November 1929.
66 *Communist Review* September 1929 pp 495-509

67 *Communist Review* October 1929, pp 560-67
68 Dutt to Central Committee 3 August 1929, Dutt papers in British Library
69 One such, Margaret McCarthy, recalled it thus – the new approach "accorded completely with our mood of frustration and despair, with our lack of confidence in the recognised labour leadership, our desire for something short, sharp and spectacular to end the hopeless stalemate…" Cited in 'To the Left and Back Again: The Communist Party of Great Britain in the Third Period' by Matthew Worley in *In Search of Revolution* by Matthew Worley (ed) (London: 2004) p 65
70 Worley (2002) p 135
71 Worley (2004) p 65
72 *Resolutions of the 11th Congress*, CPGB (London: 1929) pp 18, 20
73 See Branson (1985) pp 339-40 for lists.
74 Worley (2002) pp 141-42
75 *Resolutions of the 11th Congress* p 4

Illustration overleaf
For Soviet Britain
The Communist Party programme adopted at the XII Congress of the party

FOR SOVIET BRITAIN...

Resolution adopted by the XIIIth Congress of the Communist Party

ONE PENN

Chapter Six
Against Social Democracy and Empire
(1929-34)

HOW THE COMMUNIST PARTY saw the world during the "third period" was set out simply by one of its leaders: "...the war began the period of world revolution – the rising struggle of the working masses to end the rule of dying capitalism and bring in the new order of socialism. Over one-sixth of the earth the workers' revolution conquered, and today advances to socialism. The colonial peoples, in India and China... rise to free themselves from the imperialist yoke. The workers in Europe and America advance in growing mass struggles. The hour of capitalism reaches its end."[1]

There it was in a nutshell. As Palme Dutt put those words to paper, the capitalist world was still gripped in the apparently intractable crisis which had burst upon it in 1929, wiping out industries, employment, and fortunes; a crisis to which the statesmen of capitalism had no apparent solution. The hour of capital's rule did indeed appear to be in sight of a conclusion. On the other hand, the Soviet Union was then embarking on the path of epic industrialisation and the collectivisation of agriculture, a path hitherto untrodden. The new industries springing up across that vast land under Bolshevik direction and the social transformation of an impoverished and illiterate people caught the imagination of socialists within and beyond the ranks of the Communist Parties and stood in apparently vivid contrast to the crisis in the bourgeois world. The violence, hunger and chaos which attended the Soviet advance was then largely unknown and unreported, and such evidence of shortcomings as was presented was dismissed as the propaganda of a desperate enemy.

Nor was the upsurge in struggle in China, India and elsewhere in the oppressed world a figment of the imagination. The world did indeed appear to be turning. The mentality of Communists during the "class against class" period, including those in small and relatively isolated parties like the British, cannot be understood without recognising that they believed themselves to be in the midst of a world revolutionary process apparently unfolding broadly along the lines anticipated by the Communist International. If their own efforts were coming up short, the fault lay with their misunderstandings of the international line, or their irresolution in implementing it. Vast issues hung on their efforts. In the same pamphlet, Dutt warned that "fascist dictatorship and war – this is the outlook if we fail to overthrow capitalism. This is the actual alternative to workers' revolution."[2] Even if the hands on Dutt's political clock were seldom at other than two minutes to midnight, a consideration of the whole course of the 1930s does not show him wrong on that point. The full horror of fascist dictatorship was yet to be revealed in Nazi Germany, and the beginnings of a third alternative – the unfolding of Roosevelt's New Deal in the USA as a serious attempt to address the crisis within the parameters of capitalism – lay in the future as well. So too the war.

In this millennial confrontation, the CPGB was aware of its outsized responsibilities. It was at the heart of the world's greatest Empire, with a bounden duty to support movements across much of the earth threatening London's rule over the colonies. This same British imperialism was also seen as the most likely instigator of war against the USSR and thus the principal source of reaction in the world. The CPGB stood face to face with a labour movement shaped by Empire, led by politicians and officials either committed to maintaining Britain's world position, or at best pragmatically indifferent to challenging it. These two themes – opposition to Empire and to social democracy – defined the Party during the 1929-34 period, a test of its capacity to translate the insights and revolutionary synthesis of Leninism into a viable political practice.

Fighting imperialism

That there were now two distinct approaches to imperialism within the labour movement could not be doubted. One approach, associated with the Labour Party, was reconciled to colonialism and was prepared to discharge what it conceived of as its responsibilities to administer much of the world in the interests of British capital, disguised as doing an unsought favour to the oppressed peoples themselves. Its approach was ameliorative at best, was sustained by liberal notions of racial superiority and was ultimately prepared to use the same methods as the Tories and Liberals to ensure a continuity of British rule, violent ones if needs be. The parameters of the debate within the Labour Party were defined, on the right, by J.H. Thomas's enthusiastic discharge of his responsibilities as Colonial Secretary, absolutely supportive of Empire and the gunsmoke needed to sustain it and, on the left, the pacifist George Lansbury, who said that "there is no reason for breaking up the British Empire any more than there is any reason for smashing our own national institutions. Our duty is to transform the British Empire of domination into a Commonwealth of free nations."[3]

The other, the approach of Communists and a small element of the wider left, stood for the immediate end of the Empire, with self-determination for its constituent parts without exception, and the withdrawal of the British military and bureaucratic apparatus from the countries concerned. Dutt again: "The British working class, so soon as it wins power, will give full and unconditional independence to India, to Egypt, and to all the colonial peoples held under the rule of British imperialism...it is not only the international duty, but also the direct and urgent self-interst of the British working class to liberate the colonial peoples."[4] These opposed attitudes became a political line of demarcation of increasing importance, separating communism from social democracy, and the politics of world revolution from those of national reformism.

The two congresses of 1929 had outlined a robust programme of anti-imperialism by the CPGB which showed that, on paper at least, the lessons of Leninism were being absorbed. The resolution of the 10th Congress was categorical:

> "In the epoch of imperialism, the overthrow of the capitalist class in Great Britain and the victory of the social revolution are only possible with the cooperation of the oppressed masses in the colonies...All the big factors of the British working class movement are linked up with colonial struggle...the colonial question cannot be put on one side as a special task with which the ordinary work of the party is not concerned. We must say clearly that it is impossible to judge rightly our work in the trade unions and all our everyday tasks of the class struggle without seeing them in relation to the colonial struggle. In the coming period, the colonial question will occupy a more and more prominent place in our work."

The resolution mandated greater assistance from the CPGB to Communist parties in the Empire as well as cooperation "with anti-imperialist and revolutionary colonial organisations in Great Britain".[5] The 11th Congress demanded the persistent exposure of "the Labour government's imperialist policy and brutal oppression of the colonies" and the creation of "a united front of the British workers and colonial masses against the common enemy – the imperialist Labour government…" The Party, the Congress resolution stated, "must take the lead in mobilising the workers to struggle in support of the Indian revolution, which has become in the new period one of the central areas of the world revolution." Again, "one of the most important international obligations of the British working class is active support to the struggle of the oppressed colonial peoples in the British Empire… This task must be brought to the forefront of all economic struggles in Britain…"[6]

So whatever else may have been in contention in the Party's debates of 1929, that at least seemed clear. The issue, as ever, was the degree to which these accurate perceptions of Britain's particular responsibilities in the world revolution[7] were translated into activity. Here India was the main testing ground. Early attempts led by M.N. Roy to found a Communist Party in the Raj had borne very little fruit. His failures led the Comintern to assign greater responsibility for promoting revolutionary politics on the subcontinent to the CPGB, at least in part because its members could enter India more easily. As already mentioned, the Party began despatching cadre to help build up a Communist party and trade unions there, working largely underground. The most significant of these was Ben Bradley, who by 1928 had taken serious steps towards building up a textile workers' trade union. This work was also aided by the CPGB's sole MP, Saklatvala, himself of Indian origin, who toured India in 1927 to an "enthusiastic response"[8]. Saklatvala also corresponded with Gandhi, imploring him to recognise the importance of trade unionism and working-class struggle.[9] Saklatvala was to lose his parliamentary status in 1929 and thus his capacity to visit India, but maintained his agitation as a Communist for Indian independence until his death.

Although overall the Communists' efforts in India did not add up to very much, and the Communist Party of India was no more than embryonic, the overall development of the Indian peoples' struggle, under the leadership of the Indian National Congress, left no room for complacency on the part of India's British rulers. Determined to destroy the incipient Comintern agitation, the Baldwin government ordered a crackdown in March 1929 arresting thirty-one trade unionists, mainly Indian but also including Bradley and Phillip Spratt, on charges of conspiracy to "deprive the King-Emperor of sovereignty over British India." This attack was maintained after the change of administration in London, with the full approval of MacDonald and his ministers. The prisoners were not released but instead eventually went to trial in Meerut where it was "the case for the prosecution that the accused were Bolsheviks", that fact alone being sufficient for a conviction.[10]

Labour's Secretary of State for India, William Wedgwood Benn,[11] rejected all calls for an amnesty, declaring the trial was aimed at preventing Communist insurrection, while the Labour Party's international secretary William Gillies justified the case to critics by claiming that "all the arrested men were Communists.[12] Viceroy Lord Irwin opposed any amnesty but did declare he would permit a Communist to visit India to assist the accused – however, the chosen Party member, the notorious J.R. Campbell, then found himself vetoed by Wedgwood Benn, who commended Fenner Brockway as an alternative who might "help…with the Indian radicals."[13] The TUC was no better, despite the fact that the repression was mainly directed against workers trying to organise. Only in 1933, four years on, did the TUC and Labour, by then back in opposition, demand the release of the prisoners. The Communist Party mobilised in their support as best it could. Pollitt wrote to the imprisoned Bradley advising that in the recent Whitechapel by-election where Pollitt had been a candidate "no meetings do take place but what the question of India, and particularly of the Meerut prisoners, is given attention."[14]

The Meerut trial was also the subject of a major international solidarity campaign, much of it organised by the League Against Imperialism (LAI), an international body established in Berlin in 1927 by the Comintern as a united front initiative.[15] It initially drew together Communists, Socialists and many figures from the colonies later to play a significant part in the history of their countries. Its British chapter was organised by a renegade diplomat called Reginald Bridgeman who, despite not being a Party member[16], stuck with the LAI through all twists and turns over the next decade, and included leading ILP figures like Brockway and Maxton and several other MPs. The LAI, according to Hakim Adi, "tended in many circumstances to act as the anti-colonial organisation of the Communist movement in Britain."[17] Although the violent ructions of the "class against class" line drove away many allies (Maxton was expelled), the LAI nevertheless played a big part in the Meerut campaign. Bridgeman collaborated with Nehru with the result that "the India Office was inundated with protests…from various trade union branches."[18] This work was opposed by the TUC, with its General Secretary Walter Citrine accusing the LAI of "exploiting the masses of India for their own ends".[19] The LAI was of course proscribed by the Labour Party because of Communist activity within it, meaning no member could participate in its work, a move symbolic both of Labour's support for imperialism and of the cleavage in the working-class movement on the issue.

The MacDonald government of 1929-31 was undoubtedly one of imperialist exploitation. It passed a Colonial Development Act the purpose of which was not so much to develop the colonies as to assist British exports. MacDonald himself held the view that the Empire's resources should be developed by British interests exclusively. The eminent Fabian reformer Sidney Webb, then doing service as Colonial Secretary, promoted an alliance with nominally independent Iraq as "vitally necessary to secure Imperial interests…There is no other means of securing that unfettered use in all circumstances of our strategic air route, of adequately safeguarding our position at the head of the Persian Gulf…"[20] Quite willing to use the vast repressive resources of the imperial state to secure these strategic perspectives, MacDonald was however opposed to giving colonial troops access to the more advanced weaponry lest they be turned against the British themselves. He was not a fool.

Given this record, it is unsurprising that Dutt's older brother Clemens, himself a leading figure in the Comintern's colonial work, described Labour as "the most valuable ally of British imperialism" whose "hypocritical phraseology…amounts to a justification of imperialism, a complete denial of the right of peoples to self-determination, a complete denial of the elementary condition of freedom and democracy for which the Labour party professes to stand. It is nothing but an excuse for denying freedom to the oppressed races, an excuse for condoning and assisting their suppression by force."[21]

As well as the communists dispatched on mission to India and elsewhere, and the solidarity work developed in Britain itself, the CPGB's work drew on the entwining of its members with struggles across the Empire. The itinerant revolutionary syndicalist Tom Mann was a pioneer here.[22] Jimmy Shields, a Scottish worker and later the CPGB's national organiser and *Daily Worker* editor, served as General Secretary of the Communist Party of South Africa from 1925 to 1927 and advocated the introduction of black Communists into the party's leadership.[23] A still more prominent role was played in South Africa by another British Communist, Bill Andrews. He too served as the CPSA's General Secretary.[24]

As early as 1917 Andrews had declared that it was "the imperative duty of the white workers to recognise their identity of interest with the native workers as against their common masters...It is time for the white workers to deal with the native as a man and a fellow worker and not as a chattel and a serf. Only that way lies freedom and justice for all."[25] George Hardy, son of a Yorkshire farmworker, had already been active as a trade unionist in Australia, New Zealand, and the USA before becoming an organiser for the Profintern (Red International of Labour Unions) in China.[26] All this justifies the description of internationalism in action.

Special mention must of course be made of Ireland, Britain's oldest colony. Most of Ireland had gained a formal independence at the price of partition after a war with the British and then civil war following World War One. James Connolly had accurately predicted that partition – the creation of a Northern Ireland statelet as part of the United Kingdom – would lead to a "carnival of reaction" on both sides of the artificial border. Communists struggled on both sides of it, against state-sponsored sectarianism in the north, clerical reaction in the Free State, and police violence in both. Attempting to launch a mass Marxist party in the Free State depended disproportionately on the influence of the legendary trade union leader Jim Larkin, forever associated with the Dublin lockout of 1913. Unfailingly militant and supportive of the Soviet Union, as was Connolly's son Roderick, Larkin was nevertheless difficult to corral into political activity. Persuading him was the task of Bob Stewart, Dundee Communist and the CPGB's acting general secretary when its leadership was imprisoned in 1925-26. Despite the two men bonding over a militant teetotalism Stewart could not get Larkin, the leader with the greatest prestige among the Dublin workers, to endorse launching a Communist Party. "My own opinion is that Big Jim would never accept the democracy of a disciplined Marxist party. He always had to be at the centre of the stage all the time, and so to join a party where the emphasis is put on collective work was not for him."[27] The younger Connolly was more reliable and participated in faltering efforts to establish a Communist party in Ireland. The CPGB was deeply entwined with these efforts and was a principle conduit for Comintern advice and funds to the Irish comrades. The position in the Free State was further complicated by the appeal of the IRA to the republican left, and then by the accession to office of Eamon de Valera. This associate of James Connolly from 1916 led the bourgeois Fianna Fail party, associated with the defeated side of the civil war, and as Prime Minister embarked on a course of systematically dismantling British neo-colonial influence in Ireland. The CPGB attacked him relentlessly, and had to be reminded by the Comintern that its main fire should be directed at British imperialism.[28] Anti-imperialism was not, however, as popular among the working class in Belfast and there Communists focussed on unemployment and the economic crisis for the most part.

Opposition to imperialism was closely linked to the fight against militarism, and to the agitation the Party directed towards the armed forces, always a prominent Comintern imperative. A number of party members were arrested and jailed for leafletting soldiers with incitements to mutiny rather than serve the needs of Empire. One such said that "we must not murder the workers and peasants of India" but should rather turn guns on "our real enemy – the thieving, robbing, British ruling class and its lackeys, the Labour government." Another, aimed at personnel in the Royal Air Force, asserted that "the interests of British workers lie in helping the Indian workers to overthrow British rule." Those imprisoned for this heroic if barely effective anti-militarism included the future General Secretary of the party, John Gollan.[29]

Not all such agitation was well-judged. J.T. Murphy told this sad story in 1930:

"The Manchester Working Bureau put forward, among other proposals, that a number of leading comrades should on March 6 lead a march of worker on to Burnley barracks and call on the soldiers in uniform to demonstrate with the workers in the streets. Now, no member of our Party will question the desirability of propaganda amongst the troops. But when it is realised that in Burnley we had not a single Party cell in the mills, that the whole Party membership in Burnley did not muster a dozen members, that there had not been the slightest preparation for mass action of the workers, no preliminary work among the soldiers, indeed that there are no Burnley barracks and no soldiers in Burnley, then the absolutely unreal and romantic line can be seen at a glance..."[30]

More consequentially, an inept attempt to rouse opposition in the Navy in the aftermath of the Invergordon mutiny involved the dispatch of two unqualified and unprepared activists to Portsmouth. There they embarked on a hopeful "political pub crawl" by the naval docks until they encountered an unannounced police agent, a round of drinks which led to the imprisonment of the comrades concerned. The Party also established a British Anti-War Council, as part of an international Comintern-inspired anti-war movement, in 1933. Its first conference was attended by an impressive 1,510 delegates, including 27 from the Labour Party and 59 from the ILP. The effectiveness of the bans from Labour head office and Communist reluctance to collaborate with those to its right were both weakening.[31]

This record illustrates that the CPGB was at long last taking its anti-imperialist work more seriously, and certainly far more seriously than any British socialist organisations had done hitherto. There are academic critics who deny this entirely – notably Marika Sherwood, who draws justified attention to the perennial weakness in prioritising colonial work, and also highlights instances of racism in the party's membership and propaganda, but considerably overstates her case. To write that "there is no evidence of the CPGB or its Colonial Committee making any contact with the colonies" is demonstrably false and the assertion that "the British Communist party, with the exception of a very few members, is shown to be as imbued with racial prejudice and indifference to the colonies as was the rest of the population" is absurd.[32] The work of the Dutt brothers alone gives the lie to this, and there was no-one in the British population other than Communists going to prison for agitating against colonial oppression. In fact, the CPGB put resources into colonial work, often it is true at Comintern instigation, beyond what it could easily sustain. Its most influential theoretical journal, *Labour Monthly*, was, in the words of its editor, specialising in "imperial and colonial questions".[33] Its propaganda effort on the question was intensive throughout the "class against class" period. As examples one could cite *The Colonial Policy of British Imperialism* by leading Communist propagandist Ralph Fox, which asserted plainly that "the exploitation of the colonial peoples is the greatest obstacle to the freedom of the British workers" and that "a socialist Britain without a people's revolution in India is unthinkable";[34] or *British Imperialism in India* by Joan Thompson (writing as Joan Beauchamp) which argued that "the well-being of the workers and peasants of India is inextricably bound up with that of the workers of Great Britain, and the final victory can only be won if the workers of both countries stand shoulder to shoulder against the common oppressor."[35] This is not a picture of neglect, nor of condescension.

It was also in this period that pioneering anti-racists like George Padmore regarded the

CPGB as the best ally in their struggle for emancipation. Active in Britain in this period, and for much of the rest of his life, Padmore wrote the pioneering *The Life and Struggles of Negro Toilers* under the auspices of the Comintern-organised International Trade Union Committee of Negro Workers. The book powerfully restated the case for the centrality of black peoples to the revolutionary process. Its purpose was "to indicate in a general way the tasks of the proletariat in the advanced countries so that the millions of black toilers might be better prepared to carry on the struggles against their white imperialist oppressors and native (race) exploiters and join forces with their white brothers against the common enemy – World Capitalism."[36] Published in London, the book took aim at British imperialism and challenged both white chauvinism and the doctrines of Marcus Garvey, who advocated a return to Africa by black people everywhere. It was an extension of .'s own thinking on the unity of all the oppressed of the world against imperialism. Padmore later broke with the Comintern over its perceived prioritisation of anti-fascism over anti-imperialism later in the decade, something to be considered in the next volume of this work. He retained an admiration for the USSR for much longer, however. That Padmore aligned with the CPGB, not uncritically for sure, during the early 1930s is a powerful refutation of the Sherwood thesis.

It is true that the Party sometimes lacked theoretical clarity on the matter. On the one hand, Robin Page Arnot could write that "unless it strives to emancipate the Indian masses, fighting the treachery of the Social Democrats, the British working class will not be able to emancipate itself from the yoke of British imperialism"[37] and Jimmy Shields could declare that the fight for socialism in Britain "is inseparably connected with the struggle against British domination of India. The shattering of the imperialist chains which bind the Indian masses would be a severe shock to the capitalist system in Britain...solidarity with the mass struggle in India is at the same time solidarity with the workers' fight in Britain."[38] These views expressed the dynamic relationship of the socialist and national liberation struggles. Yet on the other hand, Pollitt could still tell the central committee that "the English revolution will lead to revolutions in India and other countries and it will mean the liberation of Ireland."[39] This reduced the colonial masses to bystanders, waiting on the working-class in Britain to emancipate them from afar. There is some justice in Theo Williams' judgement that the CPGB found it hard to identify the colonial masses as "workers in the same way as the European", and that it became comfortable with repeated self-criticisms at public forums for lack of activity on colonial issues, while changing rather little in practice.[40] Nevertheless all leading Communists were at one in advocating solidarity with the emancipation movement across the Empire, and the party started to forge links with many who were to become leaders of the emancipatory struggles in their own countries – among them Jomo Kenyatta, the first President of a free Kenya thirty years later.

It is also true that the Empire and its workings were largely out of sight and out of mind for the British working-class as a whole and even Communists tended to be preoccupied with crises closer to home. In the unions, they were up against entrenched attitudes which mixed chauvinism with perceived self-interest. Gupta cites a trade union leader telling a cotton tariff meeting that "he desired to see India and her people take their rightful place in the comity of nations, but not at the expense of the industrial and economic life of Lancashire and those dependent on it."[41] That such ideas might have influenced some in the Party would not be entirely surprising. Sherwood is correct to highlight that the Party had little contact with the black population in Britain, concentrated particularly in port cities, a fact it admitted and must be set against the frequent denunciations of racism in the *Daily Worker*.

But no reading of the party's propaganda and its wider record can overlook the fact that for the first time there was an organisation of British socialists making anti-imperialism a central part of its work and situating its efforts in a world revolutionary framework. The work done in these years, and the connections made, despite a frequently crippling sectarianism affecting this as other aspects of the party's activity, established the Party as a friend of those fighting for independence across the Empire in the years and decades to come.

Confronting Labour

The CPGB's militant anti-imperialism was entwined with its extreme hostility to social democracy and the official labour movement at this time. As already outlined, the Labour Party was seen as not just a third capitalist party, but as an integral part of a capitalist state apparatus itself moving towards fascism. A connecting line was drawn from the betrayal of the workers of Europe by the socialist leaders of 1914 through to the bourgeois politics of the first MacDonald government, the abandonment of the miners and constitutional loyalism in 1926 and the exclusion of Communists from the Labour Party. This was understood in a frame that encompassed the views of Lenin and others that part of the working-class could be "bought off" and integrated into the state through the super-profits accruing from imperial exploitation.

The new Comintern outlook was that social democracy was not an errant trend in the workers' movement but the "main social prop" of the bourgeoisie, the influence of which had to be broken for revolutionary politics to advance. Moreover, the most dangerous expression of social democracy was its left-wing, which in a British context meant the Independent Labour Party of Brockway and Maxton. The social function of the ILP was only to stop workers disenchanted with Labour from finding their way to the Communist Party and its satellite organisations or, as the party's 11th Congress resolution put it "the ILP is an essential element in this process of Fascisation of the whole apparatus of imperialism. The policy of the ILP must be regarded not as weak opposition to MacDonald, but as one of active division of labour in deceiving the workers and retaining them as supporters of MacDonald...the Communist Party must regard the ILP...as being the most dangerous enemies of the working class."[42] The party's press in 1930, 1931, and beyond brimmed with attacks on the ILP and its leaders. Thus in 1932 when Pollitt agreed to a public debate with Fenner Brockway he was sent a lengthy preparatory note from Brussels by Dutt, setting out the structure and tone of his contribution. The ILP "is for capitalism", the audience should be told, the CPGB opposition to it was not about "difference of tactics for a common aim." Dutt concluded with a stern injunction to Pollitt: "NO POLITENESS! No mere 'difference of opinion'. No parliamentary debate. No handshakes. Treatment as CLASS ENEMIES throughout. You speak for the holy anger of whole international working class against the foulness that is Brockway. Make that whole audience hate him." And this was at a moment when the ILP was starting to break from the Labour Party. Whether Pollitt got through the event without shaking Brockway's hand is not recorded.[43]

The second Labour government, again a minority one but this time the largest party in the Commons, did nothing to dilute the Communist analysis, flawed as it certainly was. Its election was followed swiftly by the onset of the economic crisis, a circumstance which the Labour ministers were utterly unfitted to cope with, even had one granted them good intentions. The leading lights of the government were products of the pre-war socialist movement, steeped in the assumptions of ethical socialism buttressed by a firm constitutionalism. They could readily dilate on the iniquities of the present, and expiate on the splendours of a fraternal future, but as for proceeding from the one to the other they were completely clueless. In this world before Keynesianism, they could do no better than submit all their plans and hopes to the flint-eyed scrutiny of Treasury orthodoxy. The inadequacy of this approach was pitifully exposed once the economic crisis broke, with unemployment rising to 2.5 million workers by the end of 1930. All but the most limited and ineffective schemes were vetoed by a Treasury concerned solely with the value of the pound and the security of investors' interests. Oswald Mosley proposed more imaginative solutions breaking with this sterile thinking and, when he could not persuade his Cabinet colleagues, he left government and the Labour Party, setting on the path that would shortly lead him to fascism and a role as Britain's putative dictator. Altogether, the aimless drift of reformism in office contrasted once more with the purposeful planning based on the socialised production of Soviet industrialisation.

The straw that finally broke the back of the already feeble Labour camel was the demand by the bankers, in London and New York, for economies in public expenditure, to be effected primarily by means of a ten per cent reduction in benefits paid to the burgeoning numbers of unemployed. Given resistance from around half the cabinet, MacDonald persuaded himself that the "national interest" now required a "national government". Unable to convince the Labour Party of this course he embarked on it anyway, taking a few of his colleagues, Chancellor Phillip Snowden and the reprehensible Jimmy Thomas eminent among them, into coalition with the Tory party and large fractions of the Liberals. This was in effect a conservative government presided over by the hapless MacDonald for the primary purpose of making the most impoverished section of the working class bear the burden of the economic crisis. Here was a further confirmation, it seemed, of the CPGB's predictions and its assessment of reformism. The new government speedily decided to seek a mandate from the electorate for this rearrangement, so again the two lines within the labour movement were put to the test.

The election, now pitting a Labour Party that had just lost its long-time leader against a united "national" bloc, was derided by Dutt. "The Labour Party in office prepared the whole programme of the National Government; its former leaders lead the National Government; it approved nine-tenths of the cuts carried out. The electors are offered the glorious choice between ten-tenths cuts and nine-tenths cuts."[44] Gallacher called the new government the "first stage in the development towards a fascist dictatorship."[45]

The pre-election temperature was raised further by a substantial muniny in the Royal Navy at the port of Invergordon in Scotland. The causes were strictly economic – pay cuts of ten per cent had been ordered for all, but some ratings saw their pay cut by 25 per cent. The action immobilised several ships and alarmed the Admiralty, which backtracked on the deeper reductions. The Communist Party played no part in initiating the movement, but several of the movement's leaders, including Len Wincott and Fred Copeman, subsequently joined the Party, which saw the mutiny as the harbinger of a deepening revolutionary crisis. Rust declared to the central committee that "the revolt of the sailors…is an outstanding event, one of the most dramatic revelations of the revolutionary spirit of the workers shown in this country."[46] However, the movement did not spread further, despite unfounded rumours of a revolt in the Black Watch.[47]

Nor did it impede the National Government's re-election. It secured the most overwhelming majority in the history of universal suffrage in Britain, winning 554 seats with over two-thirds of the vote. Labour lost two million votes and was reduced to a parliamentary rump of 52, including three ILP MPs. The Communist Party was not the beneficiary of this collapse, however. Its vote inched up to 70,000, only a modest improvement on 1929. Arthur Horner secured the highest share of the vote in Rhondda East, with 32 per cent, followed by Gallacher in West Fife with 22 per cent.

The imprisoned Indian revolutionary Usmani was this time nominated in St Pancras, but secured just 332 votes. Even in what might seem the most favourable of circumstances, the line of independent leadership in the electoral field failed to yield results. As Matthew Worley notes, the outcome "demonstrated again the disparity between the CPGB as an agitational presence in the labour movement and as a viable political alternative to the Labour Party in the minds of the working class."[48] The Political Bureau asserted that "this defeat of the Labour Party was the chief feature of the election" but added that "…it is nevertheless a matter for the most serious concern that the Communist Party…did not succeed in bringing under the banner of the revolutionary fight a much greater number of the disillusioned workers." This failure to convince workers to vote Communist was attributed to inadequately exposing Labour as "class enemies" and lacklustre denunciation of parliamentarism, amongst a litany of factors.[49]

By this stage the "class against class" line was being modified in relation to the trade unions. However, there was no slackening in its venom towards the social-democratic political parties. The January 1932 central committee resolution which enjoined a turn to working in the unions also warned that "the ILP…is an inseparable part of British social fascism. The ILP…is the most dangerous barrier between the Party and the masses who are becoming radical." It warned against a dangerous tendency in some localities to treat the ILP as "a possible ally" on occasion.[50] This was an unfortunate approach since at the same moment the ILP was itself descending into a period of turmoil which culminated in its disaffiliation from the Labour Party. While dismay at the ignominious collapse of the Labour government underpinned this decision, it was technically taken on the issue of submission to the standing orders of the Parliamentary Labour Party, which mandated a whipping system frequently obliging ILP MPs to vote against ILP policy and their own convictions.[51] The disaffiliation was seen by the Communist Party as merely a manoeuvre to maintain credibility among the workers. A more nuanced approach would surely have yielded better results.

In fact, the ILP was now embarked on a road leading to its own disintegration, as its more left-wing elements drew closer to the CPGB while others refused to leave Labour (or sought an early reconciliation) while others still sought to build it as a revolutionary, but non-Communist, alternative to official Labour. The latter, however, embarked on only the most gradual and limited rethink of its perspectives in the wake of the electoral calamity, at least initially. Its reconstruction as a party of government was to take the remainder of the decade, but its roots in trade unionism were unimpaired, and it was this last circumstance which was to complicate the Communist Party's approach to it, even more than the fact that in 1931 Labour still received more than six million votes compared to the CPGB's 70,000.

Hornerism and trade unionism

No issue vexed the party more in the "class against class" period than trade union policy. Trade unions were initially seen as part of the apparatus of reformist mis-leadership, now tending to "fascisation". Nevertheless, treating them in the same fashion as the Labour Party proved impractical. For one thing, Communists were able to be active within them and for another they did on occasion, however hesitantly, engage in strikes and other manifestations of struggle. There was never any serious attempt, as already noted, to implement the policy of setting up "red unions" as breakaways except on those two occasions when a local mass basis for such an initiative appeared, at least temporarily. Even more restricted forms of "independent leadership", which in practice meant trying to conduct the course of industrial disputes outwith and against the trade unions officially representing the workers involved, were fraught with problems and seldom led to anything that could pass as success. Only where the party had a pre-existing mass base amongst the workers could such an approach gain the slightest traction, and those places were few and far between. Party propaganda tended to give the impression that unorganised workers retained a revolutionary purity lacked by their colleagues in a trade union. That was usually very wide of the mark. The Minority Movement, the putative core of the revolutionary opposition in the unions, dwindled in influence, and such membership gains as the Party made by intervening to offer its own leadership in strikes were generally speedily lost thereafter.

Bureaucratic fantasy often substituted for a realistic evaluation of the possibilities. Bear in mind that the CPGB had only three dozen factory cells in 1930 with an average of six or seven members in each, and no sympathetic base outside a few mining districts, and then consider the structure its cadre were enjoined to erect on their shoulders, as follows:

> "The factory cell is the core of all revolutionary organisation; it is the pivot around which is formed the revolutionary organs of struggle. Its first task in this connection is to build a factory group of the Minority Movement, through which it operates for initiating and leading struggle in the factory...the MM factory group must set itself the task of forming an independent rank-and-file factory committee, composed of organised and unorganised workers...it is the permanent organ of the workers in the factory which deals with every small grievance and puts forward a policy of struggle for the workers...for the actual preparation and conduct of a strike there must be formed a committee of action...which must be of a wider mass character, bringing in new militant workers together with the best types in the factory committee."[52]

Factory cell, Minority Movement Group, independent rank-and-file committee, committee of action... the situation placed a quite unfeasible burden on a tiny number of communists when clearly it would be much simpler and far more effective simply to agitate through the structures of the recognised trade unions in the workplace. Such structures of independent leadership as were conjured into existence during a strike rapidly evaporated afterwards. The attitude towards trade unionism was the first aspect of the "new line" to be seriously modified, but not before it had almost led to the expulsion of the party's most influential workers' leader of the time.

The South Wales coalfield was one of the few areas where the party had retained a mass following in the working class. Communism had an appeal for many miners in the area, although this was not translated into stable organisation – the party could get thousands of votes in elections in the Rhondda valley, for example, yet it lacked party branches in many villages including, at one time, Mardy, the "reddest" of all.[53] Thus, when a dispute broke out in 1931 over demands by the colliery owners for further wage cuts in the context of a limited reduction in hours it seemed like a propitious opportunity to exercise "independent leadership" as against that of the South Wales Miners Federation (SWMF), the more so since Arthur Horner, the party's leading trade union member, was on the spot and enjoyed broad personal authority across the coalfield, earned during the General Strike five years earlier.

Lacking support outside the coalfield, and with its own organisation depleted to the point where it possibly represented little more than half the miners working in South Wales, the SWMF was unable to maintain the dispute. Horner had attempted to form strike committees through the Minority Movement but had failed to establish effective leadership outside the official union. When the SWMF threw in the towel, the Party leadership, including in the South Wales district, wished to continue the dispute on an unofficial basis. It complained that its independent role "was almost completely submerged during the strike, and there were not independent party pronouncements bringing out clearly...fundamental aims...in relation to the immediate strike issues."[54] Horner was denounced for having connived in this failure of leadership. Indeed, he had opposed continuing the strike at a conference of unofficial delegates, of which he was chairman.

> "I said 'you can begin a strike and build it up but you cannot carry it on in pieces after the initial strike has disintegrated. The only result of carrying on the strike unofficially in these circumstances will be to isolate the militants from the rest of the miners in the coalfields and in the present circumstances it will be perfectly easy for the owners to victimize the militants.' I warned that the result would be the miners would turn away from the leadership of the unofficial movement...This incident started the idea that I was prepared to accept bureaucratic orthodox decisions and was not ready to undertake actions against the trade union bureaucracy..."[55]

Horner based this analysis on the fundamental view that the strength of the movement must lie in the organised working class in work. "I said we must concentrate on strengthening the trade unions and then building an alliance between the employed workers and the unemployed."[56] Exposing the futility of "independent leadership" he told the Comintern that "the role of the SWMF was practically disregarded, artificial strike committees, really MM groups, were set up as alternatives to the Lodges without mass content, resulting only in our isolation."[57]

This was sufficient for the creation of "Hornerism" as a dangerous deviation, excoriated daily in the party press, and for the CPGB to attempt to expel its progenitor, a misguided project which Horner himself assisted by failing to make adequate self-criticism.[58] A statement on the matter by the Politbureau took up twelve pages of the *Communist Review* in April 1931, urging that Horner's deviation should "be thoroughly discussed in every party unit as a question of fundamental political important for it concerns...the whole question of fighting for the correct carrying out of the line of the Party at a period of life-and-death struggles for the working class, when a retreat before the Social-Fascists will have disastrous consequences; it concerns the fight to uproot opportunism in our ranks and to crush once and for all the remnants of the old leadership, who continue an obstinate struggle against the line of independent revolutionary leadership of the working class by the Communist Party."[59]

Horner told the central committee considering his expulsion that "...the suggestions which have been made for my expulsion from this movement have a very, very serious meaning for me...it is life and death for me...in the sense that to be outside of the revolutionary working-class movement is something that I have never thought about...".[60]

In the end, he made sufficient acknowledgement of mistakes".[61] for the Comintern, markedly reluctant to endorse his exclusion, to bring the matter to an end after summoning Horner to Moscow and determining that he "was wrong in not observing the discipline of the Party, but the Party was unjustified in trying to make out that my deviation was a philosophy. They said that the difference between us was a tactical argument and that there was no such thing as 'Hornerism'."about...".[62] This judicious approach left Horner free to stand again as Communist candidate in Rhondda East in the October 1931 election, to revive the radical left in the South Wales coalfield and, indeed, to go to prison the next year for obstructing bailiffs going about their work seizing the property of the poor.[63]

Experiences like this certainly nudged the party towards a reconsideration of its trade union line, in particular its preference for working outside the official structures, notwithstanding that the latter retained the loyalty of most workers. Pollitt was particularly exercised by the absurdity of this approach and, with Comintern support, worked towards an incremental revision of it. The landmark here was the party's central committee of January 1932. Pollitt told this meeting that "a pernicious doctrine has cropped up in our party that it is our purpose to destroy the unions...it is nothing of the kind." The Party had, he said "carried on no systematic revolutionary mass work in the reformist trade unions" while the Minority Movement had become "a small organisation boxed up in itself, and thereby isolated from the masses in the factories and the trade unions."[64] The resolution itself stated that "the Party has not yet overcome its chief weakness, namely isolation from the masses of the workers", indeed a crippling defect for a revolutionary party.[65] Great emphasis was now to be placed on activity in trade union branches, even as the Labour party and the ILP were still anathematised in the familiar terms.

A contradiction was left unexplored here. If it was granted as possible to win trade union branches for Communist leadership, and to work within them to that end, why should it be regarded as out of the question for the unions as whole, at regional and national level, to be won over? Surely the resistance from the reformist officialdom would get fiercer the more their authority was challenged, but given that unions retained rulebooks guaranteeing conferences and elections, an accumulation of local advances in party influence could lead in the direction of a deeper transformation. This corresponded to reality in the trade union movement. The biggest trade union official of all, the T&GWU's Ernie Bevin, was forced to backtrack in his handling of a London bus dispute by a powerful rank-and-file movement within the union in 1932. When the AEU executive expelled half a dozen of its leading left critics from the union following a pay dispute in 1931, the union's appeals court reinstated them. The bureaucracy was not immovable.[66]

There was a still more far-reaching consideration which was not, however, considered at this stage. While it remained a fact that affiliated unions effectively controlled the organisation of the Labour Party and could, if they exerted themselves in that direction, shape its policy, surely the acknowledgement of the potential for giving a lead through local union organs had implications here too? Of course, the structural obstacles to bringing Communist influence to bear on Labour were much more severe, but once the official, established, labour movement was recognised as a site of contestation, the Labour Party could not be left out of the picture entirely.

This was not addressed at the time, since that would have risked prejudicing the whole turn to the unions by getting bogged down in what the Comintern would have regarded as a heretical turn against "class against class" and the unequivocal confrontation with social democracy at its base. Whether the Labour Party and social democracy were always and inevitably exactly the same thing was too hot a potato to be handled in 1932.

Nevertheless, controversy rumbled on around union policy. Many members did not seem to grasp the new approach straight away. When Pollitt proclaimed in August 1932 that "every ounce of our energy is to try to make the trade union organisations strong and powerful weapons in their daily fight...The Communist Party is for a powerful trade unionism, is for the strengthening of the organised power of the workers which they have built up through their trade unions" he drew a rejoinder from Dutt that "...to speak of a 'powerful trade unionism' today means to speak of a powerful united reformist trade unionism. Does the Communist party stand for this? Of course not. We stand for a powerful united revolutionary trade union opposition, firmly based on the trade union membership and the lower trade union organs..."

Dutt in turn was rebuked by Gallacher who argued that "we have only just started in a real effort to break through our isolation and to make an effective approach to the work in the unions, and now Dutt comes along and puts forward a line that will destroy all that has been done, and damn us to complete futility...Dutt's line is for independent leadership in the sense of being independent of the trade union movement..."[67]

Pollitt was surely right in his approach. A *vanguard* party, and that was what the CPGB aspired to be, cannot possibly play its role if it self-isolates from the organisations of those it seeks to lead. If "independent leadership" meant, as Gallacher argued, independence from those organisations then futility was indeed what lay in prospect. Idris Cox, once one of the strongest advocates for the new line and an antagonist of Horner's in South Wales, now acknowledged that despite having the correct policy "in general" without "close contact with the masses" the Party was "like a newly-polished locomotive engine without steam."[68] The experience of the preceding three years seemed to indicate that Communists could not play a genuine leading role by relying on special organs of struggle created by the Party itself and often arising spontaneously during a strike with no preceding organisation or roots.

The problem was only compounded by the tendency to repel any worker who did not endorse the full line of the Party and by introducing extraneous demands, as when "Defend the Soviet Union" and "Hands off India" were added to the slogans used in the Yorkshire woollen strike of 1930.[69] The trade unions were by-and-large embedded in the working class, in the major industries in particular, and while workers were frequently frustrated by the leadership offered there was scant sympathy for tearing their organisations down and starting again, or even doing without altogether. The CPGB came to recognise this, with Comintern backing, and never again turned away from the unions, as organisations to be won for revolutionary leadership rather than discarded.

The Party at work 1930-32

What were the characteristics of CPGB in this period? It was surely a formation unprecedented in British politics and the British left historically, marked out by its theoretical passion, the strength of its international connections and the demands it made on its members.

Firstly, it remained a small party. As the new line started to bite its membership, drifting down since the General Strike, reached a nadir of 2,300. It briefly ascended to 9,000 in 1931, largely as a result of campaigning amongst the unemployed, before settling down to between 5,000 and 6,000. Members joined and left in large numbers. One estimate had 2,500 joining in early 1932 but 2,000 leaving in the same period. The largest number of members was in London, but to judge by election results, the party had a mass following in the South Wales and Fife coalfields – a similar base in east London was to develop later in the decade.

It was a proletarian party, indeed it was proud of being the most proletarian in the International. But it was a party of the unemployed proletariat – as much as sixty per cent of the membership were out of work.[70] It was therefore not a party strongly implanted in the factories, despite repeated exhortations.[71] As Pollitt pointed out this was a weakness shared with the mighty Communist Party of Germany, which was likewise rooted in the unemployed, with the factories remaining the strongholds of Social Democracy for the most part.[72] Internationally, "class against class" appealed most to those workers unable to participate in the main organisations of the labour movement, rather than to those in the trade unions which, the perception went, the Communists wanted to break up. One historian describes the Party as "small and isolated with a highly fluctuating and largely unemployed membership" while another writes that those members were "young, militant and less 'encumbered' by the traditions of the British labour movement."[73]

It was a party with a united leadership. That is not to say that there were no internal disputes, but the leading group was established and coherent. The Comintern had enjoined the Party in August 1930 to regard Pollitt as its leader[74], and indeed his authority only grew throughout this period. The influence of Dutt is more of a moot point. He remained in Brussels until 1936 and became a figure of some mystery to many of his comrades. He could play little part in the day-to-day running of the Party, although he corresponded endlessly with Pollitt and with the party's leading bodies, and was charged, by either the CPGB or the Comintern, with drafting most of the Party's major statements and documents. As the most capable theoretician in a party which was taught to treasure ideological rectitude, his influence was significant, but maybe not more so than that of Gallacher. At any event, in this period what was to become the party's historic leadership took shape. Apart from the relatively minor issue of J.T. Murphy, whose case is discussed below, the leadership suffered no splits until the outset of World War Two, and even then, a clear political division led to no defections. By way of contrast, the French Communist Party suffered multiple defections from its Political Bureau, including five individuals that subsequently became fascists, collaborators and, in one case, a likely police agent.

The CPGB was preponderantly male. It estimated that 800 of its members were women, of which 600 were working-class housewives. Special appeals to women workers were limited, and there were few women in the party leadership, and those that did reach the central committee did not last long at that level. Clearly the "working-class housewife" was not going to be pivotal in building factory cells, and the party's heavy proletarian emphasis meant in fact emphasis on the male industrial worker. Isobel Brown seems exceptional in this period in playing a leading part in industrial disputes. One of the party members of the time who has left us her memoirs, Mary Docherty from Fife, reports carrying out administrative tasks for her branch, until she asked to be given political responsibility for running the party's children's groups in a part of the country where its large following made such a thing feasible. The group campaigned against the use of the strap in schools, against religious education and in favour of free school meals for needy children, as well as the teaching of history from a working-class standpoint. [75] Gender roles were not challenged.

Intellectuals drawn to the Party were welcomed but not exactly indulged either. The great influx of intellectuals to the Communist movement in the 1930s is mainly associated with the later popular front against fascism, but already some were attracted by the evident contrast between capitalist crisis in the west and the achievements of Soviet planning, the apparent advance of a new society. David Guest and John Cornford, alongside former Labour MP John Strachey, were among those who either joined the CPGB or operated in its orbit during the latter stages of the "class against class" policy. At any event enough joined to start taking steps towards self-organisation within the party, sufficient to call forth stern warnings from Dutt as to how intellectuals should be expected to conduct their work in a well-known article "Intellectuals and Communism" published in the *Communist Review*. Dutt wrote that until recently the Party had little contact with intellectual strata due to the more backward development of such groups, their relative isolation from international influences and "their much greater domination and corruption by imperialism." Now, however, there was a "new vogue or fashion of Marxism' or what passes for 'Marxism'." This was welcomed in so far as "the Party has hitherto been very short of a useful proportion of professionally-trained intellectual elements" but he emphasised that "there is no special work and role of Communists from the bourgeois intellectual strata. There is only the work and role of all Communists, the propaganda of Communism, the fight for Communism…" Intellectuals' role was to use their skills in that fight, not to sink into debating their specialisms with other like-minded thinkers.

> "The intellectuals ought to be, from their training, widely read, versed in fields of knowledge not accessible to workers without special training, used to handling arguments, and able to express themselves clearly; and they have no need to hide all this, or be ashamed of it, but bring it into play for the service of the party" and its fight against capitalism, without expecting that their skills made them leaders more competent to determine the party line. The intellectual Communist "should forget that he is an intellectual and remember only that he is a Communist."[76]

To underline the point the same issue of *Communist Review* carried a scathing review of a book on the Soviet economy by Maurice Dobb, then the CPGB's leading figure in academia. Dobb was told that his book was of no use to workers!

Yet, if lukewarm about intellectuals, the party placed the highest value on the study of Marxism and a grasp of theory. Few things distinguished it more sharply from both the traditions of the British left and from the contemporary practice of the deeply pragmatic Labour Party. The works of Marx, Engels, Lenin, and to an increasing extent Stalin, were at the heart of this, and the study of them was an individual and collective responsibility for Communists. The Party furthermore maintained two theoretical journals and a book publishing house.

The whole party worked in a high state of mobilisation, with its core activists using most of their spare time for party work. Mass work focussed heavily on the unemployed movement, reflecting the nature of the Party's membership and the most visible and searing consequence of the intensified capitalist crisis. This was led by Wal Hannington, who built the National Unemployed Workers Movement into a mass national organisation with tens of thousands of members.[77] It organised hunger marches of the unemployed from South Wales and elsewhere which were so successful in highlighting the issue that the official labour movement was forced to abandon its indifference to organising the out-of-work and instead copy the initiative, with its own Jarrow March. Memoirs of the period generally dwell heavily on campaigns against the Means Test, and the obstruction of the eviction of unemployed workers from their housing.

Street meetings and workplace sales of party newspapers and literature were staples of the party's activity, as was regular Marxist education. While aspiring to be a party "of a new type" and actually in many respects being one, the CPGB was also the product of ordinary and frail human beings. One life-long party member left this account of the party cell he joined in the early 1930s. "There were seven people and we spent our first evening talking about distributing leaflets, which did not arrive, and who would speak at a street corner meeting on Saturday. This raised some argument since most believed it was useless to stand in the cold addressing themselves. It was agreed to wait till the weather was warmer. Daunting to think that this material was going to change the social order...It took months to get a membership card. Meetings were not prepared and ended in the pub on the corner."[78]

Such lack of disciplined fervour was not exclusive to the base of the party either. At one meeting of the Political Bureau in 1930 Willie Gallacher laid into Walter Tapsell on the grounds that the latter had got out of running a meeting by claiming illness and yet had been seen going to the cinema the same day![79] Surely the Bolshevik party itself had similar stories to tell, behind all the chest-thumping mythologies.

The party's lack of a daily newspaper, like its weak implantation in the workplace, had been a central issue in the polemics around its insufficient Bolshevisation and general lassitude. It is true that Lenin had urged the creation of a Communist daily in Britain as far back as 1921, yet this injunction had gone unheeded, in large part because maintaining such a venture was and is a stupendous undertaking which would have taxed the resources of a party much bigger than the 1920s CPGB.

Nevertheless, the impossible happened and the *Daily Worker* saw light of day on January 1, 1930. Extraordinarily, it remains in existence to this day, as the *Morning Star*. Considerable Comintern prodding was required to get the Party to the point of publishing, and still more considerable Comintern subventions. The subsidy was, however, well spent, in that publishing a daily paper immediately restructured the work of the Party. For one thing, it mandated responding to all the issues of working-class life on a more-or-less immediate basis, itself requiring the transformation of the leadership's way of working. As the paper's first editor Bill Rust put it in his history of the paper's early years:

> "It meant that the Communist Party was now able to advance from the stage of general propaganda to the handling of daily political events as they occurred, to give a daily and direct answer to the problems before the people as they arose and to organise action in support of its policy."[80]

For a second thing, the organisational and financial effort required to sell the paper and it in being demanded a step-up in terms of party work at all levels, and gave a clear focus to the efforts of branches and individual Communists. These demands were only exacerbated by capitalist efforts to abort this new venture more-or-less immediately. Initial Conservative hopes that the government might act against it, largely on grounds of articles commending resistance to British rule in India,[81] came to nothing. The newspaper wholesalers, which distributed all daily papers to newsagents, soon began to boycott the *Worker*, ostensibly on grounds relating to libel insurance. This left an enormous gap in the paper's distribution which only the party itself could fill. As per Rust:

> "The challenge was taken up and throughout the country our energetic supporters were to be found in the small hours of the morning collecting parcels at the railway stations and delivering them to newsagents or direct to readers....It was a great test and the paper came through with flying colours...Close, unbreakable ties were established between the paper and its readers...great public interest and sympathy was aroused in the fight of a gallant little paper which was beset on all sides."[82]

However, the new demands – political, practical, financial – involved in sustaining a daily newspaper did have a deleterious impact on other aspects of the small party's work. It could hardly be otherwise – at one point four of the five members of the central secretariat of the party, the core of the new leadership elected at Leeds, were involved in either writing, editing, or managing the *Worker*. As a consequence, at the party's industrial and colonial departments both temporarily ceased to function.[83]

The paper's contents of course reflected the narrow perspectives and isolation of the party at the time. It was subjected to regular scathing review both within the Party and by the Comintern. These problems were worsened by the lack of any relevant professional experience on the party of most of the staff and by a view that having such skills brought with it the threat of bourgeois attitudes. In 1932 *The Party Organiser* published a scathing speech by an "Islington Comrade" speaking on behalf of local members at a conference to promote the paper. The comrade took the paper to task for every conceivable sin over five pages before concluding "apart from these points we think the paper is all right." The speaker advised that "even members of the CP buy the *Daily Worker* for propaganda and the *Manchester Guardian* or *Telegraph* for news".[84] There was particular controversy relating to sports coverage, which was dropped shortly after the launch, to the approval of Dutt, whose views as to the unsuitability of covering such activities in a Communist paper would only have been intensified had he known that the racing tipster wished to sign his notes as "Nilats", being Stalin spelt backwards. Nevertheless, the *Worker* survived (and sports coverage returned), and gradually began to extend its influence, and the strength of the Communist Party with it.

Two internal disputes, neither of great significance, affected the Party in the course of 1932. J.T. Murphy, a member of the party leadership, was expelled for publishing an article in the *Communist Review*, of which he was editor, advocating increased trade with the USSR in order to assist with unemployment in Britain. He did this in spite of Pollitt explicitly opposing the policy as being an attempt to ameliorate the situation for British capitalism. Murphy endeavoured to resign from the party, an impermissible act for one of its leaders. He had little following in the party and seemed to work as something of a loner.[85] He took no following with him out of the party and his expulsion seemed to be generally welcomed – in his native Sheffield only two members out of 76 at an aggregate meeting dissented. Rumours spread that he had been a police spy, for which no evidence was ever adduced beyond the suspicions aroused by him affording to have his son educated privately while living on occasional payments for articles in *Pravda*. Murphy, the Political Bureau wrote, had "passed over to the camp of the enemy."[86]

The second ruction involved a small group of members in Balham, south London, who, frustrated at the party's lack of progress which they bizarrely attributed to a drift to the right, had made contact with Leon Trotsky, by then in exile from the USSR and in the first stages of establishing his Fourth International. This group, the first organised manifestation of Trotskyism in Britain, was expelled without much public fuss. Hitherto, the divisions between Trotsky and the Stalin-Bukharin leadership of the CPSU over "socialism in one country" and the purported bureaucratisation of the Soviet state and party had caused very few ructions in the CPGB.[87] It was to be a long time before Trotskyism was to gain any serious following in the British labour movement or pose a threat to the Party's position on the left, although it was not so long before some Trotskyist views started making their influence felt within the ILP.

12th CPGB Congress

The Party's twelfth congress, held in London in November 1932 was an occasion to review the progress it had made in the three years since the definitive triumph of the new line and its associated leadership. The party's membership had stabilised at around 5,400 or twice what it had been at its low point in 1930. However, sixty per cent of the membership was unemployed, which meant that the Communist base in the factories was necessarily fragile. There were only eighty factory cells across the country, with 550 members in them. Only two Communists had been chosen as union delegates to the TUC Congress that year (out of around 700).[88] This was no strong foundation for giving leadership to a movement of millions in the throes of an enormous crisis.

By the time of the Congress, Pollitt was the party's unchallenged leader, and he had been using this enhanced position to move away from the wilder shores of "class against class". In particular, he sought to have the Party embed itself properly in the trade union movement, curbing the fantasies of "independent leadership" while remaining strongly critical of social democracy, as we have seen. Addressing the Congress, he advised delegates that the "main tasks" were "first, to overcome the sectarianism and the isolation from the mass struggles now taking place...secondly, to establish unbreakable bonds with the working masses in the factories and in the trade unions" as well as strengthening democracy within the Party and renewing its leadership at all levels.[89]

This turn required starting at quite a basic level. "The first essential...is...that every Party member eligible for membership in the trade unions must join the union" to become "organisers of the workers' fight in fact and not in resolutions." This was "not trade union legalism, but directing our attention to simple elementary things."[90] Pollitt acknowledged something which was later to become a much more serious problem for Communists in trade unions: "There are many good trade union comrades who are in danger, and serious danger, because they voluntarily cut themselves off from Party activity and Party life because of the trade union activity they carry through."[91] Casting this turn as directed against the domination of the right-wing leaders, he stated that the "objective must be that our mass work in the factories and unions is for the purpose of building up mass influence and winning the positions in the factories and unions, for us to lead the daily struggles and economic struggles, and to get that backing which gives them power for independent organisation and leadership to become a fact. Precisely on the basis of what we have done in the factory and the union can we carry on a struggle independent of the reformist leaders."[92] There was no more talk of forming "red" unions, rather the perspective was of a militant opposition *within* the unions.

This did not mean any reconciliation with the Labour Party. "They say that they have 'recovered their soul' because they have got rid of MacDonald, Thomas and Snowden... This is their demagogy, but in deeds they carry out the same policy as when Labour was a government. They now come forward with all their schemes of 'Socialism', with their Socialist phraseology, when in daily practice, in daily work, their role is to disorganise the workers' fight against every phase of the capitalist offensive..."[93] Ridiculing schemes for regulation of industry and control of banks, Pollitt said that "they ignore, and studiously ignore, the basic question of how to win power, how we can really commence to build socialism in this country....they do not admit...that...before Socialism can be established or commenced in this country there must be a revolutionary overthrow of capitalism and the complete destruction of the political power of the capitalists, and the setting up of the dictatorship of the working class..."[94] As for the ILP, now disaffiliated from Labour and on a course towards disintegration, Pollitt sought to draw "in ILP workers in every phase of united front activity" against unemployment, reformism, and war, exposing the policy of the Maxton-Brockway leadership. "We want to win these workers, and when we once get the impression across to the ILP workers that we want to win them for the revolution, then we will make a big step forward."[95] Here was the beginning of a serious return to united front politics, although Pollitt also noted that "our average party member drops down dead with fright if in an anti-war committee or NUWM branch or anything associated with united front work, a non-party member is elected as Secretary or Chairman, they have a special LPC in order to know how to break down this big danger to the social revolution, and this is the foisting of mechanical Communist leadership on to the united front..."[96]

Pollitt also situated the party's work in the wider struggle against imperialism. "Everywhere the hand of British imperialism has meant mass poverty, disease, shocking housing conditions, illiteracy, persecution, prison, bombing, death, and the loss of all economic and political rights."[97] Only the Communist Party, he said, "wages ceaseless war against colonial oppression", recalling that under the late Labour government, tens of thousands had been imprisoned in India and [99] "defenceless native women" killed in Nigeria in an anti-tax protest.

> "Only our Party is in a position to build up the bonds of daily solidarity with the colonial workers, and it is vital that our Congress and party shall do much more decisive anti-imperialist work than we have done in the past...we have to put the question in the way of convincing the working masses of this country that the only line of advance for them and for our Indian comrades is by common struggle against British imperialism. It is through these class bonds of solidarity that we can help each other in times of strike...and make the demand for the withdrawal of the troops from these countries and the right of complete independence...Only our Party stands for the waging of this struggle, and we have ourselves to begin to realise how strong are many imperialist illusions in the minds of the workers."[98]

As for leadership renewal, nineteen members of the outgoing central committee were not re-elected, and the new committee of thirty included just two women.[99]

Rise of Nazism, Comintern response

The perspectives of the 12th Congress, and the Comintern as a whole, were speedily overtaken by events in Germany. In January 1933 Hitler came to power and instituted a reign of terror, in the first instance directed against the Communist Party. Hitherto, fascism had been regarded as a danger in mainly less advanced or peripheral countries in Europe. Now it had conquered in one of the great imperialist powers, with a powerful state and advanced industry at its disposal. Hitler not only aimed at establishing a dictatorship actuated by antisemitism and anti-Marxism, he also sought to scrap the Versailles treaty by force if necessary and, beyond that, aimed at war directed towards the Soviet Union, in the interests of securing Germany "living space."

It is now scarcely disputable that the Comintern misread the Hitler threat very considerably. Until the very end of the Weimar Republic and indeed beyond, it insisted that the main enemy was social democracy, with its paralysing and counter-revolutionary influence on the working class. While not at all oblivious to the possibility of Hitler coming to power, the Comintern and the KPD held that this would constitute a sort of last gasp for the German bourgeoisie, a violent interlude before soviet revolution and the conquest of power by the working class. "After Hitler, us" was the slogan expressing this illusion, which was hard to die. Responsibility for Hitler's ascent rests in the first place on the German ruling classes who placed him in power, believing that more conventional conservatives would control the Nazi leader, using him first of all to smash the workers' movement. That too was an illusion. In the labour movement, the KPD's sectarianism was echoed by social democracy's anti-communism, support for the state and political passivity in the face of the threat. However, there is no denying that the Comintern played its part in the calamity, its strategic myopia masked by the KPD's apparent growing strength right up until the last moment.

As Hitler clamped down, driving the Communist Party underground and the SPD into exile, while suppressing or suborning the trade unions, taking the first measures against Germany's Jews, and reducing the Reichstag to a rubber stamp, the Comintern made its first tentative call for a workers' united front internationally against the advance of fascism. In Britain, the ILP wrote to the CPGB proposing joint action, drawing a positive response from the party's Secretariat, which urged a common fight on a detailed list of proposals. Pollitt, severely realistic as he usually was, acknowledged in the Political Bureau that "the proletariat had suffered a terrific defeat as a result of the triumph of fascism in Germany".[100] By March 17, a joint meeting was held with the ILP and by April a joint demonstration. This was a definite departure from the hardest line interpretations of "class against class." However, unity was hard to sustain, as first the ILP's Fenner Brockway made public criticisms of the Comintern, and the *Daily Worker* did not desist from denouncing ILP potentates.[101] Correspondence was impeded apparently by Stalin's decision to personally supervise from Moscow the CPGB's approach, and the initiative petered out, although it was to resume the next year.[102] The Labour Party was still less pliable, greeting the advent of Nazism with a declaration "Democracy vs. Dictatorship" which made clear Labour's opposition to communism and fascism alike.

This drew a response from Dutt, constituting the first considered British Communist response to the new situation. In *Democracy and Fascism* Dutt pointed out that the Labour Party statement had attacked Communism or Bolshevism more times that it had fascism. He ridiculed Labour's claim to stand for democracy.

"Face the facts. The Labour Party in office has shown what it means by democracy when it has ruled as the Government of the British Empire...The Labour Party ruled and held in subjection these four hundred and twenty million colonial slaves...by armed violence, shooting and imprisoning all who dared to resist and to claim democratic rights."[103]

He argued that "fascism is the outcome of reformism" and that "the democratic path to socialism" would end in a fascist victory to which, he claimed, the Labour party would adapt itself, detailing the instances of SPD leaders in Germany trying to come to terms with Hitler. "Fascism arises when the working-class movement has grown to a point of strength when it should advance to the seizure of power, when the bankruptcy of the old regime is revealed, but the working class is held in by reformist leadership." His conclusion that "if the British workers put their faith in the Labour party as the defence against fascism, they will suffer as cruel an awakening as the German workers" showed the limitations of anti-fascist unity from the Communist perspective.[104] The answer to fascism was socialist revolution and nothing else.

The Comintern's adaptation to this disaster, and consequently a new lead to its sections, was indeed ponderous. It was doubtless reluctant to acknowledge, or even incapable of doing so, that the ascent of Nazism put an end to any perspective of continuing world revolution for an indeterminate period. It may now be clear that such a perspective had been out of joint with reality since 1923 at the latest, but the whole "class against class" line, reinforced by the fact of world capitalist crisis, had been based on its continuing viability. Thus, when the ECCI considered Hitlerism, it did so initially through red-tinted spectacles. "A new upsurge of the revolutionary mass movement in Germany is beginning," the leadership of the KPD declared in October 1933[105]. In fact, the party was starting to crumble under the blows of the dictatorship, which had already sent tens of thousands of communist cadre to the concentration camps. While the KPD maintained a heroic underground resistance throughout the Nazi dictatorship, its clandestine networks had basically been crushed by the end of 1934, reducing the Comintern's strongest European section to ineffectuality.

The KPD's leader Wilhelm Pieck (Ernst Thalmann had been imprisoned by the Nazis) told the ECCI that the Party had "launched a sharp struggle against the Social-Democratic swamp ideology, against the view that the proletariat had suffered a decisive defeat at the hands of fascism"; moreover, "the establishment of the fascist dictatorship was only possible for the bourgeoisie in consequence of the sabotage of the class struggle pursued by Social Democracy, its disorganisation and disarming of the proletariat and its ever more pronounced fusion with the capitalist state apparatus."[106] It was at this meeting that the Comintern first adopted the formula that "fascism is the open, terrorist dictatorship of the most reactionary, most chauvinist and most imperialist elements of finance capital", a definition which lasted better than the plenum's declaration that "Social democracy continues to play the role of the main social prop of the bourgeoisie also in the countries of open fascist dictatorship", an entirely misguided position which undermined the calls for unity which the Comintern also issued.[107]

These views guided the CPGB's own analysis, of course. They were embodied in Dutt's *Fascism and Social Revolution*, a book length analysis of the phenomenon which was intended by its author to be an update of Lenin's *Imperialism*. Curiously, the mechanisms of international exploitation and the struggle in the colonies are one of the few salient features not explored in his book, which can be described as a masterpiece of Third Period Marxism-Leninism, and one of the last.[108] Dutt locates the rise of fascism in the whole post-war development of capitalism, and its growing inability to develop the forces of production. The first chapters deal with this socio-economic background – the whole crisis of bourgeois society in decay – before turning to the rise of fascism itself. This he saw as the instrument of the ruling circles of finance capital, and scored theories that it was a middle-class movement, as opposed to a form of ruling which endeavoured to secure a new mass base for the ruling class, mainly among the middle classes.

Its main features, Dutt argued, were "the basic aim of maintaining capitalism in the face of the revolution…the consequent intensification of the capitalist dictatorship; the limitation and repression of the independent working class movement…the increasing supersession of parliamentary democracy…state monopolist organisation of industry and finance", the integration of each imperialist bloc into "a single economic-political unit" and "the advance to war as the necessary accompaniment of the increasing imperialist antagonisms."[109] Dutt saw these trends at work throughout all capitalist politics, and therefore at one point or another cites US President Roosevelt and John Maynard Keynes as advocating proto-fascist views on account of their seeking a strengthened role for the state.

Fascism did not have a specific ideology, rather it "developed as a movement in practice, in the conditions of threatening proletarian revolution, as a counter-revolutionary mass movement supported by the bourgeoisie, employing weapons of mixed social demagogy and terrorism to defeat the revolution and build up a strengthened capitalist dictatorship."[110] Dutt turns the then-fashionable theory that fascism arose as a response to Communism on its head, asserting that it arose as a result of the failure of socialist revolution, not its success. It "arises when the breakdown of the old capitalist institutions and the advance of the working class movement has reached a point at which the working class should advance to the seizure of power, but when the working class is held in by reformist leadership."[111] Here the responsibility for the rise of fascism is placed squarely on social democracy once more. Defending the use of the term "social fascism", albeit in a somewhat muted way (acknowledging it had given rise to "indignant resentment and much misunderstanding"), Dutt cites extensively internal briefing papers circulated in German bourgeois circles as describing how the ruling elite had turned to first social democracy and then fascism to split the working class and ensure the maintenance of capitalism in the post-war period.[112]

However, Dutt then strayed into what should, even in 1934, have been implausibilities:

> "Fascism never becomes the main basis of the bourgeoisie…because Fascism never wins the main body of the industrial workers with traditions of organisation – the sole power that can overthrow capitalism. Here the role of Social Democracy remains of decisive importance, even after the establishment of the fascist dictatorship."

Social democratic ideological influence among the industrial workers remained the key to allowing fascism to remain in power.[1.3] Indeed, Dutt went further, seeing germs of fascism in the ideology and practice of social democracy after the war, as it had increasingly become absorbed into the bourgeois state. He did also acknowledge the role of national-chauvinist ideology and of antisemitism. He did not perhaps give the latter the weight he might have done a few years later, dealing with the question in a lengthy footnote, concluding that "antisemitism, the typical degrading expression of a tottering system, is developed in its decaying stage in proportion as the class struggle grows acute",[114] a somewhat mechanical formulation.

Foreshadowing the disputes of 1939, Dutt located fascism's heightened aggressiveness internationally not in its specific nature but in the fact that it had taken hold in "hungry" imperialist powers, disadvantaged in the international distribution of colonies and markets, while Britain and France, in particular are "relatively 'sated' imperialist groups, gorged with world-plunder and seeking above all to hold what they have...This is the working of the law of unequal capitalist development which underlay the last war and drives to the next."[115] To this he added the already evident desire of the British ruling class to direct German (and Japanese) imperialism into war against the USSR. Britain's own democracy, he argued, was merely a reflection of its imperial strength. "The 'democratic freedoms' of western imperialism have been built on the foundation of colonial slavery."[116] And, in a dialectical unity, the same experience of colonial rule was one of the main bases for the development of fascism in Britain. "The British bourgeoise is trained for generations on the basis of its rule of India, Ireland and the colonial empire to methods of violence and despotic domination, at the same time as on the basis of parliamentary and electioneering humbug in Britain to the technique of mass deception – the two together constituting the perfect combination for fascism."[117]

If one recalls the anti-democratic agitation of Milner, Cromer, Curzon and other imperialist leaders before the first world war, it is clear that Dutt was not far off the mark here. It is a shortcoming, however, that he did not expand on the violence of Britain's colonial rule – there are only passing references – since it underlined that in the 1930s Britain's capitalists merely "exported" the fascist methods which their German and Italian confreres deployed at home.

In terms of the fascist menace in Britain, Dutt identified both the National Government and Mosley's new British Union of Fascists as threats, the latter having acquired the support of *Daily Mail* proprietor Lord Rothermere for his movement. He made great play of the roots of the BUF in the Labour Party, with Mosley having served in MacDonald's second government and his intermediate venture, the New Party, having secured the support of a dozen Labour or ILP MPs before its open development into fascism. Mosley's influence was thanks to "the Labour Party and the Independent Labour Party, which in this way characteristically performed the role of Social Fascism." Dutt did not omit to cite statements by Brockway supporting Mosley in his pre-fascist period. [118] Listing the authoritarian measures taken by the National Government, Dutt claimed that it marked "the process of bourgeois concentration and intensified dictatorship for the carrying through of measures of an increasingly fascist character."[119] Indeed, it became increasingly clear that the advance of dictatorial government in Britain would lie through the National regime rather than Mosley's movement, which remained an intermittent street force but otherwise became marginalised. The fight against fascism, Dutt concluded "cannot be conducted on the basis of trusting to bourgeois 'democracy' as the defence against fascism." Rather, "the workers' dictatorship is the only alternative to the capitalist dictatorship, which at present is increasingly passing from the older 'democratic' to fascist forms." [120] The united workers' front against fascism had to have socialism as its objective.

Dutt's work is a masterpiece of research and erudition, and is the strongest argument presented for the arguments of "class against class". Nevertheless, it underestimated the durability and depravity of the fascist regimes and over-estimated the drive against democracy – in Britain and the USA at any rate. It failed to sufficiently differentiate between different positions within the ranks of the Labour and Social democratic parties, attributing the arguments of the right-wing to the whole. By 1934 that was no longer tenable, even to the extent it ever had been. Nevertheless, it outlined an alternative approach for the Communist Parties to fight fascism, one located in the perspectives of socialist revolution, quite different to the one eventually followed.

There is a more fundamental point yet, that Dutt did not acknowledge, because no-one did, in the Comintern or outside it – that is that the advent of Nazism in Germany marked the definitive shift of centre of the world revolutionary process from Europe to China, a shift which shapes the history and theory of socialism to this day.

For Soviet Britain

This chapter should conclude with a note on the party's programme, *For Soviet Britain*. This was adopted somewhat after the period we are considering, at the 13th Congress in 1935. However, in spirit and approach it belongs to the earlier period – its adoption was an echo of a phase by then passing. The campaign for soviet power then constituted the general slogan of the Communist International and its affiliates, but it was scarcely to be foregrounded for very much longer. Indeed, the CPGB itself was drafting a different programme a mere four years later. So, *For Soviet Britain*, the first party programme drafted in Britain itself, should be outlined here. It was prepared by Robin Page Arnot, who also introduced it to the Congress in a speech that heavily focussed on Lloyd George's contemporary campaigns for no very compelling reason. The fact that this task of introduction was left to him rather than undertaken by Pollitt as general secretary perhaps reflected a feeling that it was not going to be central to the party's public presentation.

The party had previously produced works addressing strategic questions of the progress to socialism. The most notable were *Capitalism, Communism and the Transition* by rising Communist propagandist Emile Burns, working with Pollitt at the Party Centre, and *The Coming Struggle for Power* by John Strachey, one of those Labour MPs who had joined with Mosley on his break with MacDonald only to abandon the incipient fascist and be drawn to Communism under the influence of Dutt in particular. Without every formally joining the Party, Strachey became one of its most effective and popular advocates in the 1930s. Burns' book drew heavily on Soviet experience and mandated both the creation of Soviets as well as the development of armed struggle to crush capitalist resistance in advancing to socialism.[121] In relation to the mechanics of imperialist exploitation, Burns outlined the principles of unequal exchange, perhaps for the first time in a Communist publication.

> "In capitalist society, trade with technically backward countries is always unequal: machine made products are sold in the colonial country at a price but little below the cost of production by handicraft methods. The product of perhaps one day's labour in Lancashire is sold in Africa at a price which is the equivalent or but little below the price of a product of perhaps three or four days' labour there. In this way the advanced country is always exchanging less labour for more labour."[122]

Strachey's popularisation of the Communist case, published in 1932, maintained the position that the trade unions and Labour were "a part of the machinery of capitalism" but did allow that "social democracy, like the British Empire, has very great defensive strength", a rare acknowledgement at the time.[123] His book is notable for taking on the theories of not only Keynes but also F.A. Hayek, then a fairly obscure economist, more than a decade ahead of the latter's publication of the disastrously influential *Road to Serfdom*.[124] On those grounds Strachey's work, the fruit of a very recent and rapid conversion to Marxism, can be considered remarkable. It was, perhaps, the first engagement between Marxism and what became neo-liberalism.

For Soviet Britain itself set out the views of Communists on a range of issues which have bedevilled socialists ever since. It is therefore a theoretical document of some interest. Its main purpose was to show what a Soviet government would do in Britain, explaining in detail the policy of the putative revolutionary workers' government which the CPGB had championed for the preceding six years. A lot of its text therefore outlines policies for the major industries and for social welfare, alongside exposes of the capitalist crisis and the bourgeoisie's attempts to find a way out through fascism or war.

As far as the road to revolution went, the programme was unequivocal:

> "The Communist Party declares that it is not possible to end capitalism and establish Socialism in Britain by the election of a majority in the House of Commons."

The matter was never put so clearly again in CPGB programmes.

> "The capitalist class will never allow itself to be gradually expropriated by successive acts of parliament…without breaking the power of the capitalists it is impossible to get rid of capitalism or to build socialism. It is a question not of votes but of power… there is no such 'peaceful, gradual' way… It is nothing less than a crime to delude the workers with the false hope that the capitalists will quietly lay down their powers and privileges if only sufficient Labour members of parliament are elected."[125]

The answer, the programme continued, was a "workers' revolution. But that revolution is not a single spontaneous act, coming like a bolt from the blue. It is a continuous process. It begins with the victorious struggles of workers uniting to win their elementary demands: the struggle against wage cuts, the struggle against high rents, the struggle against speed-up and wholesale dismissals. The fight against hunger is the fight against the capitalist class. The fight against fascism and war is the fight against the capitalist class. The struggle for colonial liberation is the fight against the capitalist class.

> "By every victory in that struggle on a united front against the capitalist class, the workers step by step develop unity, power and organisation. Bit by bit the workers become more and more conscious of what they have to do and how they can do it. Out of their own ranks there develops in the course of struggle a working-class party that can lead the whole class in its day-to-day struggles and therefore in the final struggle for the overthrow of capitalism and the establishment of workers' rule. This party is the Communist Party. Not only is this the way by which the workers can and will win: **but there is no other way**. The choice put by capitalism to the working-class today is not some imaginary alternative of Socialism by parliament or socialism by revolution, but the grim choice of 'starve or rebel'."[126]

This stark presentation was accompanied by an emphasis on the inevitability of civil war on the road to socialism because of armed resistance by the capitalist class.

The workers, the programme declares: "will not maintain the present parliamentary system...for the parliamentary system has not brought any real democracy to the overwhelming majority of the British people...[it] is a form of political organisation which the capitalist class in Britian has worked out to serve its own needs. While parliament registers formal decisions, it is the whole elaborate machinery of government, from the cabinet at the top to the Public Assistance Committees at the bottom, and including the civil service, the military, naval and air high commands, the judges, the magistrates and the police, by which the capitalist class manages its affairs and maintains its rule over the working class..."

"It is quite impossible for the workers to take over this machinery and use it for their own entirely different purposes. The workers will have an altogether different job in hand, and they will have to fashion different tools for the doing of it...in the moment of need that will arise when the workers are getting ready to take over power, the British working class will create its own instruments to hold and maintain this power," which would be Workers Councils, based on the factories, mines, depots, and offices etc. These would become the basis of the new state apparatus.[127]

These new organs of power would find a place for "those substantial sections of the population, such as technical and professional workers, whose interests are today being sacrificed by the present dictatorial rule of the great capitalists." For *Soviet Power* averred, in a phrase that would in later programmes mushroom into a far more extensive consideration of class alliances. Nor would the petty bourgeois be suppressed. For big capitalists, however, there was only a promise of dictatorship. "The capitalists will sabotage industry, conspire with foreign capitalists who may still be in power and will not hesitate to betray their country to them" the programme warned in an interesting quasi-patriotic note. "Hence it is essential that the workers establish and maintain their dictatorship over the capitalists so long as there is any remnant of capitalism left in the country."[128]

On the matter of imperialism, the programme struck a somewhat contradictory note, with ill-thought-out eurocentrism coexisting with internationalist formulations. The latter were clearly expressed: "After taking power, the British Workers' Councils will immediately proclaim the right of all countries now forming part of the British Empire to complete self-determination up to and including complete separation." They would "hand over, free of charge, all docks, buildings, railways, factories, plantations, canals, irrigation works etc etc, that have been constructed from the sweat and blood of the colonial workers and peasants. The immediate guarantee of this will be the withdrawal of all British armed forces and police, and the cancellation of all the claims of British imperialist finance...in spite of the deep hostility that imperialism has generated in the colonies, there will be friendly relations with the British Soviets and fraternal interchange of products, whether in fact these former colonies also set up Soviet governments at once or not." This friendly perspective would prevail "only in so far as the British workers repudiate imperialist rule and imperialist ideology **now**."[129]

However, this programme of post-imperial socialist cooperation was somewhat vitiated on the next page, where one could read the following assurance that a blockade of a Soviet Britain by other capitalist countries would not succeed: "For example, the Argentine would face immediate ruin if it interrupted its trade with Britain in foodstuffs and raw materials in return for British manufactured goods." This attempt to reassure British workers of the integrity of post-revolutionary export markets actually betrays an assumption that the fundamental economic relations between industrial countries and semi-colonial countries would remain unaffected by socialism, the latter serving as appendages of the former. The Argentines of the world would still hand over food and raw materials in return for industrial products, and should they not do so would face penury.[130] This was in fact the policy of neo-colonialism at a later stage. The bombastic claim that "the building of a free Socialist Britain will lead the whole human race forward" likewise betrayed traces of a chauvinism more usually the stock-in-trade of British social democrats.[131]

The programme also celebrated the achievements of Soviet Russia – "going from triumph to triumph" – and spelt out the role of the Communist party itself.

> "Without such a party all the other conditions for a revolution may be present, but the capitalists will not finally be overthrown...the revolutionary party should embrace the best elements, those whose revolutionary spirit and devotion to the cause of their class have made them a *vanguard* for the working class in its struggle. But to be a *vanguard* means not only to struggle, but to know how to struggle...therefore, the revolutionary party is based on the work of those who first taught how society develops and changes, on the revolutionary science of Karl Marx and Frederick Engels, developed and enriched both in theory and practice by Lenin and Stalin. The revolutionary party has no interests apart from those of the working class as a whole...In Britain this party is the Communist party – the British Section of the Communist International, which unites the revolutionary working-class parties in all countries."[132]

For Soviet Britain was the last programmatic document of the Communist Party to base itself on the experience of the October Revolution and on the assumption that the road to socialism in Britain would run along similar lines. That assumption was not explicitly discarded for some years yet, but it was implicitly assumed that things would go differently before the programme was very old at all. The perspective of smashing up the capitalist state, the preparation for civil war, the idea of workers' developing their own governmental apparatus, and the unabashed foregrounding of internationalism were all of their time, and not for much longer.

Conclusion

The "class against class" period in Communist history has had an almost universally bad press, both in Britain and internationally, as previously noted. That is hardly surprising. It left the Communists at best unable to effectively oppose the advance of fascism and in most countries, including Britain, it led to a marginalisation of the party from the mass of the working class. A recovery in influence followed on the dilution and then abandonment of the Third Period approach.

There are other views. One measured assessment from Fred Westacott, who joined the Party in these years, was written years later and ran thus: "That the policy was mistaken, there can be no doubt. It was sectarian, it falsely believed that socialism was on the agenda, it condemned the Labour Party as being 'an auxiliary apparatus of the bourgeoisie', ended the campaign for affiliation and urged trade unionists not to pay the political levy to the Labour party and not to vote Labour. As a result it alienated thousands of Labour supporters..." Yet the line had support. "I suggest two reasons. Firstly, in many areas the policy was never applied to the letter. There is plenty of evidence of continued good working relations with local Labour Party organisations and individuals throughout the period. Secondly, the policy did have some basis in reality, at least in the worst-hit areas of places like South Wales, where the struggle was sharp and clearly defined, and really was class against class…I have never experienced such optimism and mass enthusiasm, as that which then existed in the localities where I was active." Why the drop in membership then? There was a "particularly stringent attitude to the admission of members in those areas. It was not easy to join." If the mass party concept that came later had applied many more would have been recruited in places like Blaina and Nantyglo. One active member of the NUWM was refused because he was "not yet ready" for membership.[133]

Some of what Westacott writes is contestable. That socialism was not on the agenda is a judgement of hindsight, it was far from unreasonable to champion it at the time, in the midst of an unending crisis of capitalism. However, his emphasis on the ebullient militancy – in the South Wales coalfield at least – strikes a chord. Those who joined, and stayed, in the Party at this period threw themselves into the mass struggle and connected it closely with the perspective of world revolution. The main characteristics of the CPGB, in its best years, where shaped in this period.

Still, there was indeed no socialism. The British working class settled under the hegemony of the Labour Party and the trade unions, the more easily so because they were products of its own making. Moreover, it acquiesced in its own organisations' acceptance of the parameters of capitalist rule, while often rebelling against the consequences. "Class against class" showed no way through this conundrum. But that masks two extraordinary aspects of the CPGB's development up until 1934.

The first was that here was an organisation of the British left which situated itself entirely within an international framework, not as an ethical invocation, but as a theoretical and practical imperative. There was no separation of the struggle in South Wales from that in South Africa, of Stepney from the Soviet Union. This was manifest in the detailed supervision of the CPGB, like other Communist parties, by the Communist International, which was at its most demanding and intrusive in day-to-day matters during the Third Period. But this itself was only a reflection of the desire for a disciplined internationalism shaping the conduct of national tasks. This was a world away from the platonic internationalism of pre-war British socialists.

What was also novel, and this is the second aspect, was the cleavage of the labour movement over imperialism and its consequences. Again, while there had long been disputes on the issue of the Empire as we have outlined, the division between the attitude of the Labour Party, exemplified by the conduct of the MacDonald governments towards the oppressed peoples, and the Communist Party admitted of no precedent. Lenin had identified wartime chauvinism with pre-war opportunism from 1914 on, and in the Labour Party that fusion was made flesh, even more starkly than it was in the German SPD which, post-war, had no colonies to oppress any more. The CPGB, on the other hand, rejected not just the class collaboration of the Labour and TUC leaders, not just their support for the state and their commitment to no more than ameliorative reforms within capitalism, it worked to undermine the base for such a strategy in imperialist exploitation, as it declared its solidarity with both the workers of the Soviet Union and the oppressed of the Empire in struggle against the British ruling class. Such attitudes had been present pre-1914 for sure, but the Communist Party raised them to the level of strategy.

These were the days when world revolution still appeared a practical, material, reality. It can now be judged that that moment had in fact passed a few years earlier, but it is given to few individuals or organisations to exactly calibrate the nature of the times they are living through whilst living through them, down to the day or even the year. Between 1919 and 1933 the British ruling class had faced the most substantial challenge to its position since the days of Chartism, and world capitalism had been swept up in a crisis both cyclical and structural without precedence. The old parameters of working-class politics would never have fitted that time, even had the CPGB not taken the shape and followed the trajectory it did.

World revolution did not disappear as a motivating political project in 1933-34, but it was substantially redefined as a reality. The politics born of its anticipated imminence receded in the face of the reality that capitalism might not only endure a while, but might get still worse while it did so, its depredations taking still more alarming and destructive shape. That is the story of the next volume. As in the earlier period, it will be a story of crisis, war, and revolution globally, but the pillars of the social order will not be shaken as violently in Britain as they were in the years covered by this one. Nor will the connections between imperialism and socialism ever be posed as starkly again, with the exception perhaps of the years 1939-41.

In the times of greatest tumult, there was a party in the British working-class movement that placed its international obligations at the centre of its work, and measured itself by the extent to which it could discharge them and bring the lessons of struggles elsewhere to bear on the politics of Britain. The CPGB left behind flawed but indigenous traditions for the most part, embracing instead more apparently successful ones minted in other lands. In the heart of the greatest centre of imperialist exploitation in history, it was the party of world revolution.

As matters stood in 1934, that was the enduring significance of the CPGB and its bolshevisation.

Notes

1 *Capitalism or Socialism in Britain* by R.P. Dutt (London: 1931a) p 6
2 *Ibid.* p 19
3 *Rajani Palme Dutt* by John Callaghan (London: 1993) p 104. Lansbury's view somewhat anticipated the position taken in the first edition of the *British Road to Socialism*, to be discussed in volume two of the present work.
4 Dutt (1931a) pp 30-31
5 *The New Line*, CPGB (London: 1929) pp 110-113
6 *Resolutions of the 11th Congress*, CPGB (London: 1929) pp 15-16, 28
7 Not all perceptions were accurate. In a 1929 pamphlet pointing out that "the handful of white exploiters in the City of London dominate and draw their profits from four hundred and fifty millions, or more than one-quarter of the human race" Dutt then claimed that British imperialism was concentrating on organising wars against the USSR and the USA, neither of which happened. *The Coming War* by R. Palme Dutt (London: 1929) pp 10, 12.
8 John Callaghan in *In Search of Revolution* by Matthew Worley (ed) (London: 2004) p 326
9 Saklatvala by Mike Squires (London: 1990) p 154. The correspondence is reproduced in Is India Different? (London: 1927) with an introduction by Clemens Dutt describing Gandhi's teaching as "socially reactionary and Gandhi himself is…the ally of class exploitation." (p 5).
10 *History of the Communist Party of Great Britain 1927-41* by Noreen Branson (London: 1985) p 59
11 Father of Tony Benn.
12 *Ben Bradley – Fighter for India's Freedom* by Jean Jones (London) pp 16-17.

13   *Imperialism and the British Labour Movement 1914-1964* by P.S. Gupta (London: 1975) p 204
14   Pollitt to Bradley 16 December 1930, in PHM CP/IND/BRAD/4/5
15   The most comprehensive history of the League is *Willi Munzenberg, The League Against Imperialism and the Comintern 1925-1933* (2 vols) by Fredrik Petersson (Ceredigion: 2013)
16   Bridgeman was very close to the Soviet Union. He stood as Labour candidate for Uxbridge in the 1929 election and, having been expelled for his association with LAI, as a Communist-supported "Workers' Candidate" in 1931, in both cases unsuccessfully. "As a first step in the class struggle I demand freedom for the colonial countries," he told the Uxbridge electors in 1931.
17   *Pan-Africanism and Communism* by Hakin Adi (Trenton, N.J.: 2103) p 258
18   Gupta (1975) p 203
19   *The League Against Imperialism* by Jean Jones (London: 2012?) p 24
20   Gupta (1975) p 165
21   *Labour and the Empire* by Clemens Palme Dutt (London: 1929) pp 9-10
22   See *Yours for the Revolution* by Phil Katz (Croydon: 2023) and *Tom Mann's Memoirs* (London: 1967 [1923]). Chapter headings in the latter give a sense of his international involvement – "New Zealand", "First Years in Australia", "New South Wales, New Zealand Revisited", "South Africa".
23   *Fifty Fighting Years* by A. Lerumo (Michael Harmel) (London: 1971) pp 52, 57. Strangely, Shields' role is ignored in many histories of the SACP, although he remained involved in Comintern guidance to the party through the 1930s.
24   See *Comrade Bill* by R.K. Cope (Cape Town: n.d. 1940s) for details of Andrews' turbulent path in the Communist movement.
25   *Moses Kotane* by Brian Bunting (London: 1975) p 19.
26   *Those Stormy Years* by George Hardy (London: 1956)
27   *Breaking the Fetters* by Bob Stewart (London: 1967) p 154
29   Branson (1985) pp 61, 66-67.
30   *Communist Review*, June 1930 pp 244-46
31   *Labour-Communist Relations 1920-1951* Part 1 by Noreen Branson and Bill Moore (London: 1990) p 64
32   'The Comintern, the CPGB, Colonies & Black Britons' by Marika Sherwood. Paper presented to Communist history conference 1990s.
33   Dutt to Political Bureau, January 4 1930, Dutt papers, British Library.
34   *The Colonial Policy of British Imperialism* by Ralph Fox (Oxford: 2008 [1933]) p 133
35   *British Imperialism in India* by Joan Beauchamp (London: 1934) p 222
36   *The Life and Struggles of Negro Toilers* by George Padmore (London: 1931) p 7
37   Cited in *Rajani Palme Dutt: A Biography* by Dr Panchanan Saha (Kolkata: 2004) p 35
38   *Communist Review* February 1932 p 77
39   *Communist Review* March 1932 p 133
40   *Making the Revolution Global* by Theo Williams (London: 2022) p 45
41   Gupta (1975) p 219
42   Branson and Moore (1990) p 54
43   Dutt to Pollitt 14 April 1932, Dutt papers in British Library.
44   *The Workers Answer to the Crisis* by Rajani Palme Dutt (London: 1931b) p 4
45   *The British Communist Party and Moscow 1920-43* by Andrew Thorpe (Manchester: 2000) p 180
46   *Communist Review* October 1931 p 417
47   See *Mutiny at Invergordon* by David Divine (London: 1970) for an account of this episode.
48   *Class Against Class* by Matthew Worley (London: 2002) p 280
49   *Communist Review* November-December 1931 pp 493-95, 500
50   *Communist Review* February 1932 p 57
51   See *Under Siege* by Ian Bullock (Edmonton, Canada: 2017) pp 177-188 for details.
52   *Building the Party in the Factories*, CPGB (London: 1930) pp 15-16
53   See *Little Moscows* by Stuart Macintyre (London: 1980)
54   *The Fed* by Hywel Francis and David Smith (London: 1980) p 178
55   *Incorrigible Rebel* by Arthur Horner (London: 1960) p 110
56   *Ibid.* p 111
57   *Communist Review* April 1931 p 153
58   The party leadership was itself divided on the issue of sanctioning Horner, with Pollitt and Arnot

wanting to retain him within the Party and Rust pushing for expulsion. See *Arthur Horner* volume 1 by Nina Fishman (London: 2010) pp 210-26 for a detailed account.

59 *Communist Review* April 1931 p 145
60 Branson (1985) p 87
61 Apparently after an intervention by veteran syndicalist and CPGB member Tom Mann.
62 Horner (1960) pp 111-12
63 Francis and Smith (1980) p 180
64 *Communist Review* March 1932 pp 125-27
65 *Communist Review* February 1932 pp 55-59
66 *The British Communist Party and the Trade Unions 1933-45* by Nina Fishman (Aldershot: 1995) pp 53-54, 40-42.
67 *Daily Worker* August 20, September 19, September 21 1932. It is notable that at this stage members of the Political Bureau of the party could argue out their differences openly in the party press.
68 *Communist Review* December 1932 p 576
69 Worley (2002) p 172
70 Worley in Worley (2004) p 72
71 It did however gradually improve its position. By early 1931 it claimed that pit and factory cells were producing 46 papers, usually fortnightly, with an aggregate circulation of 17,000. *Communist Review* April 1931 p 140.
72 *Communist Review* March 1932 p 125
73 Thorpe (2000) p201; Worley (2002) p 259
74 Worley in Worley (2004) p 71
75 *A Miners' Lass* by Mary Docherty (Cowdenbeath: 1992) pp 52-53
76 *Communist Review* September 1932 p 421
77 In 1933 the NUWM had 20,000 members in 349 branches, with 36 district councils and 34 women's sections (Worley in Worley (2004) p 82).
78 *Breakfast with Mao* by Allan Winnington (London: 1986) p 34
79 Thorpe (2000) p 164
80 *The Story of the Daily Worker* by William Rust (London: 1949) p 10. Rust begins his account by outlining how "eight men" produced the paper's first issue. In fact one of the eight comrades was Kay Beauchamp, a woman. She was still telling the story into the 1980s. Another of the eight was future MP Willie Gallacher.
81 The first front page, appearing on January 1 1930, had "Revolution in India grows" as its second headline (the main headline was about the woollen strike in Yorkshire). See *Is That Damned Paper Still Coming Out?* by Mark Howe (ed) (London: 2001) p 17.
82 *Ibid*. p 13
83 *The British Communist Party and Moscow 1920-43* by Andrew Thorpe (Manchester: 2000) p 158
84 The *Party Organiser* September 1932 pp 18-23. The next issue featured a response from the Party Secretariat repudiating the Islington comrade for abusing the principle of criticism and self-criticism in a negative way.
85 See *To Struggle is to Live* volume two by Ernie Benson (Newcastle: 1980) pp 77-78 for an example of Murphy's obnoxious and dishonest behaviour towards local comrades. Benson was secretary of the Leeds branch at the time.
86 See *The Political Trajectory of J.T. Murphy* by Ralph Darlington (Liverpool: 1998) pp 206ff for an account of this episode sympatheic to Murphy.
87 Supporters of the "right" in the Comintern and the CPSU (B) had formed factions and separate organisations after their defeat in 1929, for example in the USA and Germany. Yet in the CPGB the "right" acquiesced in their removal from leadership without splits or further struggle, and set to work in more humble positions for the party.
88 Branson (1985) p 90.
89 *The Road to Victory* by Harry Pollitt (London: 1932) p 4.
90 *Ibid*. pp 45-46
91 *Ibid*. p 46
92 *Ibid*. p 47
93 *Ibid*. p 19

94 *Ibid.* p 20
95 *Ibid.* pp 24-25
96 *Ibid.* p 40. An LPC was a Local Party Committee, equivalent to a Branch Committee later on.
97 *Ibid.* p 31
98 *Ibid.* pp32-33
99 Branson (1985) p 340
100 Thorpe (2000) p 202
101 See PHM CP/Ind/POLL/14/09 for correspondence
102 Thorpe (2000) p 204
103 *Democracy and Fascism* by Rajani Palme Dutt (London: 1933) p 8
104 *Ibid.* pp 12, 13, 21
105 *We are Fighting for a Soviet Germany* by Wilhelm Pieck (London: 1933) p 5
106 *Ibid.* pp 11, 57
107 *Theses and Decisions, Thirteenth Plenum of the ECCI* (London: 1933) pp 6, 8. The definition of fascism is often attributed to Dimitrov who was, however, in prison in Germany at the time and therefore not at the plenum.
108 Edwin Roberts, in his *The Anglo-Marxists* (Lanham, MD: 1997) argues (p 69ff) that Dutt makes the case for the popular front in this book. In my view he does no such thing and his analysis is much more clearly rooted in a class confrontation perspective. The Popular Front did not become Communist policy until eighteen months after the first publication of *Fascism and Social Revolution*.
109 *Fascism and Social Revolution.* by R. Palme Dutt (London: 1934) p 92
110 *Ibid.* p 95
111 *Ibid.* p 108
112 *Ibid.* pp 170-74
113 *Ibid.* p 175
114 *Ibid.* p 203-4
115 *Ibid.* p 235-36
116 *Ibid.* p 255
117 *Ibid.* p 258
118 *Ibid.* p 286
119 *Ibid.* p 264
120 *Ibid.* p 296, 308
121 *Capitalism, Communism and the Transition* by Emile Burns (London: 1933) see Chapter Seven in particular.
122 *Ibid.* p 269
123 *The Coming Struggle for Power* by John Strachey (London: 1934[1932]) p 333
124 *Ibid.* pp 88-130. Strachey polemicises with Keynes in the text and Hayek in the footnotes
125 *For Soviet Britain*, CPGB (London: 1935) pp 19-20
126 *Ibid.* p 21
127 *Ibid.* pp 23-25
128 *Ibid.* pp 26-27
129 *Ibid.* p 44
130 *Ibid.* p 45
131 *Ibid.* p 46
132 *Ibid.* pp 46-47
133 *Shaking the Chains* by Fred Westacott (Chesterfield: 2002) p 80. Westacott joined the Party in South Wales and later served as a full-time worker for many years.

Workers of the World Unite!

DAILY WORKER

No. 1 — WEDNESDAY, JANUARY 1, 1930 — One Penny

WOOLLEN WORKERS TAKE THE FIELD

REVOLUTION IN INDIA GROWS
Congress Chiefs Feel Mass Pressure

The All-India National Congress, which opened at Lahore yesterday, adopted by 942 votes, against 79, the resolution moved by Gandhi, deploring the throwing of a bomb at the Viceroy and congratulating him on his escape. The minority, waving Red Flags, raised angry protests. Ghandhi's second motion is to deal with the new manoeuvre of withdrawal of "Dominion status" in favour of independence.

The reports of meetings of the Congress Committee in Session since Christmas Day, shows that the enormous rising tide of the Indian masses, led by the heroic Indian proletariat, whose determined fight, masked by mass political strikes, is the enormous motive force which has compelled the leaders of the Indian bourgeoisie, who have in the past two years gone over to the side of British Imperialism, to make a desperate attempt to retain their hold on the masses by a show of opposition.

The resolution of the bourgeois nationalist leaders in favour of independence and boycott of legislature significantly leaves the campaign for civil disobedience and non-payment of taxes to the discretion of the Congress Committee, "as and when necessary."

At the Sikh Conference meeting yesterday, also in Lahore, Kharal Singh, the president, stated that out of thirty-one recent death sentences on revolutionary Indian nationalists, twenty-seven were Sikhs.

When Sir Frederick Sykes, Governor of Bengal, visited Ahmedabad two days ago he was met by a demonstration outside the station waving flags and with shouts of "Frederick Sykes, go back."

SIXTY DEATHS IN CINEMA FIRE
Many Children Amongst The Victims

A fire which broke out at the Glen Cinema, Paisley, near Glasgow, during a children's matinee, yesterday afternoon, caused a panic, resulting, it is feared, in about sixty deaths.

As soon as news of the fire spread frantic mothers ran to the Cinema and began searching for their children.

One hundred and fifty people were taken to hospital.

It is certain that at least six children are dead.

FASCISTS WOUND WORKERS

Berlin, Tuesday.—On Sunday night sixteen armed Fascists attacked a group of workers who were leaving a Party local in a demonstration working-class quarter.

The Fascists fired on the unarmed workers and wounded four of them seriously. As usual, the police arrested two Communists.

PRINCE'S JAUNT
To Travel into Impenetrable Jungle — By Train
WITH HIS VALET!

On Friday the Prince of Wales will again start a jaunt that will cost thousands of pounds of the money the workers have earned for him.

He is going to Capetown, and from there will journey into the jungle—by train!

There he will display his intrepidity against the wild beasts of Africa. His valet is to accompany him; probably to hold the rifle.

An official of the "Kenilworth Castle," on which he is to travel, states that he is expected to play a prominent part in the "strenuous" deck games which are to be played on board.

"Otherwise, he will use an ordinary first-class cabin with the usual dressing-room."

SHOOTING THE UNEMPLOYED
Social Democrat Police Chief Orders Massacre in Cologne

Berlin, Tuesday.—Yesterday evening 10,000 unemployed workers demonstrated in front of the Cologne Town Hall in order to support the proposal of the Communist faction for winter assistance for the unemployed.

The social democratic Police President, who was in charge of large forces of police, who tried to prevent the demonstrators from reaching the Town Hall. At first the police used their batons, but when their efforts proved ineffective the Social Democrat gave the order to fire.

Many workers were wounded by the police bullets and over 100 arrested, including the Communist, W. Deputy Kolven. The Communist proposals in the Town Council were rejected.—Inprecorr.

CLOSING THE RANKS
Woollen Workers Consolidate Against Wage Cuts
From Our Own Correspondent.

Shipley, Tuesday.—Rank and file conferences are to be called in the textile area to consolidate the workers' resistance to the threatened wage cuts.

To counter the proposed woollen wages' enquiry, the Bradford district committee of the Communist Party issued to-day a statement to all woolworkers.

The statement compares the statement with the Lancashire arbitration, which served the same purpose of breaking the workers' resistance.

The woollen textile workers are advised not to return to work, but to extend the struggle, and to build up strike committees of action to fight against the strike-breaking court of enquiry proposed by the Labour Government.

MASS STRIKES AGAINST WAGE REDUCTIONS
Police Attack Pickets
ALL WORKERS SOLID AND DETERMINED TO WIN FIGHT

OVER two thousand woollen textile workers are on strike. The attempt to cut wages is meeting with real mass resistance. The workers are in a militant mood and maintain the utmost solidarity against employers, Labour Government, trade union bureaucrats and police.

The young workers are especially active and are giving increasing support to the Communist Party Campaign for rank and file Committees of Action.

BONDFIELD, SCAB;
Labour Prepares to Smash Wool Strike
(From Our Own Correspondent.)

Bradford.—The council of the wool textile employers has not yet commented on the letter of the Minister of Labour proposing to set up a court of enquiry into the situation in the woollen industry under Part 2 of the Industrial Courts Act, 1919.

Before availing themselves of the offer to impose the wage reductions by means of arbitration, the woollen bosses are anxiously watching the strikes which are repeatedly breaking out and being carried on with remarkable determination.

I understand that Margaret Bondfield is going ahead with the setting up of the Court and that the constitution and terms of reference will be announced shortly.

DYE WORKERS STRIKE
Lightning Strike follows Dismissals

There was a lightning strike of 160 dye workers at the Kirk Lane Dye Works on Monday. The strike was due to the dismissal on the Saturday of 100 men.

Pickets were placed on the gates in the early morning and only the office staff and the key men on the mechanical side remained at work.

So far there is no news of a settlement and the works remain closed.

VOTE AGAINST WAGE CUTS

The strike at the Prospect Mills, Pudsey, continues. In answer to the opening of the mills in an attempt to impose a reduction of 1s. 6d. in the pound, a well-attended meeting of strikers held at the Trades Hall decided unanimously to resist any cut in wages for any section of the workers. A strike committee was elected and pickets appointed.

All operatives, union and non-union, are out.

DEPIANT SPIRIT
Determined to Resist Lower Wages
(From Our Own Correspondent.)

Saddleworth.—The attempt of the Saddleworth millowners to break the strike is now nullified with a wage cut of two shillings in the pound has completely failed. Although the mills were opened on Monday morning not one of the thirteen hundred strikers, mostly women and girls, returned.

The police have repeatedly attacked the pickets and some arrests have been made. The defiant attitude of Lily Hutton, a young women worker, when "on trial" for assaulting a burly police inspector, typifies the spirit of the workers.

A long period of short time and low wages has made them determined to resist to the utmost.

Tom Thuelbeck, who was fined £10 or two months on a charge of assaulting the police at the mill gates, has now been released, the workers having collected sufficient money to pay his fine.

GREENFIELD STRIKE
Employers appeal to Labour Govt.

The operatives of the Kinders Mill, Greenfield, Yorks, are on strike and pickets are operating at the mills.

The employers' secretary has sent the following telegram to the Home Secretary:—

"Operatives of Messrs. Buckley and Co. (Greenfield), Ltd., Kinders Mill, Greenfield, Yorkshire, are being prevented by pickets from entering the mill, and are being otherwise intimidated at their homes. I am to ask that you will take such steps as will obviate intimidation of the workers and afford them adequate protection."

"DAILY WORKER" PRIZE DRAW

INDEX

Bulow, Bernhard von, 40
Beauchamp, Joan, (Thompson), 144, 166
Beauchamp, Kay, 170
Allison, George, 102
Anderson, Kevin, 35, 54, 55, 59, 78
Andrews, Bill, 114, 143, 169
Beer, Max, 31, 32, 44, 45
Bevin, Ernest, 119, 151
Biel, Robert, 38, 54, 55
Blatchford, Robert, 23, 24, 25, 35, 83
Bradley, Ben, 102, 141, 169
Brailsford, H. N., 121
Branson, Noreen, 131, 136, 137, 169, 170, 171
Brewer, Anthony, 47, 51, 56, 57
Bridgeman, Reginald. 142, 169
British Socialist Party (BSP), 14, 21, 22, 26, 27, 28, 32, 76, 82, 88, 91, 93, 94, 98, 105
British Worker (The) , 111
Brockway, Fenner, 115, 141, 142, 146, 158, 159, 163
Call (The), 76
Campbell, John Ross, 1, 105, 115, 131, 133, 135, 141
Carr, E. H., 84, 101, 113, 114, 115, 120, 136, 137
Carson, Edward, 15
Casement, Roger, 75, 79
Challinor, Raymond, 29, 32, 33
Chamberlain, Joseph, 23, 24, 32
Chicherin, Georgi, 88, 113
Citrine, Walter, 142
Clemenceau, 89
Clyde Workers Committee 27
Communist (The), 115, 150, 154, 157
Communist International 1, 2, 3, 17, 22, 26, 27, 29, 31, 35, 40, 52, 55, 59, 60 - 63, 65, 68, 71, 74, 77, 82, 83, 88, 89, 90, 91, 92, 93, 94, 95, 96, 98, 100, 101, 102, 103, 105, 106, 110 - 115, 117- 124, 126, 127 - 137, 139 - 146, 150 - 153, 155, 156, 159 - 163, 166, 168, 169, 171
Connolly, James, 20, 57, 59, 73, 74, 75, 79, 86, 143
Connolly, Roderick, 143
Cook, A. J., 108, 109, 115, 119, 125
Copeman, Fred, 147
Cornford, John, 154
Cox, Idris, 127, 135, 152
Crossley, James, 102
Councils of Action, 83, 109, 111, 113
Daily Mail, 21, 24, 33, 106, 162

Daily Telegraph, 19
Daily Worker, 99, 134, 142, 146, 155, 156, 159, 170, *172 (Illustration)*
David, Edgar, 40, 42
De Leon, Daniel, 21
de Valera, Eamon, 143
Dobb, Maurice, 154
Docherty, Mary, 154, 170
Donald, Moira, 67, 78
Douglas, E., 101
Easter Rising 1916, 73, 74, 75, 79, 84
Dutt, Clemens, 169
Dutt, Rajani Palme, 1, 2, 9, 30, 31, 33, 87, 98, 99, 100, 103, 104, 106, 107, 113, 114, 115, 118, 121 - 124, 126, 127, 128, 130 - 137, 139, 140, 142, 144, 146, 147, 152, 153, 156, 159, 160, 161, 162, 163, 168, 169, 171
ECCI/Executive Committee of the Communist International 160, 171
Fabian Society, 16, 18, 19, 23, 24
Farrow, Sam, 28
Fineberg, Joseph, 88, 89
First Congress of Representatives of the Peoples of the East. 92
First International, 38
Foster, John, 20, 32, 113
Fox, Ralph, 113, 144, 169
Gallacher, Willie, 1, 22, 27, 33, 96, 109, 115, 125, 133, 135, 155, 170
Gandhi, 85, 141, 169
Garvey, Marcus, 145
General Strike 1926, 115, 117, 118, 135
George Bernard, 25
Gillies, William, 141
Glading, Percy, 102, 114, 136
Gollan, John, 1, 144
Guest, David, 154
Hannington, Wal, 106, 115, 135, 154
Hardie, Keir, 15, 18, 26
Hardy, George, 143, 169
Hegel, 36, 38, 54, 59, 77
Hildebrand, Gerhard, 68
Hilferding, Rudolf, 36, 39, 45, 50, 52, 53, 54, 56, 66, 67, 68, 69, 70
Hitler, Adolf, 159, 160
Ho Chi Minh, 100
Hutt, Allen, 119, 135
Hyndman, HM, 19, 20, 21, 23, 24, 25, 26, 27, 28, 32, 33, 62, 84, 94, 113
Independent Labour Party (ILP), 17, 18, 19, 21, 25, 27, 29, 31, 33, 74, 76, 93, 96, 98, 104, 113, 121 - 125, 132, 136, 142, 144, 146, 148, 151, 157 - 160, 162

Inkpin, Harold, 103, 114, 115, 131
IRA, 43
Irish Worker, 74
Irwin, Lord, 141
Jackson, Tommy, 75, 135
Johnstone, Thomas, 124
Justice, 20, 28
Kahan, Zelda, 21, 24
Kama, Bhikajee, 42
Karski (Julian Marchlewski), 42
Kendall, Walter, 32, 33
Kenyatta, Jomo, 145
Klugmann, James, 94, 108, 109, 110, 114, 115, 121, 135, 136
Kol, Hendrick van, 41, 42
Kuusinen, Otto, 120, 126, 127
Labour Monthly, 98, 99, 137, 144
Larkin, Jim, 143
Ledebour, Georges, 24, 41, 42
Lenin, V. I., 1, 2, 3, 10, 11, 15, 20, 21, 23, 27, 30, 33, 36, 39, 42- 51 54, 55, 57, 59, 60 - 73, 75 - 79, 82, 83, 84, 86, 87, 88, 89, 90 - 102, 106, 114, 117, 129, 130, 131, 145, 146, 154, 155, 160, 161, 166, 167 114, 16
Leninism, 2, 10, 49, 59, 60, 78, 88, 98, 121, 123, 140
Liebknecht, Karl, 40, 86, 98
Liebman, Marcel, 60, 78
Litvinov, Maxim, 27
Lozovsky, Solomon, 109, 111
Lucas, C. P, 14, 31
Luxembourg, Rosa, 35, 43, 49, 52, 54, 56, 57, 61, 62, 86,
MacIntyre, Stuart, 16, 31, 136, 170
MacManus, Arthur, 101, 115
Mahon, John, 103, 114
Manuilsky, 100, 101, 133, 135
Marchlewski, Julian, (Karski), 32, 42, 96
Marx, Karl, 10, 16, 19, 35-40, 42, 49, 50, 54, 55, 56, 59, 83, 154, 166
Marxism-Leninism, 1, 61
Maxton, James, 125, 142, 146, 158
McLaine, William, 91, 97, 113
Mclean, John, 27
Meath, Lord, 14
Miners Federation of Great Britain (MFGB), 108, 109, 111, 112
Minto, Lady, 18
Morley, Lord, 18
Morning Post, 24
Moseley, Oswald, 121
Murphy, J. T., 91, 96, 107, 110, 115, 118, 125, 126, 127, 131, 135, 144, 153, 156, 157, 170

Nation, Craig, 33, 65, 71, 78
National Minority Movement (NMM) , 106, 107, 107, 158, 167, 170
National Unemployed Workers Movement
Nehru, 142
Newbold, J Walton, 100
New York Tribune, 36, 54
Padmore, George, 145, 170
Page Arnot, Robin, 110, 113, 115, 118, 127, 130, 132, 122, 135, 145, 163, 169
Pankhurst, Sylvia, 27, 33, 75, 76, 94, 96, 97, 98
Pannekoek, Anton, 51
Petrovsky, Max, (Bennett), 126, 127, 136
Pieck, Wilhelm, 160, 171
Plekhanov, 62
Pollitt, Harry, 1, 3, 32, 82, 83, 84, 99, 102, 103, 104, 106, 107, 113, 114, 115, 130 - 136, 141, 145, 146, 151, 152, 153, 156, 157, 158, 159, 163, 169, 170
Pradella, Lucia, 35, 39, 54
Pravda, 89, 157
Pyatakov, Yuri, 72, 73
Quelch, Harry, 21, 22, 55, 91, 93, 113
Radek, Karl, 56, 73, 74, 75, 91, 110, 113
Redmond, John, 15
Reginald, 142 169
Rhodes, Cecil, 23, 32, 69
Roberts, Lord, 15
Robson, R. W., 135
Rothermere, Lord, 162
Rothstein, Andrew, 126, 131, 132, 133, 135
Rothstein, Theo, 20, 21, 32
Roy, M. N.,90, 91, 100, 102, 141
Rust, William, 115, 131, 132, 133, 135, 147, 155, 156, 170
Rutgers, S. J., 88
Saklatvala, Shapurji, 100, 114, 133, 136, 141, 168, 169, 174
Samuel, Herbert, 109
Second International, 17, 25, 32, 37, 40, 43, 54, 59 - 65, 67, 71, 73, 77, 78, 82, 84, 89, 92
Shaukat Usmani (Sukander Sur), 126, 127, 132, 136, 148
Sherwood, Marika, 144, 169
Shields, Jimmy , 135, 142, 145, 169
Shinwell, Manny, 27
Snowden, Phillip, 25, 121, 147, 158
Social Democratic Federation (SDF), 5, 17, 19, 20, 21, 22, 25, 32, 33, 94
Socialist Labour Party (SLP), 21, 22, 27, 32, 73, 74, 93
German Social Democratic Party (SPD), 5, 26, 40, 43, 49, 55, 59, 61, 68, 114, 159, 160, 168

Spratt, Philipp, 102, 141
Stalin, Joseph, 57, 88, 111, 112, 115, 120, 154, 156, 157, 166
Stewart, Bob, 110, 143, 169
Strachey, John, 121, 154, 163, 164, 172
Sukander Sur, (Shaukat Usmani) 126, 127, 132, 136, 148
Sunday Worker, 125
Tapsell, Walter, 131, 135, 155
Terwange, Modeste, 41
Thalmann, Ernst, 160
Thomas, Jimmy, 105, 108, 147
Thompson, Basil, 87, 144
Thompson, Joan, 144
Tingfu Tsiang, 15, 31, 33
Trade Union Congress (TUC), 11, 14, 31, 68, 74, 106, 109, 110, 111, 115, 119, 124, 125, 141, 142, 157, 168
Trotsky, Leon, 51, 57, 74, 79, 88, 89, 111, 112, 120, 157
Ulbricht, Walter, 133, 135
Usmani, Shaukat, (Sukander Sur) 126, 127, 132, 136, 148
Vanguard, 28
Vaughan, Joe, 28
Webb, Sidney, 25, 33, 142
Wedgewood Benn, William, 41
Wilkinson, Ellen, 99
Wedgewood Benn, William, 141
Williams, Theo, 145, 170
Willis, Fred, 76
Wincott, Len, 147
Worley, Matthew, 136, 137, 148, 169, 170
Workers Weekly, 101
Wyndham, George, 23
Young Communist League (YCL), 100, 131, 133
Zetkin, Clara, 98
Zimmerwald Conference, 27
Zinoviev, 64, 88, 92, 93, 101, 106, 112, 120

Illustrations

Cover   Communist MP Shapurji Saklatvala speaks in Trafalgar Square. *Communist Party image*

ii   The British Empire in 1921 at its height. *Vadac. Creative Commons*
Daily Worker Thursday May 8 1930. The second week of publication. *Communist Party image*
Leaflet protesting the imprisonment of trade unionists in India. *Communist Party image*

iv   Stowage of the British slave ship Brookes under the regulated lave trade act of 1788.
US Library of Congress Creative Commons

4   Detail of a Mural Depicting 1919 Amritsar Massacre, Jallianwala Bagh, Amritsar, India
Creative Commoms

34   Vladimir Lenin in 1920. *Photographer Pavel Zhukov (1870–1942) Creative Commons*

58   James Connolly *David Granville. Creative Commons*

80   Women's demonstration for bread and peace in 1917. *State Museum of Political History of Russia. Wikimedia Commons. Licensed under CC BY Public Domain Mark 1.0*

116   Welsh unemployed workers on the march. *Communist Party image*

138   *For Soviet Britain* 1935 Programme of the Communist Party of Great Britain. *Communist Party image*
172   First issue of the *Daily Worker*. *Morning Star image*

176   *Sunday Worker* May 16 1926 reporting on the betrayal of the General Strike. *Communist Party image*

Back Cover Pamphlet protesting at the imprisonment of trade unionists in India. *Communist Party image*

FINAL EDITION

Tom Mann on Unity
Page 5

Sunday Worker

LABOUR'S SUNDAY NEWSPAPER

Lansbury's Message
Page 3

No. 62 SUNDAY, MAY 16, 1926 [Registered at the G.P.O. as a Newspaper] Twopence

MINERS WILL FIGHT—BACK THEM

FIRST ROUND OVER

General Strike Dead, But Miners' Fight Continues

WORKERS' FINE RALLY

Men Were on Verge of Victory When Battle Was Called Off

By A. J. COOK
(Special to the "Sunday Worker")

A. J. Cook

The General Strike was the greatest struggle in the history of British Labour. It began with the lockout of the miners. And although the solidarity of the industrial masses was daily overcoming the opposition of the government and the owners, the General Strike was suddenly called off without any consultation with the miners. But the lockout of the miners continues. We are still in the storm centre of the industrial struggle.

Every miner in the country thanks the Workers of Britain for their amazing [illegible] in responding so readily to the call of the General Strike. In the streets and in their Trades Councils they, at least, displayed both courage and initiative. The wide range of their activity, and the solidity of their resistance against the lies and attacks of the government, made the ruling capitalist class afraid.

A Confession

Even the "Times" confessed:—

There was always a risk that the government in its sincere desire for peace might somehow become entangled in conversations which favoured fresh concessions to the mining industry for the abandonment of the general strike.

Despite everything, the general strike prevented the owners from enforcing their brutal and exploiting proposals upon the miners. Greater triumphs might easily have been won, but at this moment I have no desire to indulge in [illegible].

Can Still Help

A million miners are still locked out. Those who rallied so splendidly to our assistance, two weeks ago, can still help us in many ways.

At our conference yesterday we placed the Baldwin proposals before our men. It was decided to refer the matter to the districts, and to have the whole problem thrashed out at a further delegate conference on Thursday.

The general strike [illegible] revealed that a bold lead [illegible] the masses.

The action of the British rank and file thrilled the Workers of the world. Never were the Workers of other lands so keenly interested in a struggle; never did they respond so loyally and with such an abundance of offers of assistance.

Their generosity was even greater than the courage of some of our leaders.

Still Bear Brunt

The miners still bear the brunt of the struggle. They are led by Herbert Smith, whose determination is only equalled by his steadfast pluck. Both he and Comrade Swales [illegible] well.

With the assistance of the industrial masses the miners can achieve their right to a living wage.

Risked All

I am not [illegible] that during the last fortnight many Workers risked everything to help us. See with what readiness our men and women suffered [illegible] by [illegible] to stop blacklegs.

The miners know that hundreds of Workers are now in prison for no other reason than that they desired to help to defend the mine workers and themselves against capitalism. We must see to it that these comrades are not forgotten. As always, the SUNDAY WORKER is giving a splendid lead in this direction.

SUPPORT OF RANK AND FILE IS ASSURED

Tremendous Opposition to Baldwin's Plan of Attack

THOUSANDS OF WORKERS STILL OUT

Cook and Smith Give Thanks for Splendid Display of Solidarity

Although the General Council have called off the General Strike, the miners will continue the fight against starvation wages and longer hours.

They can still count on the support of the rank and file, who, indeed, were full of fight when the call came to resume work.

Hundreds of telegrams continue to pour into the office of the Miners' Federations from all districts pledging support to the miners.

Thousands of Workers are still on strike. A.E.U. men and dockers are still firm.

Baldwin's offer to the miners is shown by Arthur Horner to imply wage reductions, compulsory arbitration, and greater unemployment still.

The miners' conference yesterday adjourned to Thursday, when great opposition to the terms will be forthcoming.

Herbert Smith, in an interview printed below, declares that Workers imprisoned for strike activities must not be forgotten by the Trade Union Movement.

BALDWIN'S TRICK TERMS

Wage Cuts and Compulsory Arbitration

By ARTHUR HORNER
(Executive Committee, S.W.M.F.)

(Special to the "Sunday Worker")

An examination of the new Baldwin proposals to the miners reveals many serious dangers.

In Clause 2 the government pledges itself to introduce a number of bills dealing with all kinds of good things (fuel and power, pit committees, pithead baths, housing, etc.). In clause 4 the necessity for mines to [illegible] power, merely by disagreeing with the advisory committee which has to examine such bills, and reporting his disagreement to parliament, to make these bills a mere farce. So much for the sugar on the pill.

The miners are to suffer a reduction in wages, percentage and duration unstated. Those who don't get reductions, under clause 3, will be thrown out of work altogether by the closing down of pits which the owners will refuse to work. We can safely say that at least 100,000 miners will be added to the permanent unemployed.

Ambiguous Term

Clause 6, section 2, says that the national wages board shall decide wages, taking into consideration trade, reorganisation, "and other relevant factors." What are these factors? Do not they mean "district conditions"? Does not this clause open the way again to district settlements?

Throughout, the memorandum says the wages board "shall **decide** the minimum percentage; shall **decide** what the districts shall be; shall **issue its decision** within three weeks" (not "submit its recommendation"). In the event of disagreement on wages, "the **decision** shall rest with the independent chairman" (a wonderful [illegible]).

These sentences mean nothing if not compulsory arbitration, despite the fact that in clause 2 the board is described as "on the lines of the Railway Wages Board," whose decisions are not compulsory.

The memorandum opens the way, in clause 7, for a revival at a later stage of the attack on the 7-hour day.

As for the proposed £3,000,000 subsidy, that would last only a few weeks.

It is clear that all those in the coalfields who have the freedom of our Workers at heart would do well to demand immediately, through their districts, the reaffirmation of our "Three Points"—**no reductions, no longer hours, no district settlements—with a fourth, No Compulsory Arbitration.**

The other Workers will stand by us, in spite of their leaders.

Fighting Lead to Railmen

A fighting lead to railmen is given by the London Central Strike Committee of the N.U.R., which yesterday passed a resolution viewing the strike settlement with "profound suspicion and disgust," and instruct the executive committee of the N.U.R. that if at the end of the present week all men have not been reinstated, to take the necessary steps to call a national railway strike to secure their return.

Further, demand was made that the General Council of the T.U.C. take the necessary steps to secure the re-employment of all men who took part in the strike, and the release of all those who were imprisoned for acts committed during the strike.

TRANSPORT MEN WILL NOT GROVEL

Demand Former Wages and Conditions

Although in many parts of the country the Transport Workers have secured their status quo, there is still a huge number who are stopping out until attempts to cut wages and retain scabs have been withdrawn.

The union officials concerned are all acting [illegible] and are determined to back the men until wages and conditions are guaranteed.

In London the T. & G.W.U. has secured a satisfactory settlement and all tram and busmen have returned.

London Dockers are still out, as are dockers in Leeds. Railmen are remaining out in Hull until [illegible] are reinstated, and the threat of the Electricity Committee to prosecute union leaders is withdrawn.

Thirteen hundred bus Workers in Sunderland, after doing one day's work, have again struck until their status quo is assured.

Tram-men Decide To-night

The Manchester tramwaymen are still out and will take a decision tonight.

At Portsmouth strikers in all industries are staying out until the transit men are reinstated.

The "Scottish Worker" says that over 100 tramwaymen have been refused reinstatement in Glasgow and measures are being taken to secure their fair treatment.

It is reported that the union has secured reinstatement without qualification in Edinburgh.

Aberdeen tramway Workers with long service have been told they will only be taken back as new entrants. None will return until this has been [illegible].

HERBERT SMITH'S VIEW

Rank and File Unflinching—Prisoners Must Be Freed

(By Our Industrial Correspondent)

I managed to see Herbert Smith for a few moments before he ascended the platform at the miners' conference held in the Kingsway Hall, yesterday. Despite the tremendous energy he has displayed during the last few weeks, in conducting the miners' struggle, he looked as solid and determined as ever.

In answer to my inquiry regarding his opinion of the General Strike he stated:—

"As President of the Miners' Federation I sincerely thank the millions who have helped us in our great conflict with the owners in order to secure a living wage for all mine-workers.

Great Reception

"For two weeks I have been in London and have been addressing meetings. I know, from the reception accorded to Cook and myself, that the rank and file Workers, many of whom never saw a coal pit, were solidly behind us. They knew that the miners' fight was their fight.

"Whatever may be the final result of the struggle we know that the Workers did not flinch at the cruellest moment of the conflict."

"They rallied to us during a crisis and they will do so again if necessary."

When asked his opinion about the men and women imprisoned during the strike, he replied:

"Those now in jail were brave fighters. Some of our best lads are in prison and we must get them out. The employers may try to victimise them, but I for one shall insist upon their reinstatement. We would be cowards if we did not stand by them.

"Finally you can tell the readers of the SUNDAY WORKER that the miners are determined to struggle to secure a decent living wage, not only for themselves, but for all Workers."

MINERS' DECISION

The miners' delegate conference yesterday sat only for half an hour and then decided that the government proposals were so obscure that it would be necessary for the Executive Committee to approach the government and obtain a proper explanation. In the meantime the districts are to be consulted.

The conference therefore adjourned until Thursday next.

A resolution was passed expressing profound appreciation of the self-sacrificing loyalty displayed by all trade unionists, and pledging the conference to render all possible assistance to any organisation confronted with difficulties when the strike stops.

HOW MINER[S] TOOK NEWS

Rhondda Valley Men S[till] Undaunted

"WE NEVER FORGET"

"Workers All Right—We Don't Blame Them"

(By a Special Correspondent)

In the Rhondda Valley there [are] practically no pickets and no spe[cial] police.

They are not needed because th[ere] are no scabs.

The solidarity of the Workers [in] this South Wales mining area is [so] complete that there is no question [of] blacklegging. The trams are [not] running, nor the trains. No bl[ack]legging could take place in this [illegible] district. Therefore, the [illegible] differs somewhat from that of [a] large mixed industrial centre.

This was the position when the [illegible] news came that the Trades U[nion] Congress had called off the strike.

Seldom have I witnessed a [more] affecting scene. Never have I ex[peri]enced such an intensity of [illegible] feeling.

Heroes of Industry

Not that there was a theatric[al] affecting scene. That would be [im]possible among these heroes of [in]dustry, who have suffered so [much] and who have fought so well.

As fact it was not believed. A[fter] the magnificent display of [illegible] shown by millions of Workers, [the] miners could not believe they [were] again left alone to pursue their [illegible] road.

"The T.U.C. would never do [it]," they said, clustered round the [illegible] shops, where the latest bulletin [was] shown.

For, among the miners, the [illegible] T.U.C. had become something [of a] magic talisman. It spelt salvat[ion] and to spell real solidarity—a gua[ran]tee that they would not be deserted [by] their fellow workers.

But it was true, as they were [to] realise. It was the shattering [of a] hope, the death of a splendid [illegible]tion.

Determination Firm

Even this did not lessen the [mi]ners' determination. Nor did it [illegible] feeling against the [illegible] other Workers. The miners [illegible] that these Workers were all for [illegible]. On every side you may hear the [illegible] comment: "It's not the Work[ers], they're all right. It's the lea[ders]. We never forget."

And so the men have taken [their] belts in their belts and set [their] teeth still a bit more firmly. [They] are grimly resolute. Whatever [may] happen, however they may be [illegible] by others, they have their own [organ]isation, they have their [illegible] themselves. In these narrow val[leys] there have been many hard strug[gles] testing men to the utmost, [and] with abounding courage, the [illegible] are preparing for [illegible].

Whatever may happen in the [illegible] of the valleys, we shall never [forget] how the other Workers threw [in their] help. And, when they in their [turn] need help, we shall be ready.

Despite the abandonment of [the] general strike, a fraternal [illegible] feeling has been forged between [the] miners and the other Workers [illegible] no set-backs and no [illegible] machinations of leaders can ever br[eak].

GOSSIP ASKS GENERA[L] COUNCIL TO EXPLAIN

We are informed that Alex. Gossip, General Secretary of the Amalgamated Furnishing Trades Association, [has] written to the General Council of the T.U.C. demanding that a conference of all Trades Union Executives [be] immediately summoned in order to hear an explanation regarding the conditions under which the General Strike was called off.

BOB STEWART ARREST[ED]

Bob Stewart, acting secretary of [the] Communist Party of Great Brit[ain], was arrested on Friday night. [illegible] of going to press the charge was [not] known.

www.ingramcontent.com/pod-product-compliance
Lightning Source LLC
Chambersburg PA
CBHW060836190426
43197CB00040B/2635